INSTRUMENTS IN THE HISTORY
OF WESTERN MUSIC

by Karl Geiringer

BRAHMS
HIS LIFE AND WORK

HAYDN
A CREATIVE LIFE IN MUSIC

THE BACH FAMILY
SEVEN GENERATIONS OF CREATIVE GENIUS

JOHANN SEBASTIAN BACH
THE CULMINATION OF AN ERA

The Concert. Two ladies, playing a flute and a lute, and a singer. They are performing a French chanson by Claudin de Sermisy (the music and text are clearly visible in the original painting). By the Master of the Female Half-length, around 1530. Rohrau, Gallerie Harrach.

KARL GEIRINGER

Instruments in the History of Western Music

New York
OXFORD UNIVERSITY PRESS
1978

LIBRARY OF CONGRESS CATALOGING IN PUBLICATION DATA

Geiringer, Karl, 1899-
    Instruments in the history of Western music.

    1943 and 1945 editions published under title:
Musical instruments.
    Bibliography: p.
    Includes index.
    1. Musical instruments—History.   I. Title.
ML460.G4 1978   781.9'1'09   78-14802
ISBN 0-19-520057-7

FIRST PUBLISHED AS "MUSICAL INSTRUMENTS.
THEIR HISTORY FROM THE STONE AGE TO THE
       PRESENT DAY" IN 1943
          SECOND EDITION 1945
          THIRD IMPRESSION 1949
        FOURTH IMPRESSION 1959
          FIFTH IMPRESSION 1965
THIRD (REVISED AND ENLARGED) EDITION 1978

Printed in the United States of America

To the memory of
HENRIK A. WESTEN
ever a devoted friend of the arts

PREFACE

As the title of this book implies, it is organized in a somewhat unconventional manner. Authors of works on musical instruments like to present the facts in systematic order, based on groups of instruments, beginning with primitive percussion and working up to highly sophisticated stringed and wind, and possibly electronic instruments. In the present book, however, the material is arranged in historical order. The instruments of the West are discussed within the great epochs of history, from prehistoric times into the second half of our own century. The interrelation of their development with that of the history of music is traced, and their true role as tools of the art is brought to the fore.

Each chapter begins with an introduction offering a bird's-eye view of the musical trends of the period, with special emphasis on their general cultural and artistic aspects. Then follows a description of the instruments in use during that particular epoch. They are dealt with in approximately the same order in every chapter, which should help the reader's orientation. Each section of the book attempts to draw the obvious parallels between a phase in the history of music and the implements which were used in its development. However, the reader who prefers to follow the course of an instrument through the centuries can do so with the help of the table of contents and the index.

Musical instruments were made in countless shapes, often deviating only slightly from each other. It seems obvious that in a book of this kind the author had to resist the temptation to describe every form of instrument known to have existed, every deviation created by the inventive mind of an ancient instrument maker. The same is true of the various names given in the past to a single instrument. Here it seemed advisable to choose only the most characteristic names (usually with their translations into French, German, and Italian) and to leave out those which appeared to be less significant, or were even ambiguous. Finally, I have avoided leading the reader into the labyrinth of the various tunings of stringed instruments or the range of wind instruments. In these the subjective inclination and the technical skill of the performers played an important part and it would far surpass the scope of this book to mention all those known to have been employed. Usually a single tuning or range which seemed particularly representative is mentioned, but the reader should keep in mind that in many cases others too were in use.

A few important acoustical principles have been outlined in a special section, in order to relieve the text of too many technical details. These brief remarks have been assigned to an Appendix, and they can be passed over by the reader without detriment to his understanding of the historical chapters.

My interest in musical instruments is not of recent date. More than half a century ago, while I was studying in Berlin, the great Curt Sachs, one of the founders of the modern science of musical instruments, opened my eyes to the wonders of this fascinating field of research. In 1941 my first book on musical instruments was published and went through two editions and seven printings in London and New York. In the meantime, while I was working in quite different areas of musical research, my long-held conviction grew that instruments should not be considered as independent objects of study, but as an essential part of the history of music. This induced me to completely re-shape and update my earlier book and give it its present form.

This book could not have been completed without the generous assistance of various colleagues. I should like to single out here my late friend Mr. W. F. H. Blandford in London, who placed his wide knowledge and experience fully at my disposal. Hofrat Dr. Victor Luithlen, former director of the collection of early musical instruments at the Kunsthistorisches Museum, Vienna, offered valuable replacements for various plates in my earlier book. Dr. Kurt Wegerer, his successor in office, likewise provided fine photos of the treasures in his care. I feel equally indebted to Dr. J. H. van der Meer, curator of ancient musical instruments at the Germanisches National-museum, Nürnberg, who provided me with several significant illustrations; to Dr. Emanuel Winternitz, former curator of ancient instruments in the Metropolitan Museum, New York, for valuable help; and to Mr. Klaus G. Roy, Director of Publications of the Cleveland Orchestra, who furnished illustrations of contemporary instruments. The firm of Allen & Unwin in London, which has published my books for more than 40 years, proved again most co-operative. I feel greatly obliged to its director, Mr. Rayner S. Unwin, and to the editorial staff, who made numerous valuable suggestions. My wife, Dr. Irene Steckel Geiringer, has once more been my unfailing helper, exercising constructive criticism through every phase of my work.

KARL GEIRINGER

Santa Barbara, October 1977.

CONTENTS

CHAPTER IV

CHAPTER V

LIST OF PLATES

VII/2   Crwth.
Vienna, Gesellschaft der Musikfreunde; at
present Kunsthistorisches Museum.

VIII   King David with his musicians.
The king holds a lyre. His musicians perform on
horn, vielle, cymbala, and organ. Psalter of St.
Elizabeth, 13th century. Cividale del Friuli,
Museo Archeologico.

IX   King David with his musicians.
The king tunes his harp, the musicians perform
on cymbala, two types of vielle, double shawm
and transverse flute (?). In the lower corners are
bells, a psaltery, and an organistrum. Psalter of
the 12th century. Glasgow, University Library.

X/1   Oliphant from southern Italy, 11th
century.
The inscription is probably a later addition.
Vienna, Kunsthistorisches Museum.

X/2   Players of pipe and tabor.
Cantigas de Santa Maria, Spain, 13th century.
Monasterio de Escorial.

XI   Angels playing on straight and folded
trumpet, portative, harp, and vielle.
Hans Memling, c. A.D. 1480, Anvers, Musée.

XII   Angels playing on psaltery, tromba
marina, lute, folded trumpet, and
pommer.
Hans Memling, c. A.D. 1480, Anvers, Musée.

XIII   Angel playing the portative.
Detail from Hans Memling, Marriage of St.
Catherine, A.D. 1479. Bruges, Hôpital de St.
Jean.

XIV   Angel playing the mandola (detail).
Bartolommeo Vivarini, A.D. 1474. Venice,
Santa Maria dei Fiori.

XV   Virgin and Child, with angels playing
the rebec and double recorder.
Marcello Fogolino, 15th century. Milan, Museo
Poldi Pezzoli.

XXVI   Mounted musicians playing on trombones and pommers.
Hans Burgkmair, around 1500. Detail from Triumphal Procession of Emperor Maximilian.

XXVII   Dulzian, 16th century.
The upper brass rim bears the engraved inscription (in German):

> I am called a Dulzian
> Though not well known to every man.
> And if to play me well you yearn,
> You first my fingering must learn.
> (Trans. C. Zytowski)

Vienna, Gesellschaft der Musikfreunde, at present Kunsthistorisches Museum.

XXVIII   1. Recorders of different sizes; 2. four "Dolzflöten"; 3. three transverse flutes; 4. Swiss pipe; 5. two tabor-pipes; 6. tabor.
From Michael Praetorius, *Syntagma Musicum*, 1618.

XXIX   A player on the crumhorn (detail).
Vittore Carpaccio, early 16th century. Venice, Accademia.

XXX/1   Tenor rackett by I. C. Denner, around 1700; silver-gilt trumpet in fancy form by A. Schnitzer, Nürnberg, 1598; ivory cornetto of the 16th or 17th century.
Vienna, Gesellschaft der Musikfreunde, at present Kunsthistorisches Museum.

XXX/2   Bible regal, in front of it a regal pipe, around 1600.
Formerly: Berlin, Staatliche Sammlung alter Musikinstrumente (lost during the war).

XXXI   Silver trumpet by Anton Schnitzer, Nürnberg, 1581.
Vienna, Kunsthistoriches Museum.

XXXII   Double spinet by Martinus van der Biest, Anvers, 1580.
Nürnberg, Germanisches Nationalmuseum.

Between pages
176 and 177

XXXIII   Positive organ with four registers, around 1600.
Berlin, Musikinstrumenten-Museum des Staatlichen Instituts für Musikforschung, Preussischer Kulturbesitz.

XXXIV **Allegory of Hearing.**
Among the numerous instruments represented
are (from l. to r.): harpsichord, trombone, kettledrum, 3 viole da gamba of different sizes, mandola,
pochette, shawm, lira da braccio, lute played
by woman, various kinds of horn. In the background l. a group of musicians; on the wall r., a
painting showing Orpheus surrounded by animals. Jan Brueghel, A.D. 1618. Madrid, Prado.

XXXV **Clavicytherium with two 8' registers.**
The folding doors are painted with religious and
musical subjects. Italy, 17th century. New York,
Metropolitan Museum of Art, the Crosby Brown
Collection of Musical Instruments, 1889.

XXXVI **The Family of Jacques van Eyck.**
Represented are bass viola da gamba, positive,
and guitar. Gonzales Coques (1614–1684).
Budapest, Museum of Fine Arts.

Between pages
192 *and* 193

XXXVII **Lid of a spinet, made for the Nürnberg
patrician Lukas Friedrich Behaim in
1619 (detail).**
Behaim is portrayed playing the bass viol. The
center is occupied by the composer Johann
Staden, who performs on a positive organ with
his left hand, and with his right hand on the
spinet from which this lid is taken. Next to him
sits a player of an alto-tenor viol; in the background stand performers on violin and viola.
Nürnberg, Germanisches Nationalmuseum.

XXXVIII **Musicians playing (from l. to r.): guitar,
viola, recorder, theorbo lute, violoncello, spinct.**
David Ryckaert III, 17th century. Vienna,
Czernin Gallerie.

XXXIX **Players of theorbo lute and cittern.**
Jan M. Molenaer (1610–1668). London,
National Gallery.

XL **A lady at the spinet, in the foreground
a bass viola da gamba.**
Jan Vermeer (1632–1675). London, National
Gallery.

XLI/1 Musicians playing on pochette and dulcimer.
F. P. von der Schlichten, 17th century.

XLI/2 Player of the tromba marina.
From Filippo Bonanni, *Gabinetto Armonico*, 1722.

XLII Viola d'amore with seven melody and seven sympathetic strings.
18th century. Private property.

XLIII Musicians of the French court holding bass viola da gamba and transverse flutes.
Attributed to Robert Tournières, 1705–1715. London, National Gallery.

XLIV/1 Chitarra battente, 18th century.
Formerly: Berlin, Staatliche Sammlung alter Musikinstrumente (lost during the war).

XLIV/2 Hurdy-gurdy (vielle à roue). France, 18th century.
New York, Metropolitan Museum of Art, Crosby Brown Collection of Musical Instruments, 1889.

XLV/1 Player of the chitarrone.
From Filippo Bonanni, *Gabinetto Armonico* 1722.

XLV/2 Hook harp.
Vienna, Gesellschaft der Musikfreunde, at present Kunsthistorisches Museum.

XLVI/1 Fretted clavichord with "short" lowest octave and "broken" F♯ and G♯ keys (detail).
Germany, early 18th century. Nürnberg, Rück collection in Germanisches Nationalmuseum.

XLVI/2 Alto oboe, oboe da caccia, English horn.
18th century. Vienna, Gesellschaft der Musikfreunde, at present Kunsthistorisches Museum.

XLVII/1 Double bassoon by Anciuti. Milan, 1732.
Salzburg, Museum Carolino Augusteum.

LIV/2　Octobass by J. B. Vuillaume. Paris, 1849.
Vienna, Gesellschaft der Musikfreunde, at present Kunsthistorisches Museum.

LIV/3　Lyre-guitar by Lupot. Orleans, 1778.
New York, Metropolitan Museum of Art, Crosby Brown Collection of Musical Instruments, 1889.

LV　Alice Chalifoux of the Cleveland Orchestra playing the double-action pedal harp.
Photo G. Landmann, Courtesy Cleveland Orchestra.

LVI　Members of the Vienna Philharmonic Orchestra performing an oratorio.
In the third row a player of the kettledrums; in the second row players of bassoons, trumpets, trombones, bass tuba; in the front row players of flutes, oboes, and horns. Photo A. Fischer, Wiener Neustadt.

LVII　Oboe, oboe d'amore and English horn of the 20th century.
Courtesy Cleveland Orchestra.

LVIII　Bassoon players of the B.B.C. Orchestra.
By kind permission of the British Broadcasting Corporation.

LIX/1　Serpent, 18th century.
Salzburg, Museum Carolino Augusteum.

LIX/2　Stanley Maret of the Cleveland Orchestra playing the double-bassoon.
Photo Hastings-Willinger & Associates. Courtesy Cleveland Orchestra.

LX　Bass clarinet, B♭ and E♭ clarinets.
Courtesy Cleveland Orchestra.

LXI/1　Player of the contrabass saxophone.

LXI/2　Player of a contrabass trombone by Boosey, London.
By kind permission of Mr. A. Falkner, London.

LXII　Myron Bloom of the Cleveland Orchestra playing the French horn.
Courtesy Cleveland Orchestra.

FIGURES IN THE TEXT

I
PREHISTORY AND ANTIQUITY

Stone Age

The function of music in prehistoric times was quite different from what it came to be in later periods. Music was not made to provide pleasure and aesthetic enjoyment. Its purpose was to help man in his struggle against the overwhelming forces of nature. For primitive man musical sound, whose origin he did not quite understand, had a mysterious quality, and he attributed magical effects to it. Quite often music was intended to induce fear and terror not only in man, but also, and above all, in evil spirits. While driving away hostile forces it furthered, preserved and propagated the powers of life. Played at funeral services it was intended to assure rebirth. Strong taboos were often attached to musical instruments and dire punishment threatened the unauthorized who dared to use or even touch them.

On the basis of excavations and the archeological interpretation of pictorial evidence it appears that in Europe some kind of musical activity can be traced back some 15,000 years, or even further. During the early Stone Age (Paleolithic era) man learned how to cut notches in a bone and to produce rasping noises by rubbing such a "scraper" with a stick. He fastened a thin, fish-shaped bone to a thong, and by whirling this "bull-roarer" swiftly through the air, he produced weird moaning sounds. He blew across the sharp edge of a hollow bone or bored through the foot-joint of a reindeer, thus fashioning a primitive flute or whistle with a penetrating sound. These instruments might also have been used by hunters to attract a prey, to imitate the voices of birds or to produce signals.

During the later Stone Age (Neolithic era), which began in Europe around 10,000 B.C., man started to use clay in the construction of musical instruments. He made clay bells, as well as clay drums shaped like a cup or, occasionally, like an hour-glass and even provided with eyelet holes for lacing on the skin (Pl. I/1). His bone flutes had now made considerable progress and were furnished with finger-holes so that several notes could be produced on them (Pl. I/2). He cut a hole in the center, or later in the side, of a marine or snail shell and used this natural object as a kind of trumpet. Wood, too, must have been used as material for musical instruments, as for instance in the musical bow, for which a string was stretched between the ends of a flexible rod, producing a hollow sound when the string was plucked. However, materials like reed, wood or bark decompose in the course of centuries and we can only deduce the past existence of such instruments from the fact that wide use is made of wooden instruments by primitive tribes of our own time, who are culturally on the same level as the Stone Age men of Europe.

The instruments used in the Stone Age were inseparably bound up with extra-musical ideas. The notched bone of the scraper, which resembled a phallus, became the instrument of the love-spell, as it still is today among countless primitive peoples. For similar reasons the flute was used as an instrument of the fertility-spell. To increase its magic power, vessel-flutes (somewhat similar to the modern ocarina) were sometimes constructed in the shape of various animals. The whirring sounds of the bull-roarer symbolized the voices of dead ancestors, in whose former vital energies their descendants wished to share. The magic strength of the implement was increased by the fish-shape, as fishes, on account of their abundance of roe, were considered to be symbols of fecundity. The occasional use of red paint added to the magic properties, as red was the color of life-giving blood. Round drums, with their suggestion of the female body, were considered to be instruments of great holiness and were employed in various cults. Confirmation of the magical functions of early instruments may be found—to take only a single example—in a famous rock drawing of the Stone Age (in the *Trois Frères* cave, Ariège), which shows a kind of flute played by a masked dancer who is wrapped in the skin of a wild beast, which turns him into a horrible and diabolic figure.

From these supernatural implications musical instruments have never been wholly freed. In spite of the ever-growing importance of the aesthetic aspects of sound, which has been brought about by technical improvements in construction and manipulation, the symbolic values of the instruments have continued to carry weight up to the very threshold of the present age.

Bronze Age

Ritual usage still occupies the foreground when we consider the most important instrument of the Bronze Age in northern Europe, the *lur* (Pl. I/3)—from the Norwegian word for horn—which was in use from the twelfth to the sixth century B.C. all over Scandinavia and northern Germany.

Very early in the Bronze Age men began to bind the open ends of natural horns with metal, and their next step was to fashion the whole horn in this material. Instruments shaped like the horn of an ox became plentiful, and the tusks of elephant and mammoth also were imitated. In Ireland, metal horns that have been found in graves not only follow the curved shape of an elephant's tusk, but are also provided with a blowing hole in the side, a relic of the days when the solid end of the ivory tusk could not be pierced. Primitive ivory horns of Africa still retain this feature. The form and proportions of the mammoth tusk served as the model for the peculiar S-shaped lur. The fact that this instrument has been found in pairs, twisted in opposite directions, may also be attributed to its origin in the tusks of the pachyderm. It is noteworthy that at the time the metal lur was used, the mammoth had ceased to exist. Possibly ancient, unearthed tusks served as models for the instrument's shape.

The slightly conical and boldly curved lur, which uses a kind of trombone mouthpiece and ends in a handsome, ornamented disk, forms one of the most distinguished creations of the Bronze Age. When played by a modern performer this instrument produces a noble and solemn tone which reminds the listener of the French horn and the tenor trombone. Moreover, a skilful musician can produce up to the twelfth note of the harmonic series, so that in addition to the usual triad, consecutive notes become possible in the upper register. A further remarkable fact is that the two lurs of every pair were tuned to the same pitch with marvelous accuracy. One would be tempted to conclude that we have here the first evidence of the existence of part music, did not everything we know about the music of primitive peoples contradict this supposition. It is far more likely that the two instruments were played alternately, or in unison to increase the volume. The performers were probably bent on achieving a harsh tone and did not venture beyond the lowest partials of the harmonic series. During the Bronze era and the succeeding Iron age, the idea, previously conceived, gained ground of connecting different tubes of wind instruments so that they could be played by a single performer. In a tomb near Kattovice (Poland) a group of as many as nine bone tubes of various lengths has been found. Originally they were obviously tied together to form a kind of *syrinx* (cf. p. 37). Experiments have shown that these tubes were tuned to the pentatonic (five-tone) scale prevalent in primitive music.

Greece

While our knowledge of prehistoric music is rather sketchy and largely based on indirect evidence, we reach firmer ground when we turn to the music of Greece. Here we can draw not only on a certain number of instruments that have survived, and on pictorial evidence, but also on numerous literary sources and even on some actual musical compositions of the period, preserved in a fully developed notation.

Greek mythology emphasized the magic power of music, thus continuing the beliefs held by prehistorical peoples. Orpheus, the divine musician, could not only tame wild beasts with the sound of his lyre, but his song moved the spirits of the underworld and he was allowed to bring his dead wife back to life. The archaic belief that music miraculously bridges the gap between death and life is here still in evidence. To music was attributed also the gift of magically influencing nature and healing sickness. Asklepios, the god of medicine, was known as the son of Apollo, the god of art and song.

Ethos in Music

In historical times the doctrine of *ethos* in music, to which Pythagoras, Plato and Aristotle attributed high significance, continued similar trends of thinking. These philosophers emphasized the great educational value of music. They contended that it was beneficial for young people to hear melodies based on the right kinds of scales and rhythmic patterns and accompanied by properly chosen instruments. On the other hand, acquaintance with the wrong kind of music might lead to intemperance and moral turpitude. From the beginning it was felt, both in Sparta and in Athens, that laws had to govern the nature of music, as it exercised a decisive influence on the human character.

Vocal and Instrumental Music

The Greeks used predominantly vocal music. It was connected with every form of literature and frequently also with the dance. The ode and the epos, the dithyramb (a choral song in honor of the God Dionysos) and the drama all made use of singers, who moved to the rhythm of the music. The inflections of the poetical language were followed in the melodies of the singers, and similarly the alternation of short and long syllables determined the rhythms of the composition. But while all the literary forms were dependent on the cooperation of singers, the vocalists in turn required the support of instruments. The singer accompanied himself on an instrument, or he was accompanied by a player. Instruments were indispensable, though they were, as a rule, relegated to a subservient position. Pure instrumental music did exist. Yet it was—at least in earlier times—very rarely used. When, at the beginning of the sixth century B.C., a player of the *aulos* (cf. p 46) performed a programmatic composition describing Apollo's fight with the dragon, this created something of a sensation and was long remembered. It was only in the fourth century B.C., after Greek culture had passed its zenith, that pure instrumental music gained in significance.

The Instruments

The earliest representations of musical instruments in Greece date from the second half of the third millennium B.C. They are found in two marble statuettes of Cycladic art from the islands of Keros and Thera. One represents a player of a small harp shaped like an equilateral triangle, the other a performer on stubby double-pipes, each pipe being held in one of the player's hands.

From the Minoan culture of Crete and the Mycenaean period on the mainland pictorial representations have survived, as well as instruments found in graves. These are mostly lyres, stringed instruments with a yoke, consisting of two arms and a cross-bar, attached to the body, the strings being stretched from the lower end of the body to the cross-bar. This type of instrument, employed throughout the ancient orient, was apparently also used in Greece at an early date.

Later, when literary reports are added to the source material, a substantial number of names for musical instruments appear, some of them evidently referring to instruments of great similarity.

Lyra

Among the most important stringed instruments was the *lyra* (closely related to the *phorminx*, *chelys*, and *barbitos*). It was a primitive lyre* which might have been introduced into Greece from the Balkan peninsula. Its body originally consisted of a tortoise-shell with a tympanum of oxhide, while the arms of the yoke were of antelope horns. Later, the whole instrument was fashioned of wood. The strings were supported by a bridge and fixed to the cross-piece of the yoke by means of fatty hide (Pl. II). By twisting this hide the instrument could be tuned. The number of strings, which were originally made of hemp and later of gut, was gradually increased. Up to the seventh century B.C., 3–5 strings were generally used. In the classical period of Greek music, during the sixth and fifth centuries, seven strings were the rule. They were tuned to the notes of the pentatonic scale, with five notes (e, g, a, b, d) to the octave, omitting the semitones. It may well be that the instrument was played both with the bare fingers and with a hard plectrum, the bare left hand plucking the strings to accompany the song, and the right hand, armed with the plectrum, which was fastened with a 'thong, rhythmically sweeping across the strings to bridge the pauses of the song.

Kithara

The *kithara* was probably imported from Asia Minor via the islands of the Aegean. In the shape of its sound-box, the manner of attaching the strings, and the method of playing, it has much in common with the lyra, but in other respects the two instruments

---

*The generic term lyre is not to be confused with the name of one of its most important representatives, the Greek *lyra*.

are fundamentally different. While the lyra was always light and unadorned, the kithara had a massive and often richly ornamented body (Pl. III). Its cross-bar had a handle which made it possible to alter quickly with a single movement the tuning of all the strings, or to slacken their tension after use. The kithara did not stop at the seven strings of the lyra, but might have as many as twelve. These strings were again tuned according to the anhemitonic scale, but the player could raise their pitch by a quarter-tone, a semi-tone, or a whole-tone, by pressing a piece of hardwood against the lower end of the string. The increase in the number of strings met with much resistance. Indeed it is reported by Timotheus of Miletos that the authorities of conservative Sparta actually cut off four of the newly added strings of his kithara.

The technical differences between the lyra and the kithara not unnaturally had some influence on the employment of the two instruments. The lyra was the instrument of the dilettante and the novice, being used only to accompany singers; the kithara, on the other hand, was played by virtuosi and was eventually also employed for instrumental solos.

Despite its refinement of tone, the sound of the antique kithara must have carried a great distance; otherwise it would have been hardly possible, at the popular competition-meetings, such as the Pythian Games, for the sound of a single kithara to be heard by a large audience.

The kithara, like the lyre, was employed mainly for the accompaniment of lyric and epic poetry. The emotional mood to which they both gave expression was calm and restrained, and was aptly described as "Apollonian".

Harp

In a *harp* the plane of the strings stands perpendicular to the sound-board, not parallel as in a lyre. As previously mentioned, instruments of this type were used already in prehistoric Greece. They disappeared later and around the middle of the fifth century B.C. a different type of the instrument was introduced from the orient. In this harp—known under various names, such as *psalterion, magadis, pektis, trigonon*—the neck is attached to the body approximately at right angles. On account of its light and delicate tone the harp was the favorite instrument of Greek women, but it never achieved the popularity of the lyra or kithara.

Aulos

The *aulos* (Pls. II and IV/1), the Latin *tibia*, was an oboe-like instrument of cylindrical bore, fitted with a single or double reed (cf. p. 291). It was made of wood, ivory or metal and was usually played in pairs by a single performer. Like the Greek stringed instruments, the aulos was not indigenous to the country. As similar pipes were employed by the Egyptians, Jews, Hittites, Elamites and Assyrians, Greece could hardly have avoided adopting it.

To translate aulos by "flute," as philologists are fond of doing, is quite unwarranted. The instrument was far more like a shrill and strident shawm, whose penetrating sound had nothing whatever in common with the mild tones of the flute. It was played with such force that the musician, to protect his cheeks from being over-distended, often wore a leather band, the *phorbeia*, round his head (Pl. IV/1).

The aulos was made in several sizes. The smallest were the "girl" pipes (sopranos); then followed the larger "boys" (altos), the "perfect" (tenors) and the "more than perfect" (basses), the tenors sounding an octave below the sopranos and the basses an octave below the altos. Together the four sizes covered a range of more than three octaves.

In the course of time an ever-increasing number of finger-holes were introduced in the aulos. At first there were only three or four, but finally there were at times as many as fifteen. Since so great a number could no longer be covered with the performer's fingers, rotating rings were devised by which the holes could be opened or closed at will, thus anticipating our modern keys. Indeed, in one way these rings were more efficient than the modern keys, for by rotating a ring in such a way that a hole was only partly covered, the performer could produce intermediate tones. Further, the notes of the instrument could be wholly or partly tuned to a different pitch by fixing little cup-like tubes on to the individual finger-holes, thus lengthening the path of the air before it escaped and deepening the individual notes.

It is not surprising, in view of its high efficiency, that the aulos was given an important part in the art of the ancient world. It was used in sacrificial processions, at weddings, masquerades, athletic contests, in the performance of dithyrambs, and, most of all, in the Greek drama, where choruses and solo songs were accompanied by the aulos and interludes entrusted to it. Performers turned to the instrument whenever strong emotions— the so-called "Dionysian" mood—had to be expressed. Even extensive program music was performed upon the aulos. The above-mentioned composition describing the combat between Apollo and the dragon consisted of no less than five sections: the exploration of the field of combat, the challenge, the fight itself, the conquest of the dragon, and the hymn of victory.

There is still some uncertainty as to the role of the second pipe of the aulos, since, as a rule, two pipes were played by one musician. In the earliest times the second instrument may have sustained an unchanging high drone or bourdon-note in the oriental manner, while in later times the notes of the accompaniment may have been more frequently varied. On no account, however, must we imagine that the aulos was used to play polyphonic compositions on the harmonic basis of our modern European music; for the music of antiquity was essentially melodic, as the music of the orient still is today. Even when a performer on the lyra or kithara was accompanying a vocalist, he would only decorate and play around the melody, never adding an accompaniment in chords.

Two other Greek wind instruments were of limited significance.

Syrinx

According to Greek mythology the *syrinx* was the instrument of goat-footed Pan, god of nature and fertility. The instrument, still known today as pan-pipes, was primarily used by shepherds. It consisted of five, seven, or nine pipes without finger-holes. They were of different lengths and bound together like a raft, so that the upper ends formed a straight line (cf. Pl. VII/1). By moving the lips along it and blowing in turn across the sharp edges of the different pipes (cf. p. 290) the player could perform a simple tune. The attempt to mechanize the syrinx eventually led to the invention of one of the most important instruments of later centuries—the organ.

Salpinx

The long, straight Greek trumpet, known as the *salpinx*, was usually made of metal and equipped with a mouthpiece of horn. In blowing it, performers originally used the *phorbeia* (cf. p. 36). A salpinx from the second half of the fifth century B.C., made of ivory sections joined together with bronze rings, is preserved in the Boston (Mass.) Museum of Fine Arts. This beautiful instrument, the only one of its kind to have survived, is approximately five feet long. The salpinx was primarily an instrument of warfare and of no significance for art music.

Percussion Instruments

Among the instruments employed in the Dionysian rites were the *krotala* (Pl. IV/1), clappers made of wood or split cane, the two parts of which were hit against each other by the player's fingers. The krotala, which were mainly played by female dancers, resembled in their use the Spanish castanets of a later period. Also used in the Dionysian cult were the *kymbala*, cymbals of various sizes which could be hit harshly or with a tinkling sound, and the *tympanon*, a hand-beaten drum with a skin on either side of the frame. These instruments, which were little used at first, gained in significance during the Hellenistic period.

Etruria

The history of the Etruscans has not been fully clarified yet. They seem to have migrated from Asia into central Italy at the beginning of the first millennium B.C. From sculptures and paintings that have been preserved, the Etruscans appear to have had a great interest in music, and their instruments resembled on the whole those of ancient Hellas. There is even a tradition that the Greek salpinx was first made by the Etruscans. A remarkable exception, however, is offered by the realistic representation, on a sarcophagus found near Perugia, of a player of a transverse flute (Pl. V). Here we see an instrument introduced from the Etruscans' Asiatic homeland and not employed in Greece.

Rome

The musical life of Rome is not as well documented as that of

Greece. With the exception of an insignificant fragment, none of its compositions seems to have survived. It is known, however, that in early Rome music was considered to be quite important. Works-songs were performed by slaves digging trenches and rowing boats, by maid servants, weavers, grape-pickers and shepherds. The street cries of tradesmen and the clamour of beggars assumed a musical character. There were nursery songs, lullabies, birthday and wedding songs, and triumphant tunes to celebrate victories. In religious rites music was employed to ban evil spirits and to evoke ecstasy. Dirges resounded at the bier of the dead. Music was particularly important in comedy and drama, where it was employed in overtures, interludes between the acts, solo numbers, dances and choruses.

As Rome gradually expanded its territory, it began to absorb the culture, and with it the music, of the peoples brought under its dominion. Slave girls from Syria, Egypt, Phoenicia, Spain and other distant provinces congregated in the capital, bringing with them their songs, their dances and their instruments. Above all, Greek and Etruscan music gradually assumed a dominant position among the Romans. Most of its features, and eventually also of its theory, were taken over, but in accordance with their character, the Romans saw to it that the means at their disposal were enlarged and magnified. They constructed lyrae and kitharae as big as sedan-chairs and liked to assemble massed orchestras and choruses. They showed a definite preference for wind instruments, possibly because their tone was more powerful than that of the delicate stringed instruments.

Roman Wind Instruments

The *tibia* was the Roman form of the aulos. It held a privileged position among the Romans, as it was the only instrument admitted in earlier times to religious ceremonies. Occasionally it was made of ivory and equipped with silver rings. Later it became as dominant in the theatre as it had been in the Greek world.

In view of the tremendous importance of the army in the Roman Empire it is not surprising that various instruments were developed to meet the demands of military music. There was the *cornu* (Pl. IV/2), a large, coiled trumpet with a very narrow bore, in some ways reminiscent of the later hunting-horn. A wooden crossbar helped the player to support the long tube, which encircled his body. (Cornu fragments found on Austrian. soil seem to point to the occasional use of smaller forms of the instrument.) The cornu could be used for signals that had to be heard at a great distance, while the *tuba* directed the movements of smaller groups. This was a straight, slightly conical trumpet (Pl. IV/2) well over a yard in length, using a mouthpiece of horn or bronze. The instrument resembled the Etruscan–Greek salpinx. The *lituus*, possibly also derived from Etruscan models, was a small, straight, conical horn with an upturned bell. Related to it was the *karnyx*, an instrument used in every district inhabited by Celts, who were apparently introduced to it by Roman legionaries. In its original form the instrument consisted of a straight tube with an ox-horn fixed to one end, so as to form a sort of bell. Later the tube was bent at both ends in opposite directions, and the bell was shaped to resemble the open jaws of an animal (Pl. VI). Interestingly enough, the custom of so fashioning the bell of certain military instruments persisted into the early nineteenth century. The oriental *bagpipe* is reported to have found use in the Roman army. It consisted of a skin bag, or paunch, with openings at the extremities, into which were inserted a tube to blow the air into the skin and one or more primitive pipes with single reeds of the clarinet type (cf. p. 292). The air was forced through the pipes by the pressure of the player's arm on the windbag.

Hydraulos
Tuba, cornu and bagpipe also played an important part in the circus. And it was in the circus, too, that the popular *hydraulos* or water-organ (Pls. IV/2 and VII/1) was employed, an instrument whose invention is traditionally ascribed to the Alexandrian physicist Ktesibios, who was born between 300 and 250 B.C. In the hydraulos the principle of the syrinx and that of the bagpipe were cleverly combined. Air was pumped into a hemispherical container standing in a cylinder half filled with water, which kept the air under constant pressure. From this container a tube led to cross-channels furnished with flue-pipes, not unlike the kind used later in the recorder (cf. p. 290). These pipes were made to sound by means of an ingenious system of sliders operated with the help of large keys. In later instruments we even find several

series of pipes, and these—like the stops of later organs—could be cut out or brought in by special taps.

The hydraulos had its heyday during the Roman Empire. According to the historian Suetonius, Nero liked to play the organ, and Cicero proclaimed himself a great lover of organ music. It seems to have been used throughout the vast territories under Roman dominion. Representations of the instrument have been found on African soil and near Arles (France), while parts of a hydraulos were excavated at the site of a Roman city near Budapest, the capital of Hungary. A clay model unearthed at Carthage shows an instrument with as many as three rows of pipes and nineteen keys. During the early Middle Ages, however, the water organ gradually disappeared from musical life. The representations of a hydraulos which we find in the Utrecht Psalter from the ninth century A.D., and even in the Psalter of Edwin from the eleventh century, were probably copied from earlier models.

Pneumatic Organ

The hydraulos had a more primitive younger relation which dispensed with the complicated system of water cylinders. This instrument, known to us as the pneumatic organ, is first mentioned in the fourth century A.D., and we find it portrayed on the obelisk erected by the Emperor Theodosius (d. 395) in Istanbul. It was primarily used and developed in the eastern part of the Roman Empire and it was to this simpler and more efficient instrument that the future would belong.

Percussion Instruments

The pleasure which the Romans derived from powerful sounds may have contributed to their wide use of percussion instruments. Hand-beaten drums of various shapes and sizes were primarily played by women. Clappers were operated not only with the hands but also with the feet. The *scabellum* was a clapper-sandal tied to the chorus-leader's right foot; with its sharp, cracking sound it served to keep time for singers and dancers. Metal disks of various thicknesses were used for signalling purposes, and also for acoustical experiments. Cymbals, originally employed in the Bacchanal rites, played an important part in theatrical music.

II

THE MIDDLE AGES
(To 1300)

Gregorian Chant

In A.D. 313 the Emperor Constantine granted Christians in the Roman Empire religious freedom and the same civil rights as all other citizens. Centuries of persecution and torture thus came to an end and a new era began in which Christianity spread over parts of Asia and Africa as well as through Europe.

As many of the early Christians had originally been Jews, the ritual of the Hebrew synagogue supplied a model for their worship. The singing of the psalms, which was of great significance in the Judaic rite, was thus taken over by the adherents of the new creed. This chant was strictly vocal in character, meant to support and strengthen the impact of the texts. Instruments were not admitted to the service. Clemens of Alexandria stated bluntly: "We need . . . the word of adoration only, not harps or drums or pipes or trumpets." Inevitably this attitude had a fateful influence on the status of musical instruments.

Toward the end of the fourth century, the Roman Empire was divided into an eastern section with Byzantium (Constantinople) as its capital and a western part with Rome as its center. After that the western churches went their own way and Latin became the universal liturgical language. The Roman liturgy served eventually as model for the ritual of other churches and the Roman chant was adopted throughout the greater part of European Christendom. This liturgical music was revised, substantially improved and codified by St. Gregory, Pope from A.D. 590–604. The music of the Roman liturgy is thus rightly known as "Gregorian chant," though the medieval conception that St. Gregory "invented" the tunes is by no means justified. Gregorian chant or "plainsong," as it is often called, was widely used throughout the Middle Ages and still is in modern times. This venerable body of tunes belongs to the greatest treasures of western music.

Polyphony

The negative attitude toward musical instruments gradually changed with the advent of polyphony. Traces of medieval polyphony may be observed on western soil as early as the fourth century. In one form, known as *organum* (the name might have been derived from the instrument), a Gregorian melody was accompanied by a lower voice in parallel fourths or fifths. On solemn occasions both voices were doubled in octaves, thus creating an imposing tonal structure in which instrumental as well as vocal sounds might be represented. The development of polyphony made only slow progress. An important stage was represented by the *melismatic organum* from the first half of the twelfth century. Melismas, groups of notes sung on a single syllable, accompanied a long-held note of the plainsong, or *cantus firmus* as it was now called. The organum of the Notre Dame school in Paris (ca. 1150–1250) became richer and more complicated. Most of the time the notes of the cantus firmus were greatly prolonged, a second voice, and eventually even a third and fourth, being added. It seems probable that instruments were used to perform the excessively long notes in the cantus firmus (often also called "tenor", from Latin *tenere* = to hold). The most significant form of the time was the *motet*. Its tenor was based on a melismatic passage taken from a Gregorian chant. It was forced into a peculiar rhythmic pattern consisting of three notes followed by a rest. The origin of the melody was indicated, but no text accompanied the notes, which were probably performed by instruments. A second voice introduced a text. It was called *motetus*—"the one with words" (from the French *mot* = word). There was also a third voice with text and at times a fourth. It was one of the strange features of the motet that two and even three different texts were often employed in the same piece, and the simultaneous use of different languages in one composition was not unusual.

Obviously the lack of clarity resulting from the simultaneous use of different texts in a motet was avoided when not only the tenor, but also one or two of the upper voices were entrusted to instrumentalists. At times, moreover, the texts are completely missing in a manuscript, thus clearly indicating that the particular piece was intended exclusively for players. Instrumental music came fully into its own in various polyphonic dances, which appear in early sources.

Vernacular Monophonic Songs

In spite of the rise of polyphony, monophonic music remained a vital force throughout this era. It was used not only in Gregorian chant, but also widely in non-liturgical music. Thus in Spain, at the court of Alfonso X, King of Castille and León (d. 1284), the *cantiga* was cultivated as a form. There were *Cantigas de Amor* (love songs) as well as the important *Cantigas de Santa Maria* in praise of the Holy Virgin. The manuscripts recording them are provided not only with texts and melodies, but also with more than a thousand miniatures vividly depicting music-making and the musical instruments of the time (see Pl. X/2).

In southern France, the 12th and 13th centuries saw the rise of the *troubadours* (from the Provençal *trobar* = to find, to invent). These were amateurs who dabbled in poetry and music. They were to be found in all classes of society, from simple folk to noblemen and even crowned rulers. Troubadour songs deal with various topics. Quite often they express platonic love for a *domina*, a high-born married lady who is admired and desired from afar. There is the *pastourelle*, voicing the love of a knight for a shepherdess; there are songs exhorting the faithful to participate in a crusade, songs of mourning after the death of a noble patron, political songs, but only rarely religious ones.

The art of the troubadours inspired in northern France the *trouvères*, and in Germany the *minnesingers* (from the German *Minne* = love). They used similar forms of one-part music and by and large chose the same topics as the troubadours. However, religious songs appear here with greater frequency than in southern France. The works of the minnesingers display in general an emphasis on narration, as well as a more serious character, than those of their Gallic neighbors. It is also noteworthy that in some manuscripts containing music of the minnesingers a prelude, obviously intended for an instrument, precedes the vocal section.

Troubadours and trouvères often relied on the help of a

jongleur, who sang the tunes and accompanied them on instruments such as the vielle, organistrum, cittern, or harp. The jongleurs were selected from a large group of foot-loose people moving freely through the lands. They also appeared as actors, dancers, acrobats and trainers of animals. Socially they were for a long time outcasts, but in spite of the general contempt they had to bear they made a significant contribution to the musical culture of their time. They were performers of unusual versatility; individual players were apt to master three, six, and at times even up to nine different instruments. By introducing the instruments to ever-larger circles of music-lovers, they greatly added to their dissemination. Some of the jongleurs dropped the spectacular part of their show and appeared in public as musical performers only. They even succeeded in being appointed to specific courts as *menestrels*, performing both their own and their patrons' works. Eventually these professional musicians formed guilds of menestrels which secured their members a certain prestige.

The Instruments

The turmoil caused by the migration of barbaric hordes into Europe jeopardized the existence of many of the highly developed instruments of the ancient civilizations. As already mentioned, the hostile attitude of the early Christians toward instrumental music added to their neglect. For a long time instruments were considered by the adherents of the new creed to be relics of pagan worship. This twofold attack on musical instruments produced a kind of vacuum in the middle of the first millennium, which was only slowly filled during the following centuries through the advent of newcomers from distant lands.

An observation which was made in our discussion of the instruments of antiquity applies equally well to the Middle Ages; the home of our occidental instruments lies beyond the borders of Europe. The instruments were developed in Europe, and brought to their present stage on this continent; but their roots go back to the east. We owe our modern instruments to importations from Asia.

A few may have come from the north, along the Baltic coast; many more through the south-east, via Byzantium. One after another, now peacefully through merchants and wandering

tribes, now in the train of foreign conquerors, or as booty brought
back from the Holy Land by returning crusaders, the instruments
of the highly civilized orient found their way into Europe. The
occident was positively flooded with innumerable instruments,
which the western spirit was slow to assimilate. Eventually
invaders entered Europe also from the west. The Moors, who in
the eighth century occupied parts of Spain, introduced Arab
culture into Europe. From Spain their instruments spread
through France into the rest of Europe. This may have been due
largely to the activities of the jongleurs, who were constantly on
the move, taking with them the tools of their trade—and among
them musical instruments. With the social rise of the jongleurs
the instruments gained full acceptance and were used by laymen
and clerics alike. Around the year 900 the monk Tutilo of
St. Gallen, Switzerland, is reported to have excelled in his
performance on stringed instruments and pipes; he was widely
sought after by the sons of courtiers as a teacher of these instruments. Literary sources of the time often referred to them,
miniatures in illuminated manuscripts portrayed them; over the
portals of Romanesque cathedrals the statues of crowned elders
with instruments in their hands welcomed the congregation.
Clearly, musical instruments had been fully accepted into
western society.

Let us now see how far this general process applied to the
individual instruments.

Lyre

Lyres are among the earliest instruments depicted in medieval
manuscripts (Pl. VIII). Their origin is not quite clear. They
might have been derived from the lyres of Greek and Roman
antiquity, but it seems more likely that they were descended from
oriental ancestors. These instruments, which in shape are sometimes astonishingly like Sumerian lyres, are represented in
European works of art from the seventh century onward; and
since national boundaries were still unknown in the early Middle
Ages, it is not surprising that we meet them in Anglo-Saxon
countries as well as in various parts of the continent. Thus, in the
Württemberg village of Oberflacht, two lyres were found in an
Allemanic warrior's grave which date from approximately A.D.

500. They are among the extremely few instruments of the early Middle Ages which have been preserved to this day.

In its early medieval form, with tuning-pegs (which were unknown in antiquity) and five to seven string, the lyre was played as a rule with bare hands and rarely with a plectrum. The instrument was known under various names. Particularly significant is the name *cithara teutonica*, referring to its wide distribution in the German countries.

Crwth

After the year 1000 the lyre was gradually pushed into the background by the appearance of other, more efficient plucked instruments. It was only in a rare variant—not plucked, but played with a bow—that the instrument persisted in Celtic Wales, even far into modern times. When in the tenth century the vielle, furnished with finger-board and bow, appeared in Europe (cf. p. 48ff), the vogue of the new instrument was soon so great that the old-fashioned lyre fell beneath its influence. From the eleventh century on we find stringed instruments combining the yoke of the lyre with the neck of the finger-board instrument. These instruments, especially favored by the Welsh bards, were notable for a flat bridge with only one foot resting on the table, while the other, as a kind of sound-post, reached through the sound hole to the back of the instrument. The *crwth* (pronounced "crooth"), as it was called, had as a rule six strings, tuned by pairs in octaves (e.g. a a^1; e^1 e^2; b^1 b^2). The upper four strings ran over the finger-board; the lower two could not be shortened, but acted as drones, always sounding the same notes (Pl. VII/2).

Harp

Another instrument that was particularly frequent in the Celtic north-west was the *harp*, a native of Syria, so beloved in Ireland that it came to figure in that country's coat of arms. Of the most ancient European pictures of medieval harps produced in the ninth century, one occurs in an Irish work of art (the Reliquary of St. Mogue in Dublin), the other in a Carolingian manuscript (the Psalter in the University Library, Utrecht) which is strongly influenced by Syrian models.

The instrument must have been brought to England very early in its western career. The occurrence of the word "hearpe" in

the English epic poem *Beowulf* (eighth century) need not be taken
too seriously, for "harpa" or "hearpe" might have been used at
that time for any plucked instrument. But the harp may with
certainty be traced back to the tenth century in England, and it
is an eloquent fact that in a German manuscript of the 12th or
13th century we find the harp called *cythara anglica*. Ireland,
however, was regarded as the true home of the instrument. In
the fourteenth century we find an indication of this in Dante,
and as late as the seventeenth century the great German
musicologist and instrumental expert, Michael Praetorius, speaks
of the Irish harp.

The European harp of the Middle Ages consisted of three
parts (in contrast to the numerous Asiatic harps, which were
built in two parts). At the back is the sound-box, to which metal
strings are attached. Above is the neck, set at a sharp angle, often
curved a little inwards, and furnished with tuning-pins, turned
by a tuning-key. In front, supporting the neck, is the pillar,
sometimes with a slight outward curve. The shape of the whole
is heavy and squat, rather like an equilateral triangle, since
the neck is little shorter than the sound-box and pillar (Pl. IX).

Clearly, this new instrument, distributed rapidly throughout
the west, would have at once come into competition with the
lyre, since their uses were so similar. The outcome of this rivalry
left no room for doubt. The lyre possessed strings of equal length
only; if they were too thick or too loosely strung, they sounded
feebly, if they were too thin or too tightly strung they were liable
to break. The lyre, therefore, had only a small, middle compass.
The strings of the harp, on the other hand, were of different
lengths, so that the difficulty of a limited compass did not arise.
Thus music calling for an ever-increasing compass naturally had
to turn from the lyre to the harp.

Vielle or Fiddle
One of the most important stringed instruments of the Middle
Ages was the *vielle* (Fr.) or *fiddle* (MH Ger. *videle*, Sp. *vihuela de
arco*). It was not plucked like the lyres and harps of antiquity and
the Middle Ages, but played with a bow (developed in Asia).

In its original form, which was to be found in western Europe
from the tenth century on, the vielle was spade-shaped, like a

fiddle still in use today in Turkestan and Mongolia. The performer held it in front of him, supporting it on his thigh or knee.

In the tenth century there appeared also another and rather smaller type of vielle or fiddle. This was not held in front of the body, but supported on the shoulder; it was pear-shaped, the body being carved out of a single piece of wood, in the form of an elongated bowl. The strings were fastened at the base of the instrument to a special board, the tail-piece, and were stretched over a bridge. Just as in the larger vielle, there were frontal or rear pegs perpendicular to the table of the instrument. The circular sound-hole in the middle of the table, common in plucked instruments, was bridged by a small bar, running in the same direction as the strings, so that two semicircular sound-holes were formed. Precisely the same instrument is still employed to-day in the near east and the Balkan peninsula. Clearly, an instrument in widespread use among the Slavs of the Balkan peninsula had found its way into the western world. Even the name *lyra*, by which the instrument is frequently known among the southern Slavs to-day, was occasionally given to the fiddle in the early Middle Ages. But while to this very day the fiddle has remained unchanged in its original home, in Europe it has undergone manifold transformations. A clear distinction between neck and body appeared after A.D. 1200. At the same time we find the instrument assuming an elliptical shape (Pl. VIII).

The bigger fiddle, held in front of the player, was likewise significantly altered. In the twelfth century, possibly through contact with the guitar (cf. p. 52), which had entered Europe from Spain, it assumed a form approaching the shape of a figure eight, with a slight constriction at the waist (Pl. IX). This form also made it easier for the performer to control the movements of his bow.

About the middle of the thirteenth century the vielle was already so well known that a contemporary theoretician made it the subject of a study. Hieronymus de Moravia took as his starting-point the five-stringed vielle which then held the field. The information he provides concerning the tuning of the instrument is not quite clear. He seems to indicate, however, that it was tuned: d G g d¹ d¹ or d G g d¹ g¹, the d string being in both cases a bourdon or drone which could not be shortened, and which was plucked with the thumb of the left hand. For the more progressive player, who wanted his four-stringed fiddle without bourdon, Hieronymus recommended the tuning G c g d¹, thus suggesting the intervals of fourths and fifths which later became general in the tuning of stringed instruments.

Plucked Vielle (Cittern)

The increasing distribution of the fiddle throughout the west in the Middle Ages must not mislead us into thinking that the adoption of so prodigious a novelty as the bow then was could be achieved without opposition. On the contrary, again and again, throughout the whole of the Middle Ages, we meet with vielle-like instruments which were not played with a bow but were plucked in the classical manner with finger or plectrum. As early as the ninth century we find in the Lothar Psalter the representation of a spade-shaped, plucked vielle. In later centuries the larger and the smaller type, the waisted vielle and the vielle without a waist, were sometimes bowed and sometimes plucked. Indeed, in the late Middle Ages a special instrument was evolved from this plucked vielle, the pear-shaped *cittern* (Fr. *cistre*, Ger. *Cister*, It. *cetera*). It was used primarily in France, where troubadours employed it to accompany their songs.

Hurdy-Gurdy (Organistrum)

A very peculiar relation of the larger fiddle is the *hurdy-gurdy*, known during the Middle Ages as the *organistrum* or *symphonia*, which appeared in sculptures since the twelfth century. The organistrum was furnished with a wooden wheel, turned by a crank, which pressed on the strings from below and set them all vibrating simultaneously. The strings were shortened, not with the bare fingers, but with the aid of wooden bridges or tangents, operated by a system of keys. At first these tangents appear to have shortened all three strings together. As the strings were tuned to the intervals of a fourth and a fifth, the instrument produced the typical early-medieval organum progressions of parallel fifths and octaves. Later, however, the lowest string at least was allowed to sound untouched by the tangents, as a bourdon or drone. The instruments of the thirteenth century were equipped with 6–8 tangents, which provided them with a range of approximately one octave. Any personal expression on the part of the performer was out of the question in either system;

all the more so as in the early Middle Ages the organistrum was often operated by two performers (Pl. IX), one holding the instrument on his knees and turning the handle, the other working the boxed-in wooden tangents by means of a keyboard.

In the hurdy-gurdy the early medieval ideal of music was perfectly realized. The organistrum spoke with inflexible, super-personal energy, and was therefore held in such high regard that it was often portrayed in the hands of kings. In the Portico della Gloria of the cathedral at Santiago de Compostela, one of the richest representations of twelfth-century musical instruments, the organistrum is given the highest place in the very center of the portal.

Lute

The plucked *lute* is an instrument whose significance was only fully realized in later centuries. Initially it appeared in different shapes, which might also have entered Europe from different sides. Manuscripts of the ninth century depict instruments with two or three strings, a neck considerably longer than the body and a disk with rear pegs. The early lute, which is related to the Russian balalaika, may have come to Europe by way of Byzantium and the Balkans. It never achieved wide distribution in its new home, as it failed to compete with a smaller and handier lute. This newcomer at first showed a certain similarity in shape to the vielle. There was the same pear-shaped body, with a shallow bowl, and a neck growing out of the body with no definite line of demarcation. But whereas the strings of the fiddle were fastened to a tail-piece and led over a bridge, the lute used as string-holder a cross-bar which was glued directly to the table. Even more important was the position of the tuning-pegs. In the lute, in order to offset the direct pull of the strings, the peg-box was at right angles to the end of the neck, and the pegs were parallel to the table of the instrument, while in the vielle they were perpendicular to it. There were three to five strings, which were usually plucked with a little rod, and only rarely with the bare fingers. Here, as everywhere, the early Middle Ages avoided as far as possible any direct personal influence upon the quality of the tone.

This smaller type of instrument was introduced into Europe by the Moors of Spain. Its very name (Eng. lute, Ger. *Laute,*

Fr. *luth*, It. *liuto*, Sp. *laud*) shows its kinship to the Arabian instrument *al'ûd* ("the Wood"), with which it also has a close structural affinity. The lateral position of the pegs is likewise a characteristic feature of stringed instruments brought to the west by the Moors. An ivory sculpture from Cordoba, dated 968, seems to be the earliest representation of the pear-shaped lute on European soil, but the instrument did not reach its prime in Europe until the Renaissance period.

In the thirteenth century—more or less when the same thing happened to the small vielle—the body and the neck of the lute were first made in two distinct pieces. At the same time, perhaps, the other most important step was taken, whereby the back of the instrument was no longer made from one piece of wood, but from a number of separate staves glued together. This meant a substantial gain in resonance, and with that the possibility of a different, subjective kind of playing, more in keeping with the spirit of a new age. The strings had now increased in number, and they were tuned in pairs to strengthen the instrument's tone. There might be six to ten strings, with the members of each pair, or "course", tuned to the same note, or in octaves.

Guitar (Guiterne)
Not long after the lute a second plucked instrument came to Europe from Arab civilization: the *guitarra latina*, or *guiterne*, which was to be found in Spain after the twelfth century. This instrument, which possessed some of the features of the modern guitar, was distinguished by a slightly incurved body with a bowl-like back and a peg-box with lateral tuning-pegs.

Mandola
The Moors introduced yet another plucked instrument and one that would seem to have been superfluous, since in size, construction and method of playing it very closely resembled the lute. This instrument, which can be traced back to the thirteenth century in the west, was club-shaped; the strings were attached to buttons inserted in the end of the body, led over a bridge, and brought to a slightly curved peg-box, which was crowned by a little carved head. This was the *guitarra morisca* or *mandola* (*mandora*), as it came to be called later on, an instrument whose

nearest relation may be found to this day in the Malay Archipelago.

Rebec (Gigue)
Just as the vielle was sometimes plucked instead of bowed, so there appeared a bowed equivalent of the lute or mandola. The Spanish thirteenth-century *Cantigas de Sta. Maria*, one of the richest sources for our knowledge of the musical instruments of the period (cf. p. 44), shows a narrow, club-shaped instrument with two strings, supported on the knee. It is fitted with a peg-box which is fixed at right angles to the neck, as in the lute. This bowed lute was the Arab *rabâb*, which later, as the *rebec* or *gigue*, played an important part in the development of the violin. Hieronymus of Moravia writes about this instrument, and according to him the two strings were tuned at an interval of a fifth.

Psaltery
Some idea of the almost limitless capacity of the Middle Ages to absorb new instruments is afforded by the fact that after the harp, the lyre, the cittern, the lute, the guitar and the mandola had been accepted, yet another plucked instrument found its way to the west. In early illustrations one sometimes sees King David holding an instrument resembling in outline a harp or a lyre, but with a sounding-board at the back of the strings. The instrument occurs also in triangular and rectangular shape; the former was probably the *rotta* or *chrotta*, to which medieval literature often refers. This confusion of forms was reduced to order by the Moors, who introduced into Europe a new kind of instrument—still distributed throughout the east under the name of *qânûn*—more or less trapezoid in shape (Pl. IX). The *psaltery* (Fr. *psaltère*, It. *salterio*, Ger. *Psalterium*), as the instrument has been called since its first appearance in Europe in the eleventh century, was usually plucked with quills, rarely with the bare fingers. Thanks to its convenient shape, it gradually drove the older forms of the instrument from the field.

Monochord
The *monochord* (from Greek $\mu\acute{o}\nu os$ = single and $\chi o\zeta\delta\acute{\eta}$ = string) was already in use in classical antiquity. Its invention has even

been attributed to Pythagoras. It was an instrument for making acoustical measurements, consisting of a narrow, rectangular sound-box over which a single string was stretched. With the help of a movable bridge the production of various, acoustically correct, intervals was possible. From the tenth century the monochord was also used as an important aid in musical instruction. In music-making itself, however, it hardly played a role. It was a different matter in the case of the *monochord d'archet* ("with a bow"), mentioned by French authors. This will be discussed in our next chapter (cf. p. 75f).

Panpipes (Syrinx)

Among the flutes, the simplest was the ordinary vertical flute, in which the player, unaided in any way, blew against the sharp edge of a pipe. In the *panpipes* or *syrinx* a number of such vertical pipes, increasing progressively in length, and without any finger-holes, were bound together, the whole being enclosed, in the later types, in a leather case. The function of the panpipes was similar to that of the syrinx in ancient Greece. As the instrument mainly of shepherds, it appears throughout the Middle Ages, without playing any appreciable part in the music of the times. It has survived in the Pyrenees, the Balkans, and as the chosen instrument of the "Punch and Judy" show.

Recorder

Among the oriental instruments which entered the occident through Spain, there is one at least, the *recorder* (from an old meaning of the English verb "to record", to sing or warble), which was also introduced from the east through the Slav countries. The French fourteenth-century poet-composer Guillaume de Machault refers to *flaustes dont droit joues*, flutes which one plays straight, to distinguish them from the *flaustes traversaines* held across the player's face. The former are obviously recorders, instruments with a tapering bore, equipped with finger-holes and, at the upper end, with a beak-like formation, which is blocked except for a narrow channel (cf. the later German names *Blockflöte* or *Schnabelflöte* = beak-flute, and the French *flûte-à-bec*; in England the block in the beak is called a "fipple," and the instrument is sometimes referred to as a fipple-flute). Through the slit the wind is directed in a flat stream against a sharp edge, which sets up vibrations.

Pipe and Tabor
Together with the larger recorders, played with both hands, which appeared from the eleventh century onwards, we find in the twelfth century a small recorder or *pipe* (Fr. *flûtet, galoubet*; Ger. *Schwegel*) which was played with the left hand. This instrument, used primarily to provide dance music, had so narrow a bore that its fundamental note did not sound (cf. p. 294); thus three finger-holes only, two in front and one for the thumb, sufficed to bridge the fifth between the second and third partials. The one-handed pipe usually made its appearance in conjunction with a small two-headed drum, the *tabor*, played by the same performer, who generally fastened it to his forearm (Pl. X/2), his wrist or the little finger of his left hand, beating it with a drumstick held in the right hand. Sometimes also it was fastened to his shoulder, and then the performer used his own head as drumstick. Pipe and tabor were a very popular combination.

Transverse Flute
The *transverse flute*, held across the performer's face, came to Europe via Byzantium. It is the only one of the various flutes to have remained uninterruptedly in general use from classical antiquity down to the present day. The player blows directly—as in the syrinx—against the sharp edge of the mouth-hole or *embouchure* pierced in the wall of the cylindrical tube near the stopped end. The production of the tone is not mechanical, as in the recorder, so the sound is all the more variable; it is also stronger, clearer, and more penetrating. It is probably no accident that this ancient instrument, familiar in the east long before the birth of Christ—an instrument which allows the personal element considerable free play—had to wait a comparatively long time before it achieved general acceptance in Europe. During the Middle Ages it was primarily used in Germany, where it appeared for the first time in the twelfth century. It was consequently known as the *German flute* in England, the *flûte allemande* in France, the *flauta alemana* in Spain. In Germany itself, it was called at first by the old Latin name, *tibia*.

The combination of flute and drum which manifested itself

in the union of pipe and tabor has lived on, in altered form, through the ages; even today the "drum and fife" band, with its body of transverse flutes, provides an accompaniment for marching soldiers.

Shawm

The *shawm* (Ger. *Schalmei*, It. *ciaramella*, Fr. *chalemie*) was a primitive oboe with a conically-bored tube and finger-holes. It was equipped with a double reed, two laminae of thin cane bound together (cf. p. 291f). The shawm in all probability arrived in the west via Italy; at all events, the oldest known record of it comes from twelfth-century Sicily, where Arab culture played such an important role. The double reed was put right into the mouth in the eastern manner, so that the performer could breathe through his nose and play without pause, but was unable to control the tone-colour with his lips. Any suggestion of personal expression was avoided, and the sound of the instrument had all the power and astringent vigour demanded by the age.

Double Shawm

Double shawms (Pl. IX), consisting of two conical tubes of wood or bone, occasionally bound together, were used in medieval music, but they no longer held the dominant position of the antique aulos and tibia. Seventh-century Avar double shawms have been found in the burial fields of southern Hungary and northern Croatia, and various miniatures show similar instruments, often with a different number of finger-holes in each pipe. During the later part of the Middle Ages, however, this shrill and rather inefficient instrument was gradually relegated to the background.

Bagpipe

The tendency of the Middle Ages to avoid personal expression explains also the popularity of the *bagpipe*. The part played by the performer's mouth-cavity in the case of the shawm is here entrusted to a leather bag. Although we have evidence of the occurrence of the medieval bagpipe as far back as the ninth century, the instrument (Ger. *sacphîfe, Dudelsack*, Fr. *cornemuse*, It. *cornamusa*) was not fully developed until the end of the thirteenth century. It was then that, in addition to the "chanter," the pipe on which the melody is played, it was provided with "drones," pipes without finger-holes which sound unvarying low notes. In western instruments the chanter had a conical bore and was equipped with a double reed, while the drones had mostly cylindrical bores and single reeds. The bagpipe was mainly a herdsman's instrument in the early Middle Ages; for that reason it was introduced into Christmas music, and well into modern times musicians, in order to evoke the mood of the Nativity, have imitated the peculiar effect of a melody accompanied by bass drones.

Platerspiel

A variant of the bagpipe was the *Platerspiel* (bladderpipe; MH Ger. *blâterpfîfe*), which can be traced back to the thirteenth century. Here, instead of the leather bag, a bladder was used. The blow-pipe and the chanter always lay in a straight line; it is most likely, therefore, that they were rigidly connected inside the bladder. The chanter was sometimes straight, sometimes crooked. Drones were very unusual.

Horn

Among the instruments developed during antiquity in northern Europe, independently of Greece and Rome, were the various *horns*. But the lurs of Scandinavia and Denmark, and the finely-wrought horns of ancient Ireland, stood in no direct relationship to the horns of the early Middle Ages. It seems, rather, as though the far more primitive horns that now appeared in Europe were a throw-back to earlier prehistoric days, if not an entirely new beginning.

In the early Middle Ages the horn had a strongly conical bore and might be either slightly curved or straight (Pl. VIII). The curved instrument was originally the horn of the wild ox or the bison, but before long the practice arose of imitating the natural form in metal, a repetition of the prehistoric procedure. Such metal horns were to be found in all sizes, from tiny instruments only a few inches long to horns standing as high as man.

The various horns, as well as the tuba, cornetto and trumpet, to be discussed below, are instruments in which the human lips perform a role similar to that of the double reed in the shawm or bagpipe (cf. p. 291). Mouthpieces of various shapes assist in the formation of the tone. At first they formed part of the tube; later they could be separated from it.

The straight horn of metal corresponded to the curved horn in the conical shape of its tube and the lack of a bell. This instrument, too, was sometimes made very large, so that the performer had to support it on a fork half-way down its length. It was usually called the *tuba* on the strength of its similarity to the Roman instrument of that name.

In the social life of the period there was little place for the curved horn or the tuba. In their smaller forms they were used by the shepherd to call his flocks, and by the watchman in his tower to announce the approach of strangers. The large form was employed in war by foot-soldiers for signalling purposes.

Cornetto

To make the various horns suitable for anything beyond military purposes, the novel device was adopted in the eleventh century of boring finger-holes in the tube of the curved horn and the tuba. The number of these finger-holes varied greatly, but six was the favorite, as they provided the notes of the diatonic scale. England preferred a small curved horn with finger-holes; the Continent, and especially Germany, the straight form. At first natural horn was used as the material, but in later times wood prevailed. In the curved horns the tube was made of two hollowed pieces of wood glued together, over which a leather sheath was drawn to render it air-tight. Being one of the smaller horns, the instrument was called the *cornetto*, a diminutive of the It. *corno*. Similarly in Germany it was known as the *Zink*, "Zinke" being the last and smallest branch of a stag's antlers. In England it was the *cornet*.

Oliphant

Much more highly regarded than the various horns was the *oliphant*, an instrument made of an elephant's tusk, which was introduced from Byzantium in the tenth century. These valuable ivory horns, very often richly ornamented (Pl. X/1), were part of the insignia of knighthood. The oliphant was the horn that Roland sounded to call his friends when the Saracens surrounded him at Roncesvalles; and when defeat threatened, he strove to save from the foeman's grasp his most precious possessions, his sword and his horn. In England, the oliphant was also the symbol of dignity and knighthood, and someone who was granted an office or a fief received from his liege-lord not a document but an oliphant. If the instrument was made of metal instead of ivory, gold was the material used, and it is not surprising that in some representations of the Apocalypse the angels of the Day of Judgement are pictured blowing oliphants. The high value set upon the oliphant in the early Middle Ages is confirmed by the fact that far more specimens of it have come down to us than of any other instrument of the time.

Trumpet (Buisine)

To the Saracens, in their role of intermediaries, we owe also one of the most valuable wind instruments, rivalling even the oliphant in estimation. It was known in France as *buisine*, and called in Middle High German *busîne*. The first traces of the instrument, which later developed into our *trumpet*, are found in the eleventh century in southern Italy, in the immediate neighborhood of Sicily with its Arab culture. The buisine, which then had the form of a long, straight, cylindrical, or very slightly conical tube, provided with a bell, already occupied a very special place in the east, where it was reserved for priests, nobles and princes. In India monarchs would bestow it on the highest dignitaries; in Arabia it was used by the most exalted personages only, while others had to content themselves with the ordinary horn. This exclusiveness was retained by the buisine in Europe, where only members of the Court, knights and nobles used it for signalling purposes.

Organ

The Eastern Empire, heir to classical culture, also passed on one of the most important instruments of antiquity, the *organ* (from Greek *organon* = tool). It is true that the countries on the fringe of Europe—Italy, Spain and England—preserved some traditions of organ construction from antiquity, but the decisive stimulus to the development of the organ came with the introduction of a Byzantine instrument into Franconia during the reigns of Pepin and Charlemagne in the eighth century and the beginning of the ninth. This organ was not the hydraulos of antiquity, which scarcely survived the first centuries A.D. It was the simple pneumatic organ, with bellows worked by the hands or feet; in this form it quickly established itself on fresh soil. In the ninth century organs were built in Freising and Strasbourg, and Franconian organ-building was so highly esteemed that Pope John VIII summoned a master from the diocese of Freising to erect an organ equipped with the traditional flue-pipes, in Rome.

The tenth century saw the building of organs in Cologne and Canterbury. One of the largest organs of the Middle Ages was installed in the year 980 A.D. at Winchester. It possessed no fewer than 400 pipes, 26 bellows and two manuals (keyboards for the hands), each furnished with 20 sliders. One of those sliders alone caused 10 pipes, tuned in several fifths and octaves above the fundamental note, to sound simultaneously.

In spite of such imposing dimensions, these early organs were by no means satisfactory from a musical point of view. The pipes were out of tune and too loud. Sliders performed the functions of the later keys and had to be pulled out and pushed back again one at a time (Pl. VIII). Thus a melody could only be rendered in the slowest tempo, and the greatest obstacles stood in the way of anything more complicated than two-part playing. It was not until the thirteenth century that any substantial improvement was devised. Then, by degrees, the organ was given a compass of three octaves and levers replaced the sliders; but even these were so heavy and stiff that "they had to be depressed with the full weight of a clenched fist" (Praetorius).

Portative

As a counterpart to the powerful fixed organ, a small, portable and easily playable hand-organ was devised, the *portative*. This was furnished with only a few pipes, some of which, especially large, acted as drones. It could be operated entirely by one person, who carried the instrument on a strap around the neck, worked the bellows with the left hand, and with the right operated the keys, which were often just small push-buttons.

The first recorded appearance of the portative is in the thirteenth century; before long we find it distributed all over western Europe, as it had become one of the most important elements in both chamber and orchestral music.

If the portative was dedicated exclusively to secular music, the large organ came to be used more and more by the Church. From century to century the organ, soul-stirring through the immensity of its tone, established itself as the instrument of Christian worship. The leaders of the Church actively concerned themselves with organ-building, and no less a personage than the scholar Gerbert, later Pope Sylvester II, himself constructed an organ in Lombardy. By the close of the Middle Ages organ and Church had become inseparably associated.

Bell-chimes (Cymbala)

In its rigid inflexibility of tone the organ shows a certain relationship to another instrument, which perhaps also came to the west via Byzantium, the *bell-chimes* or *cymbala*, as the Middle Ages called it. As far back as the fourth century we find a late-Roman representation of an instrument consisting of a stand and four metal cups, which were struck with a small rod. In the Middle Ages such collections of little cups—hemispherical or tulip-shaped—were very popular. These early bell-chimes were tuned with a file to the diatonic major scale, hung in series from a bar, and played with hammers, wielded usually by a single performer, but sometimes by two (Pls. VIII, IX). The Christian Church, which since the sixth century had hung large, untuned bells in her towers to call the faithful to prayer, gradually came to use the cymbala as well. In the thirteenth century the instrument was first provided with clockwork. Whenever the clock struck, the chimes played a little sacred tune, with the object of turning the hearer's thoughts from earthly to heavenly concerns in a gentle and agreeable manner.

Kettledrum, Tambourine, Triangle, Cymbals

Several small percussion instruments found their way into Europe with the Saracens. All of them were soft-voiced, suitable for chamber music, the thunderous quality of percussion instruments being a development of later centuries.

The group includes: the tiny *kettledrum* (Fr. *nacaire*; Sp. *nacara*, from the Arab *naqqâra*, MH Ger. *pûke*), scarcely bigger than the fist, which always appeared in pairs; the *tambourine* (MH Ger. *rotumbes*, Old Eng. *timbrel*, Fr. *timbre*), a small, one-sided drum with a shallow frame containing little bells or jingles which was played with the bare hand; the *triangle* (Fr. *trépie*; It. *treppiede*), a suspended metal rod, bent in the form of either a triangle or a trapezoid and played upon with a second metal rod; and finally the *cymbal* (MH Ger. *zimbel*, Fr. *cymbale*; not to be confused with the above mentioned cymbala), two slightly concave plates which were softly struck together.

These four instruments were widely disseminated before the year 1300. With their light, yet insistent tone-quality, they added both precise and luminous accents to early medieval music, particularly to its dance compositions.

III
Ars NOVA AND EARLY RENAISSANCE
(1300–1500)

Fourteenth Century Italy
At the beginning of the fourteenth century music underwent substantial changes. The secular element gained in significance while sacred music lost ground. Italy, the home of Boccaccio and Petrarch, now joined France as a center of the art, and a number of gifted Italian composers wrote light and gay chamber music for voices and instruments. There was the *caccia* (hunt), a three-part composition in which the two upper voices chased each other in strict canonic imitation, while an instrumental *pes* (foot) supplied the necessary support. The text of the two voices likewise often dealt with hunting, but also with the pleasures of fishing or the happy confusion prevailing at a country fair. Another of the favorite forms of Italian secular music was the *ballata*, a lyrical composition for one or two voices of which one at least was instrumental, accompanying in a practically chordal style. Rhythmic complications abound in this highly sophisticated music, which was meant for well-trained performers and listeners. The comparatively large number of compositions that has been preserved indicates the popularity of the genre. Of its various composers, the blind organist Francesco Landini (d. 1397), whose favorite instrument was the tiny portative, achieved widest fame.

Fourteenth Century France, Ars Nova
In France, a country which could look back on a venerable artistic past, musicians were keenly aware of a radical change. Almost simultaneously two writers, the mathematician and musical theorist Jean de Muris and the poet-composer Philippe de Vitry, used the term *Ars nova* (new art) to distinguish the

style of the fourteenth century from what had prevailed previously. In particular the' use of duple time in addition to the triple time common in the thirteenth century, and the introduction of signs for more complicated and faster rhythms were emphasized with pride. But there were other innovations too, like the frequent use of the harmonic intervals of thirds and sixths, previously employed with reluctance only, and the growing reliance on *musica ficta*. This term referred to the chromatic raising or lowering of individual notes, motivated by the desire to loosen up the rather stiff tonal system of the past.

The progressive element was particularly noticeable in French secular music. The *virelai* and *rondeau* were forms of great subtlety and expressiveness, meant to be enjoyed by aristocratic music-lovers. More conservative in character was French religious music. The *isorhythmic motet* continued traditions of thirteenth-century music. Its cantus firmus, usually borrowed from a plain-song melody, was organized into a specific rhythmic pattern which, with or without modification, was repeated over and over again, thus solidifying the composition's structure.

True to the character of the earlier motet, different texts were employed simultaneously and we may well speculate that performance depended on various repetitions of the whole piece, entrusted partly to instruments. Philippe de Vitry and Guillaume de Machault, the greatest composer of the fourteenth century, wrote numerous isorhythmic motets. To Machault we owe also the first cohesive setting of the complete Ordinary of the Mass (Kyrie, Gloria, Credo, Sanctus and Agnus Dei). The absence of a text in some of its sections and the often unsingable character of the middle voices clearly indicate that to perform it the collaboration of instruments was required.

Fifteenth Century England

At the beginning of the fifteenth century English music, which had hitherto largely depended on Continental models, began to attract attention far beyond the confines of the island. In particular the compositions of John Dunstable (d. 1453) found general acclaim. He wrote mainly sacred works imbued with luxurious warmth and characterized by the typical English predilection for chordal progressions in parallel thirds and sixths. Although some of these compositions still show features of the

PLATE I

1.—Neolithic drum, found in central Germany. About 3000 B.C.

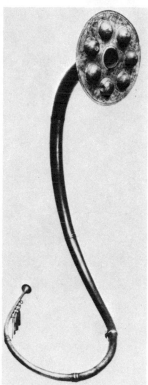

2.—Neolithic bone flute, found at Bornholm (Denmark). About 3000–2500 B.C.

3.—Bronze lur, about 600 B.C. Copenhagen, Nationalmuseet.

PLATE II

Muses playing lyra and aulos. Greek vase, middle of the fifth century,
B.C. Vienna, Kunsthistorisches Museum.

PLATE III

Flying Nike holding kithara. Greek vase, beginning of the fifth century, B.C. Vienna, Kunsthistorisches Museum.

PLATE IV

1.—Aulos-playing youth with phorbeia, dancer with krotala. Greek bowl by Epitektos, c. 520–510 B.C. London, British Museum.

2.—Players of tuba, cornu, and hydraulos, accompanying a gladiatorial fight. Roman mosaic from the amphitheater at Zliten.

PLATE V

Etruscan flutist, relief on a burial urn, c. 100 B.C. Perugia, tomb of Volumnia.

PLATE VI

Players of the karnyx. Celtic silver work from the Gundestrop cauldron, first century B.C. Copenhagen, Nationalmuseet.

PLATE VII

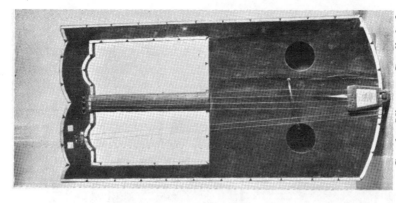

2.—Crwth. Vienna, Gesellschaft der Musikfreunde; at present Kunsthistorisches Museum.

1.—Hydraulos and case of a syrinx (?) on a Roman sarcophagus. Arles, Musée Populaire Archéologique.

PLATE VIII

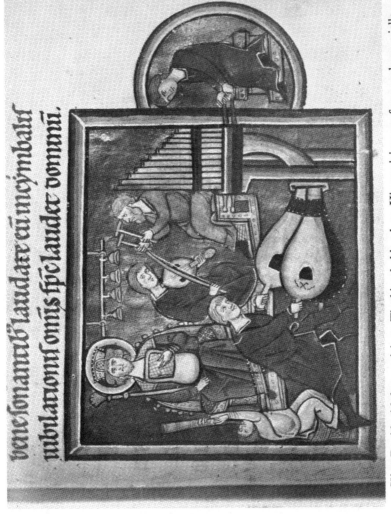

King David with his musicians. The king holds a lyre. His musicians perform on horn, vielle, cymbala, and organ. Psalter of St. Elizabeth, 13th century. Cividale del Friuli, Museo Archeologico.

PLATE IX

King David with his musicians. The king tunes his harp, the musicians perform on cymbala, two types of vielle, double shawm and transverse flute (?). In the lower corners are bells, a psaltery, and an organistrum. Psalter of the 12th century, Glasgow, University Library.

PLATE X

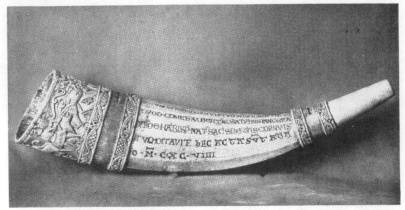

1.—Oliphant from southern Italy, 11th century. The inscription is probably a later addition. Vienna, Kunsthistorisches Museum.

2.—Players of pipe and tabor. *Cantigas de Santa Maria*, Spain, 13th century. Monasterio de Escorial.

PLATE XI

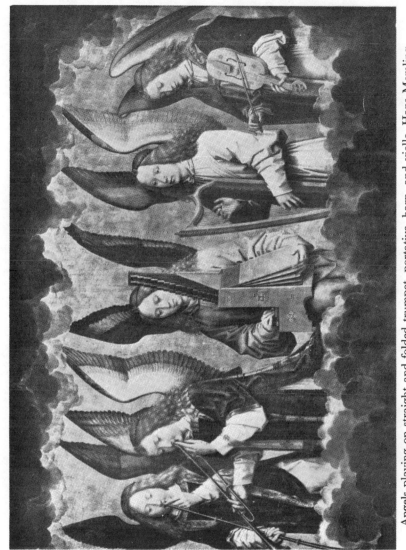

Angels playing on straight and folded trumpet, portative, harp, and vielle. Hans Memling, c. A.D. 1480. Anvers, Musée.

PLATE XII

Angels playing on psaltery, tromba marina, lute, folded trumpet, and pommer. Hans Memling, c. A.D. 1480. Anvers, Musée.

PLATE XIII

Angel playing the portative. Detail from Hans Memling, Marriage of
St. Catherine, A.D. 1479. Bruges, Hôpital de St. Jean.

PLATE XIV

Angel playing the mandola (detail). Bartolommeo Vivarini, A.D. 1474.
Venice, Santa Maria dei Fiori.

PLATE XV

Virgin and Child, with angels playing the rebec and double recorder.
Marcello Fogolino, 15th century. Milan, Museo Poldi Pezzoli.

PLATE XVI

Virgin and Child, with angels playing (clockwise, beginning at upper left) lute, tambourine, cymbals, rebec, bagpipe, harp, dulcimer, portative. Giovanni Boccati, end of 15th century. Perugia, Pinacoteca Vanucci.

PLATE XVII

Angel playing the lute. Melozzo da Forli, second half of 15th century.
Rome, Museo del Vaticano.

PLATE XVIII

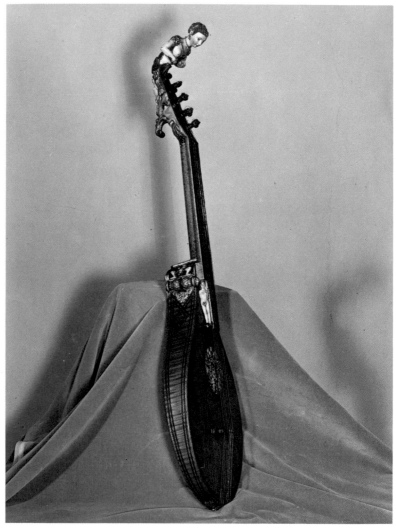

Cittern with Lucretia stabbing herself. The cittern was made by Girolamo de Virchis in Brescia, A.D. 1574, for Archduke Ferdinand of
Tyrol. Vienna, Kunsthistorisches Museum.

PLATE XIX

Men operating the bellows of the old organ in the cathedral of Halberstadt, Germany. From Michael Praetorius, *Syntagma Musicum*, 1618.

PLATE XX

Musicians playing (from l. to r.) kettledrums, cittern, tambourine,
triangle, snare drum. Bernardino Luini, around A.D. 1500. Milan,
Pinacoteca di Brera.

PLATE XXI

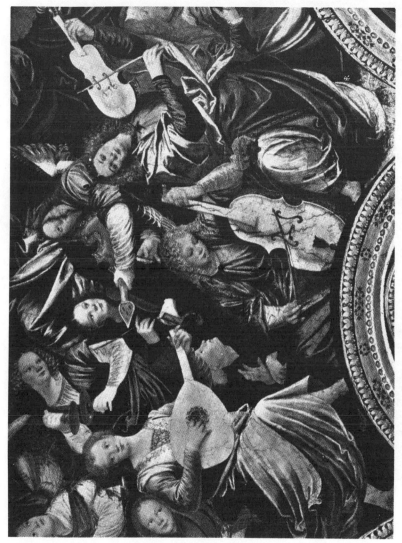

Angelic concert (detail). The angels play (from l. to r.): lute, cymbals, violin, a kind of vielle, violoncello, viola. Gaudenzio Ferrari, 1534. Saronno, Duomo.

PLATE XXII

Angel playing the lira da braccio (detail). Vittore Carpaccio, early
16th century. Venice, Accademia.

PLATE XXIII

Guitar player. Engraving by Marcantonio Raimondi, c. A.D. 1510–15.
The musician's right foot is resting on the guitar case.

PLATE XXIV

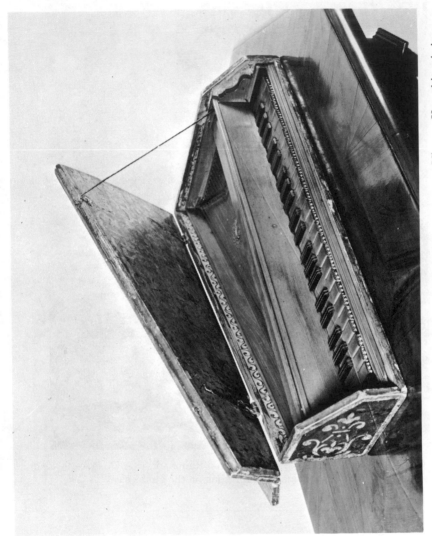

Spinettino with "short octave". Italian, 16th or 17th century. Vienna, Kunsthistorisches Museum.

PLATE XXV

Cembalo with one 8′ register. Florence, middle of 16th century. Nürnberg,
Neupert Collection in Germanisches Nationalmuseum.

PLATE XXVI

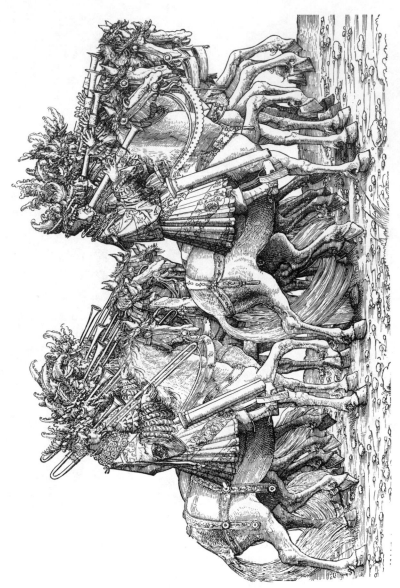

Mounted musicians playing on trombones and pommers. Hans Burgkmair, around 1500.
Detail from Triumphal Procession of Emperor Maximilian.

PLATE XXVII

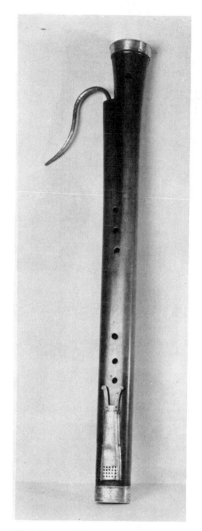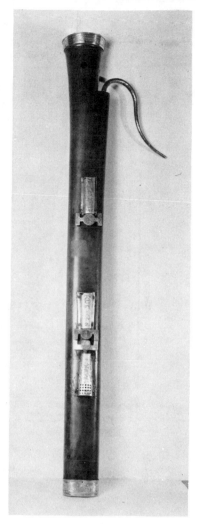

Dulzian, 16th century. The upper brass rim bears the engraved inscription (in German):

> I am called a Dulzian
> Though not well known to every man.
> And if to play me well you yearn,
> You first my fingering must learn.
>   (Trans. C. Zytowski)

Vienna, Gesellschaft der Musikfreunde, at present Kunsthistorisches Museum.

PLATE XXVIII

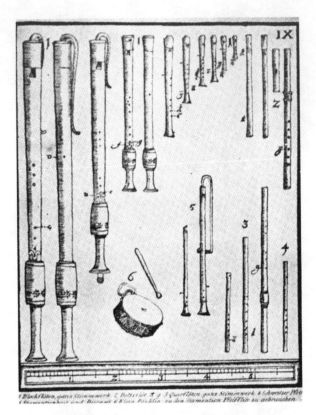

1. Recorders of different sizes; 2. four Dolzflöten; 3. three transverse flutes; 4. Swiss pipe; 5. two tabor-pipes; 6. tabor. From Michael Praetorius, *Syntagma Musicum*, 1618.

PLATE XXIX

A player on the crumhorn (detail). Vittore Carpaccio, early 16th century. Venice, Accademia.

PLATE XXX

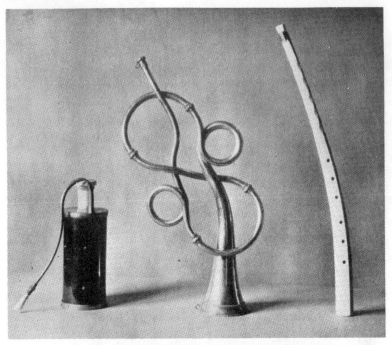

1.—Tenor rackett by I. C. Denner, around 1700; silver-gilt trumpet in fancy form by A. Schnitzer, Nürnberg, 1598; ivory cornetto of the 16th or 17th century. Vienna, Gesellschaft der Musikfreunde, at present Kunsthistorisches Museum.

2.—Bible regal, in front of it a regal pipe, around 1600. Formerly: Berlin, Staatliche Sammlung alter Musikinstrumente (lost during the war).

PLATE XXXI

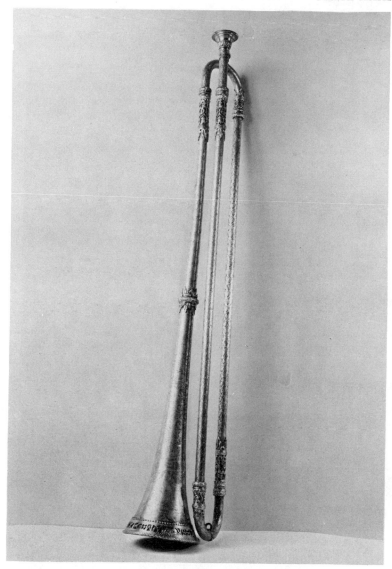

Silver trumpet by Anton Schnitzer, Nürnberg, 1581. Vienna,
Kunsthistorisches Museum.

PLATE XXXII

Double spinet by Martinus van der Biest, Anvers, 1580. Nürnberg, Germanisches Nationalmuseum.

medieval conception, others, with their careful observation of structural details in the text, and their flexible melodic lines, point to future developments.

Burgundian School

The English school of composers lost its significance after the middle of the century. Some of its main tenets were carried on, however, by composers of France and the Low Countries. Duke Philip the Good of Burgundy, one of the most important patrons of the arts, assembled eminent musicians at his court, who in turn travelled to other countries. Leaders of this international school of composers, which reached its climax after the middle of the century, were Gilles Binchois (d. 1460) and Guillaume Dufay (d. 1474). The latter spent more than a dozen years in Florence, Bologna, Torino and, most of all, as a member of the Papal Chapel, in Rome. This provided Dufay with an opportunity to become thoroughly acquainted with the spirit of the Italian Renaissance.

The Renaissance movement, which had started in Italy as an attempt to revive Greek and Latin literature, gradually changed into a trend to liberate the human spirit from the shackles of medieval scholasticism. In the field of the arts, the Renaissance aimed at achieving simplicity, clarity, and structural balance. It is true that Italy in the fifteenth century, and even in the early sixteenth century, was too preoccupied with the visual arts to produce great composers of her own. However, she invited guests from the north, who in turn showed themselves receptive to the new ideas. These taught Dufay, and before long also other members of the Burgundian school, the value of smooth melodic lines, a transparent harmonic texture and well-proportioned forms. The Burgundian composers who appropriated the aesthetic ideals of the south were active in various fields. The largest of their works were masses, which introduced a cantus firmus in long notes in the tenor and used this tune over and over again throughout the composition. This cantus firmus could be of sacred or of secular origin—borrowed, for instance, from a folk-song or even from a dance tune, the latter not seeming at all incongruous in the Renaissance period. Dufay also wrote an isorhythmic motet based on a cantus firmus and using two different texts. It was performed in 1436 at the consecration of the cathedral in Florence. A chronicler reports that a large number of singers and various players of trumpets, vielles and other instruments performed on this occasion, filling "the whole space of the temple with choruses of harmony."

Isorhythmic motets, however, were considered to be old-fashioned by the Burgundians and employed only on special, solemn occasions. They preferred a more informal type of motet with a single religious text in Latin and no cantus firmus at all, or a cantus firmus given to the top voice, where it appeared in rich ornamentation and freed from its rhythmic straightjacket.

In the field of secular music the *chanson* was the favorite form of the time. Like the fourteenth century ballata it was written for a solo singer and instruments. The text was usually in French and dealt with the eternal topic of love, preferably unrequited love, which infused the chansons with an almost romantic spirit of tender melancholy.

Franco–Flemish Composers

During the next generation the process of assimilating the northern spirit to the aesthetic ideals of the Italian Renaissance gradually slowed up. Johannes Ockeghem (d. 1495), the best composer of this group, was probably born in Flanders. He spent most of his life in France and never went to Italy. In his compositions the earlier transparency of texture gave way to a more solid and compact fabric. Compositions in three voices became obsolete and the use of four parts the rule. In exceptional cases compositions with a larger number of voices, even up to 36, were written. In performances, the handful of soloists was gradually replaced by bigger groups of vocalists and instrumentalists. Ockeghem moved the range of his compositions perceptibly downward, thus providing them with a darker and heavier character. Contrapuntal devices, which appealed more to the northern Gothic spirit than to the southern Renaissance mentality, were increasingly used and these intellectual games became more and more involved.

The mass was still one of the most important forms of the time. Ockeghem wrote masses with or without a cantus firmus, the former treating the borrowed melody quite freely. In the newly-developed *parody mass* not only a melody, but a complete sacred or secular piece was used as model and adapted, variation-like, to the changing requirements of the five movements. Motets were usually written for four or more voices, which used increasingly the same thematic material and were equal in importance.

The chanson for voices and instruments remained dominant in secular music. Here, too, the melodic material was distributed over all the voices. It demonstrates the popularity of the genre that the very first book of polyphonic music to appear in print was a collection of chansons. It was entitled *Harmonice Musices Odhecaton* ("One Hundred Pieces of Harmonic Music") and issued by Ottaviano dei Petrucci in Venice, 1501. Most of the pieces were printed without text, which indicates that the publisher considered a purely instrumental performance to be quite adequate.

Dance Music

Dance music gained in significance during the Ars nova and Early Renaissance periods. Monophonic, or two-part *estampies*, consisting of 4–7 sections, were used in fourteenth-century France and England, while Italy preferred the fast and gay *saltarello*. Dancing played a particularly important role during the fifteenth century, and dancing masters enjoyed a high esteem, even at the princely courts of the time. The choreography and the cantus firmus to a number of elegant *basse dances* have survived. Stringed, wind, and percussion instruments improvised the music on the basis of these tunes. In German sources, moreover, some elaborate four-part settings of dances with strong folk-song-like elements have been preserved and they help to convey a clearer picture of the form.

The Instruments

Thus, during the fourteenth and fifteenth centuries, instruments became a factor of the utmost importance in the musical life of Europe. They were used in polyphonic music to reinforce the human voices and to execute short introductions and interludes. Texts were completely missing in certain parts of the compositions, or else these parts were melodically unsuitable for singers. Obviously, here too instruments were required. And finally, numerous complete compositions without text have been preserved, which can only have been intended for players.

The instruments had to acquire greater handiness to meet the demands of the faster and rhythmically more complex music produced by composers of the Ars nova and Early Renaissance. Moreover, a conscious process of selection was at work. Certain instruments gained in estimation; others were gradually discarded.

Though instruments were in great demand, their role was by no means clearly spelled out. The composer never supplied exact instructions as to which specific instrument ought to be chosen. Partial exceptions to this rule were the arrangements of polyphonic compositions for keyboard instruments which the fourteenth and in particular the fifteenth century supplied. But even in these cases the performer had a choice between several different keyboard instruments available at the time.

This freedom of execution may have been related to the fact that since earliest times instrumentalists had been used to improvisation, to adapting and ornamenting the melodic line according to the nature and the technical resources of their instrument. Thus, in notated dance music, frequently no more than the skeleton of the tune was indicated, and it was left to the players to give a proper interpretation of this shorthand notation. Quite often singers performed from music, while instrumentalists played without it.

Most of the instruments of this time were rather delicate and weak. They were lightly and flimsily constructed and so only very few of them have survived. One of the main sources for our knowledge of their appearance and use is provided by the painters and sculptors of the fourteenth and in particular the fifteenth century, who seem to have felt that the banquets and dances, the tournaments and battles, and most of all, the various religious scenes they depicted needed enriching by the inclusion of musical performances. In these pictorial representations the musicians appear mostly in groups. Instruments of like tone were frequently combined; but even more numerous were groupings which provided contrast and variety. Thus a singer might be found in the company of players on a bowed stringed instrument, a plucked instrument, a woodwind, and even a percussion instrument. A multitude of light and gay sounds is suggested here, corresponding to the radiant colors of the paintings. The instruments of discrepant tone were able to differentiate the separate parts envisaged in the period of Landino, Dunstable and Dufay. Their contrasting sound-quality gave full emphasis to the polyphonic life of the compositions.

Yet two different trends, which became increasingly evident in fifteenth-century music, began to change this situation. One of these tendencies was dictated by ideas conceived in the north, the other by ideas of southern origin. Although quite different in character, they both contributed in greatly altering the prevailing picture.

The aim of the Netherlands composers of extending the range of music downward led to the construction of large wind and stringed instruments reaching deep into the bass register. At the same time northern organs were equipped with a pedal for playing low notes.

On the other hand, the growing trend toward exploring harmonic devices, which originated in the spirit of the Italian Renaissance and was paralleled by the painters' aim of creating a feeling of depth in their canvases, led to a growing interest in instruments on which several notes could be played simultaneously. The many-stringed lute, guitar and harp served this purpose to some extent, but instruments equipped with a keyboard were even more suitable. The organ was now no longer the only keyboard instrument available. The fourteenth century saw the advent of stringed keyboard instruments, which were, of course, easier to handle and less costly. Thus keyboard music slowly gained in significance. Even a particular type of notation, known as "tablature," was developed for the various keyboard instruments.

The rising interest in the different claviers and organs led to attempts to improve the method of their tuning. "Just intonation," which would have seemed ideal for this purpose, proved to be impractical for compositions which went beyond a very limited modulatory range. A new method had to be developed to meet the requirements of the time. "Mean-tone temperament", which was eventually created (cf. p. 281), represents an ingenious compromise accommodating to perfection the range of tonalities employed during the Renaissance period.

We shall now examine the specific alterations of individual instruments.

Vielle (Fiddle)

The *vielle* underwent radical changes during the fourteenth and fifteenth centuries, which enabled it to gain supremacy over the other stringed instruments played with a bow. In the smaller, shouldered fiddle, which took the lead at this time, the primitive vaulted body was replaced by a trimly built sound-box consisting of a flat or slightly curved back, straight side walls, or ribs, and a table which was usually flat. This table was pierced with sound-holes whose original, plain, semicircular shape was changed into a single slender C or two Cs, one superimposed on the other (Pl. XI). The new sound-box had the advantage of greater lightness and handiness; moreover, its resonance was infinitely superior to that of the clumsy older type. A further important modification in the construction of the small vielle concerned the adoption of the incurved waist, already found in large fiddles of the twelfth century. This waist made it possible for the musician to play on individual strings and to break away from the medieval habit of sounding several strings simultaneously. A third improvement related to the manner of fastening the upper ends of the strings. Generally speaking the vielle, throughout the Middle Ages, was furnished with five pegs, which were perpendicular to the finger-board (Pl. XI). In rare exceptions, however—under the influence of the rebec—lateral pegs were used, arranged parallel to the table, as they are in our modern stringed instruments. In this case the peg-box was usually bent back a little. The advantages of this arrangement were a greater resistance to the pull of the strings and an increased handiness of the pegs. Actually, in the early Renaissance the true value of this improvement was still far from realized, and instruments with the rebec head were rare before the sixteenth century.

Hurdy-Gurdy (Organistrum)

Significant of the artistic outlook prevalent during the fourteenth and fifteenth centuries was the fate of the *organistrum*. The size of the early medieval instrument was radically reduced, to make it easier to handle, and it was held up by a thong running round the player's neck. It could be played by a single performer, who operated the keys with his left hand and the wheel with his right. Even so, the constantly sounding drone and the rigid, unyielding tone-quality could not be abolished. The hurdy-gurdy was therefore hardly regarded as a true musical instrument; it suffered an extraordinary social decline, sinking step by step, until it finally degenerated into the stock-in-trade of the pedlar and the blind beggar.

Cittern

Both the old vielle without waist and the new vielle with waist were also used, during the fourteenth and fifteenth centuries, as plucked instruments. In the *cittern* (Pl. XIX), the pear-shaped body, the strings taken over a bridge to the rib of the instrument, and the position of the pegs in a board, all clearly indicate that this instrument was originally nothing but an old-type vielle. At the same time, the characteristics of a true plucked instrument are also clearly marked. The strings, made of wire, are arranged in pairs of courses, as in the lute, the members of each pair being tuned in unison or octaves, to strengthen the weak tone of the instrument. Fifteenth-century musicians, moreover, favored playing with the bare fingers rather than with a plectrum, and they also replaced the peg-board with a sickle-shaped peg-box with lateral pegs.

Guitar

The *guitarra latina*, *guiterne* or *quinterne*, as it was eventually called, failed to achieve wide distribution in Europe. This instrument, with its slightly incurved body and lateral tuning-pegs, was unable to compete with the more compact and fuller-sounding lute. The situation was somewhat different in Spain, which never took to the lute, although the peninsula had in fact been the instrument's homeland in Europe. There, too, the guiterne failed to win lasting acceptance, but it was replaced by an instrument which resembled it in many respects and appeared like an improved version of itself. This was in fact a waisted, plucked vielle with shallow ribs, flat back, and lateral pegs. It was only logical that the Spaniards, who referred to the bowed vielle as *vihuela de arco*, should call this instrument, whose strings were plucked by hand, *vihuela de mano*; and if it was played with a plectrum, it was called *vihuela de peñola*. Before long the *vihuela* achieved great popularity in Spain, developing there into a kind of national instrument.

Lute

Up to the thirteenth century the distribution of the *lute* was limited to western Europe. A hundred years later the instrument was

known in Italy and Germany; both Dante and Boccaccio
mention it, as well as Heinrich von Neuenstadt. Nevertheless,
the lute was used only sparsely, for it had a rival in its relation,
the mandola, which by virtue of its simpler construction was
easier to make as well as to play. During the fifteenth century,
however, the situation was reversed; the smaller, weaker and
clumsier mandola was pushed into the background, while the
lute gradually achieved a dominant position.

Various circumstances were responsible for the success of the
lute (Pls. XII, XVI, XVII). The instrument sounded most
effective both in small and large ensembles, since its dry, neutral
tone provided the happiest contrast to the human voice, the
wind and the bowed instruments. It was also favored as a solo
instrument, since it was possible to render a whole polyphonic
composition on a single lute, the clarity of its sound fulfilling the
Renaissance desire for lucidity and precision. Finally, the lute
showed a remarkable capacity to adapt itself to the needs of
Renaissance music. During the fifteenth century it underwent
important technical improvements. In order to enlarge its
compass, the number of strings was gradually increased from six
to eleven, the highest of which was designed for the clear render-
ing of the melody, while the others, arranged in pairs, or courses,
provided the accompaniment (Pl. XVII). In about 1480 the
classical stringing of the lute was: A-a, d-d', g-g', b-b, e'-e', a;
or the same one tone lower.

The Asiatic plectrum of the early Middle Ages was gradually
abandoned, being sacrificed to the needs of polyphonic playing
and flexible performance. To improve the grip of the left hand,
and thus obtain a pure intonation, loops of gut, the "frets,"
were tied round the neck, increasing in the course of time from
four to eight in number. Finally, as the demand grew for greater
beauty and volume of tone, the body of the instrument itself was
made considerably larger, and the curved shell was fashioned
of narrow staves made from precious woods or ivory; at the same
time, the little sound-holes pierced here and there in the table
of the older lutes were united in one large central hole, covered
with a beautifully carved "rose."

Mandola
Nothing better illustrates the importance attained by the lute

during the course of the fifteenth century than the position of the *mandola*. From being a successful competitor of the lute, the mandola declined during the fifteenth century into an imitator of its technically superior rival. It adopted the body-shape of the lute, with its handsomely carved central rose and its back built up from a number of separate staves. The strings were no longer carried over a bridge to the base of the body, but were fixed, as in the lute, to a cross-bar glued to the table (Pl. XIV). If the mandola had not retained its old construction, with the neck all of a piece with the body, and above all the slightly curved peg-box, with a carved scroll, it might well have been taken for a smaller variety of the lute. Tinctor, who in 1499 described the instruments of his time, went so far as to say: "It is quite clear that the mandola was derived from the lute."

Rebec

The victory of the lute over the mandola is the more remarkable as the mandola was itself victor over another instrument, which was now compelled to imitate all the modifications taken over from the lute, even though they conflicted with its fundamental character. In the Middle Ages the player of the *rebec* (also called *rubeba* and *gigue*) was already beginning to hold it, not in front of the body, but on the shoulder, in the same way as the vielle. But in this position the straight peg-box, attached to the neck at right angles as in the lute, was in the way, and it was therefore superseded by the mandola's slightly curved peg-box. The club-shaped rebec thus closely resembled the club-shaped mandola, and the history of the newly created "bowed mandola" coincided for quite some time with that of its plucked original. The rebec with its three or four strings clung as obstinately as the mandola to the unity of neck and body (Pl. XVI), although this made any technical improvement impossible. Moreover, the bowed instrument began to assume the slightly broadened body of the mandola which rendered access to the separate strings extremely difficult. Even the old sound-rose, common among plucked instruments, was retained and combined with the C-holes of bowed instruments (Pl. XV). While the vielle embodied progressive elements, the rebec displayed loyalty to tradition; it clung to its connection with the mandola even to its own detriment. Certainly there were attempts to curtail the swelling sides and to smooth away the belly, but these were not radical enough to do much good. At the end of the fifteenth century it was at last decided to break free from the cramping influence of the mandola and to return to the original club shape. The projecting sides were thus done away with, but the resulting small four-stringed instrument had a very weak tone, and it was technically too clumsy, because of its one-piece neck and body, to play a significant part in the music of the dawning new age.

Harp
The *harp* (called in French *harpe*, in German *Harfe*, in Italian *arpa*) was one of the few instruments which passed the fourteenth century without undergoing a notable transformation. In the late Middle Ages there was a tendency to increase the range of the instrument downwards, but the only result of this development was a slight change in the proportions of the three main sections of the harp's body. The sound-board and the pillar, which was occasionally curved, were lengthened, so that strings of a deeper pitch could be incorporated; and thus, from the early medieval form, roughly like an equilateral triangle, there evolved in the course of the fifteenth century a taller, more slender form, known as the "Gothic" harp, in which, moreover, all three parts—sound-board, neck and pillar—were clearly differentiated from one another (Pls. XI, XVI).

Psaltery
During the fourteenth and fifteenth centuries the strings of the *psaltery* were often arranged in pairs, or even in groups of three, to strengthen the instrument's weak tone. The somewhat clumsy trapezoid shape gave way to the more pleasing double-winged or "pig's head" form (Pl. XII); divided psalteries in the form of a single wing (Fr. *micanon*) were also used occasionally after the fourteenth century. Moreover, the plectrum or quill was often replaced by the bare fingers, which were better suited to the more personal attitude to music predominant at the time. But no basic improvement occurred and the psaltery lost ground during the fifteenth century.

Dulcimer
A variant of the psaltery was the *dulcimer* (from Latin *dulce melos* =

sweet melody), known in France as *doucemelle*, in Italy as *dolcemela*, and in Spain as *dulcema*. It was distinguished from the psaltery proper less by its construction than by the way in which it was played. The instrument was usually trapezoidal or rectangular in shape, and the metal strings, which were stretched horizontally over two bridges, were struck in the Slavo-German fashion with two padded sticks (Pl. XVI). This method of playing the dulcimer, coming from the east, can scarcely have reached Europe before the fifteenth century, and the climax of the instrument's career was not attained until some centuries later.

Tromba Marina

At about the same time as the dulcimer, what was perhaps the strangest of all the stringed instruments found its way into the west—the *tromba marina*. The position of its head, with pegs perpendicular to the plane of the table, as in the vielle, and still more the method of playing the instrument, show that it was, like the dulcimer, of Slavonic origin. The tromba marina was a truncated pyramid in shape, with either three or four sides, narrow at the base but extremely long, from three to five or even seven feet (Pl. XII). There was usually only one long main string and, rarely, a shorter second string. The main string was taken over a shoe-shaped bridge, one end of which did not quite touch the table, so that the vibrations of the string caused the free end to drum very rapidly against the table, producing a rasping sound. The method of holding the instrument was as curious as its construction. Pressing the upper end with the peg-box to his chest, the performer held the lower end sticking up in the air and drew his bow, not below his left hand, as might have been expected, but above it. Finally, one finger of the left hand touched the string very lightly, causing it to vibrate fractionally, thus producing harmonics or flageolet notes (cf. p. 284). The medieval name for this strange instrument was *monochord d'archet* (bowed single-string), on account of its one long main string and its resemblance to the ancient plucked instrument used for acoustical measurements. Later it was known by names which are not easily explicable. The English called it *trumpet marine*, the French *trompette marine*, the Italians *tromba marina*, and the Germans *Trumscheit*, *Nonnengeige*, or *Marientrompete*. The reference to the trumpet might be due to the fact that the instrument produced a series of notes similar to those sounded by a valveless trumpet; moreover, the strange rattling caused by the freely vibrating bridge gave the monochord's tone a somewhat trumpet-like quality. The instrument was used by nuns in their convents in place of the trumpet, which accounts for the German names Nonnengeige and Marientrompete. It does not seem impossible that the name trumpet marine is derived from Marientrompete; although, as we shall see later (cf. p. 139), it also had nautical associations. Europe, particularly Germany and the Netherlands, adopted this exotic eastern guest with enthusiasm, but its curious and unusual character prevented it from ever being completely assimilated.

While monochord, psaltery and dulcimer played only a peripheral role in the music of the Early Renaissance, descendants of these instruments assumed growing significance.

Clavichord

The *clavichord* is of very early origin. The Middle Ages used, at times, a combination of several plucked monochords with strings of varying tension and thickness. In the fourteenth century we find no less than nineteen monochords combined. The crude instrument of the theoreticians was now transformed into a useful instrument of music. This came about in a fashion characteristic of the times: through the adoption of important features found in other instruments. From the hurdy-gurdy it was learned that strings could be shortened by the use of tangents. From the organ the system of keys was derived which made a proper application of the tangent mechanism possible. Thus was evolved the action shown in Fig. 1. When the front part e of the key is depressed, its back part d rises and the metal tangent c is impelled against the string a–b, which is simultaneously both shortened and set in vibration. But only the section of the string marked b is allowed to sound, for section a is prevented from vibrating freely by a cloth wrapping, which serves as damper. Since the string ceases to vibrate at the point of impact with the tangent, it follows that it is quite possible to connect a single string with several keys, whose tangents strike it at different points, and thus produce notes of differing pitch. The saving of space and material implicit in this principle led to the general use of the *fretted* or *gebundenes* clavichord, as it was called. In this up to four, or even five, successive chromatic notes could be produced on a single string, or, more commonly, on a pair of strings. Mostly, however, two notes only were played on one string or a pair of strings.

The clavichord was usually built in rectangular form with metal strings running at right angles to the short, stubby keys. The instrument was small in size; it had no legs and was commonly placed on a table. Although two strings were usually tuned to each of its notes, its tone was extremely weak. Indeed, the player had to depress the keys gently, as too vigorous an attack would have increased the tension of the strings and thus raised the pitch of the notes. On the other hand, a slight shaking

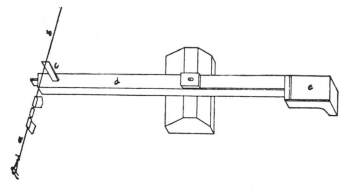

FIG. 1. Clavichord Key

movement of the fingers as they depressed the keys achieved a vibrato effect, the so-called *Bebung*, unique among keyboard instruments.

During the fifteenth century some clavichords were made with only the three most important semitones (Bb, F# and C#). However, instruments with all five semitones were also constructed and eventually this more efficient type was generally adopted. A treatise from the middle of the fifteenth century even describes a clavichord with nine pairs of strings and thirty-seven keys (compass B-b²).

The instrument was originally called, after its model, *monochord* (Fr. *manicorde*), regardless of the fact that it no longer had only one string. Then, because the device used to shorten the strings had a certain resemblance in shape to the key (Latin *clavis*) of a medieval lock, the instrument came to be known as the "key-string" instrument, or clavichord.

In addition to the gentle clavichord, other keyboard instruments were devised which employed a different principle of sound production.

Plucked Keyboard Instruments

The *spinet* and *harpsichord* were keyboard instruments in which the strings were plucked by means of a plectrum. In the fully developed instruments, a small wooden rod or jack (Fig. 2)

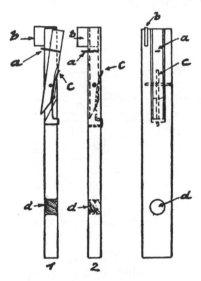

FIG. 2. Jack of the spinet or harpsichord

stood on the far end of each key. A movable wooden tongue, from which a plectrum of crow-quill or leather (a) projected horizontally, was pivoted in its upper end. A hog's bristle (c), or some other kind of spring, held the tongue in an upright position (phase 2). When the key was depressed, the jack rose and the plectrum plucked the string, which lay above it. When the key was released, a lead weight (d), let into the bottom of the jack, caused it to fall and thus return to its original position. As it did so, the tongue turned back and the plectrum slid past the string (phase 1), so that the string was not plucked a second time.

Damping was contrived by means of a small piece of cloth (b) fixed to the upper end of the jack. With plucked keyboard instruments the whole string was set vibrating, not merely a part of it, as with the clavichord, so there had to be a separate string for every note. The tone of these instruments was full and loud; it could not be modified by any variation of pressure on the keyboard, and thus had the disadvantage of inflexibility.

The *spinet* is known under various names: It. *spinetto*, from the Lat. *spina* = thorn; MH Ger. *schachtbrett*, Fr. *eschiquier*, both meaning chessboard, possibly on account of the instrument's shape; Eng. *virginal* or *virginals*, from the Latin *virga* = rod or jack. Elizabethan and Jacobean England, however, believed the name was derived from the Latin *virgo* = virgin, as may be gathered from the following title of a set of keyboard compositions: *Parthenia, or the Maidenhead of the first Musicke that ever was printed for the virginals*; the title-page of this publication from 1612–13 shows a young girl playing the virginals. In the spinet, as in the clavichord, the strings ran at right angles to the keys. Obviously, the keys could not be uniform in length; those for the lower notes were longer and harder to depress than those for the higher notes. As long as the range of the instrument was narrow this mattered little; but when the number of strings was increased, a simple expedient was adopted: the keyboard was placed at the end of the instrument instead of the side. The keys now ran in the same direction as the strings and could all be made of equal length.

The resulting instrument was the *harpsichord* (It. *clavicembalo*, or just *cembalo*, Fr. *clavecin*, Ger. *Clavicymbel*; in England the term *virginal* was at first applied also to it). The harpsichord was wing-shaped and larger and louder than the spinet.

A third plucked keyboard instrument was likewise in use at this time, the upright harpsichord or *clavicytherium*. This instrument, a sort of forerunner of the upright piano, had a perpendicular triangular or wing-shaped sound-board at right angles to the keyboard. The mechanism of the clavicytherium was rather complicated, as the jacks had to be pushed forward to pluck the strings and afterwards retracted. However, the instrument saved space and had a full tone, as the sound-board faced the listener, advantages which accounted for its occasional use.

The first beginnings of these plucked keyboard instruments

are still, for the most part, obscure. It seems that the growing interest in polyphonic and harmonic expression during the fourteenth and fifteenth centuries encouraged various experiments to increase the efficiency of the psaltery and the dulcimer by equipping them with a keyboard. Various types of plucking mechanisms and various shapes were developed before the three main forms discussed above—all rather small, without legs and meant to be placed on a table—were generally adopted. The clavicytherium and the harpsichord (the latter with a range of nearly four octaves) seem to have been known at the beginning of the fifteenth century; spinets appeared a few decades later.

Recorder
Among the woodwind instruments the *recorder* enjoyed special popularity. It was made in various sizes and had a reverse conical bore, tapering towards the lower end. The instrument was equipped with seven holes in front. The lowest of them, operated by the little finger, was duplicated, appearing both on the right and the left of the instrument, as some performers held the instrument with the left hand below the right, and some with the right hand below the left; the unused hole was stopped with wax. The tone of the recorder had a rather cool and impersonal quality, conforming to the aesthetic ideals of the time.

Pipe and Tabor
The longer, smaller-bored, one-handed recorder, commonly known as the *pipe*, was still mainly used, as in the early Middle Ages, with the drum, or *tabor*. In the fifteenth century the pipe was made in two sizes, soprano and tenor. The combination of pipe and tabor was particularly popular in western and southern Europe, while Germany was slow to accept it. In a painting of the Battle of Sinalunga in the Palazzo Publico of Siena, the infantry are preceded by men playing the pipe and drum and the cavalry by trumpeters.

Tambourin du Béarn
In France and Italy the one-handed pipe was at times also combined with a stringed instrument which consisted of a rectangular sound-box equipped with two or three gut strings tuned in tonic and dominant. It was attached to the left shoulder of the

player, who hit the strings with a stick held in his right hand. He thus produced a bourdon accompaniment to the tune of the thin pipe, which he operated with his left hand. The stringed instrument was known under various names, such as *tambourin du Béarn*, *tambourin de Provence*, *tamboril*, or *tambour de Gascogne*.

Double Recorder

Nothing more clearly illustrates the popularity of the recorder in the late Middle Ages than the fact that it completely superseded the double shawms of antiquity and the early Middle Ages. The pairs of woodwind instruments which were sometimes used during the fourteenth and fifteenth centuries were, as a rule, *two one-handed recorders*, played with the performer's left and right hands respectively (Pl. XV). This can hardly have been an original creation, however. It is far more probable that the Renaissance, in its pursuit of classical antiquity, was imitating the Greek aulos or the Roman tibia in this form of double flute. Indeed, this notion is so firmly rooted that even today the aulos and the tibia are usually, and wrongly, referred to as flutes.

Transverse Flute

The *transverse flute*, probably on account of its harsher tone, was far less used than the recorder and served above all as a military instrument. In its simple cylindrical form, with a narrow bore and six finger-holes, it became, like the one-handed flute, associated with the drum. The Swiss lansquenets, who played such an important part in the military history of the time, preferred the transverse flute, so it was often called the *Schweizerpfeiff*, or *Swiss pipe*.

The commonest flute-like instrument of the time, and possibly the wind instrument most in use, was the tiny *portative*. Because it was closely related to the large church organ, it will be discussed with that instrument (see p. 86).

Shawm, Pommer

Among the wind instruments, those equipped with reeds underwent an especially radical change during the fourteenth and fifteenth centuries. The shrill double *shawm* finally disappeared, along with the rigid Platerspiel. The single *shawm* with double reed, the group's chief instrument, on the other hand, developed appreciably. Like the recorder, it now had seven holes in front, the lowest, for the little finger, usually being doubled. Occasionally there was also a thumb-hole in the rear. The instrument was usually equipped with a tiny, cup-shaped wooden device, the *pirouette*, which separated the double reed from the tube of the instrument. The pirouette served as support for the lips of the player, who took the reed into his mouth in the ancient oriental manner.

The shawm was made in two sizes, a small soprano and a larger contralto instrument a fifth deeper (Pl. XII), called in Fr. *bombarde,* in Ger. *Pommer.* A remarkable contrivance was to be found in the bombarde. Because of the larger size, and the consequent difficulty in reaching the lowest hole, this was sometimes covered with a key protected by a little wooden barrel, known as a *fontanelle.* The upper end of this key was fitted with a double touch-piece, one side for the right hand, the other for the left. While shawm and pommer were combined in Renaissance ensembles with instruments of the most contrasting character, their sharp, clear tone rendered them particularly suitable for use with trumpets and percussion. They served also as symbols of the pastoral mood.

Bagpipe
The improvements in the shawm automatically benefited the *bagpipe.* In the fifteenth century its chanter was fashioned more carefully and provided with seven finger-holes. There were still bagpipes with a chanter only and no drones, but most instruments were made with two drones, tuned to a perfect fifth, in addition to the chanter. These drones, unlike the chanter with its double reed, were usually fitted with a single reed. Although the bagpipe was still the shepherd's instrument, it was also used for dance music and for marching tunes; and from this it was only a further step to its military associations—which were characteristic of the Roman Empire and persist in Scotland to the present day. In the later Middle Ages even crowned heads employed bagpipers. But the value placed on the bagpipe as an instrument for special purposes should not lead us to think that it played any significant part in the musical life of the time. On the contrary, the uniform and strident tone in no way corresponded to the new aesthetic ideals, and the incessantly sounding drones,

above all, prevented use of the instrument in art-music. Indeed, there was the paradoxical situation that the older form of the instrument, without drones, was preferred to the newer form on the rare occasions when the bagpipe was used in ensembles, with other instruments (Pl. XVI).

Trumpet (Buisine)

The *buisine* or *trumpet* (Fr. *trompette*, Ger. *Trompete*, It. *tromba*), as it was eventually called, continued to be one of the most highly valued instruments of the time. In contemporary paintings it is shown as an attribute of the Three Wise Men, and it is introduced at the coronation of the Virgin. Among the angels who serenade the Saviour or the Mother of God there is usually a trumpeter, although the buisine was, as a rule, an exclusive instrument, which avoided the company of ordinary stringed and wind instruments. In paintings of peasant weddings, fairs, or groups of itinerant musicians, it is never seen.

Like the shawm, the trumpet was made in two different sizes. The smaller form, which was barely as long as a man's arm, and was often made of wood, was especially popular in Italy, and its small size was clearly expressed in its name—*trombetta*, a diminutive of tromba. The parent instrument, the buisine, which stood as high as a man, was forced for practical reasons, to adopt a different shape. Its long, straight, slender tube (Pl. XI), from which a standard with the high-born patron's coat of arms was often suspended, was made in several sections, provided with ferrules or sleeves at the joints. Unfortunately, it showed a persistent tendency to lose its shape and bend. In the fifteenth century musicians finally hit on the notion of giving up the inconvenient straight form. All sorts of curved shapes were tried, until at last, in the second half of the century, the flattened loop (Pls. XI, XII) was most frequently adopted. Of course, these folded trumpets were likewise made in sections, with the joints covered by ferrules, which also served for ornamentation. In its essentials this form has persisted down to the present day.

Slide Trumpet

It appears probable that the trumpeters of the fourteenth and fifteenth centuries confined themselves chiefly to the execution of easy fanfares. Occasionally, however, the possibilities of the instrument seem to have been enriched by the use of a simple contrivance which can be seen depicted in contemporary paintings. The mouthpiece of the trumpet was fixed to a long tube, which could be made to slide in and out of the main tube. The performer held the mouthpiece with his left hand and the instrument in his right (Pls. XI, XII). By drawing out or pushing in the long tube, he could change the effective length of the instrument by as much as three semitones, and was even able to produce a chromatic scale from the fourth partial upwards (cf. p. 277f). *Slide trumpets*, which anticipated the construction of the trombone, must have persisted for a long time; at any rate the occasional use of a *tromba da tirarsi* (or *corno da tirarsi*) in the scores of Bach suggests as much (cf. p. 155f).

Horn

The regard enjoyed by the slender, cylindrical trumpet had a detrimental effect on the position of the older, conically-bored *horn* (Fr. *cor*, Ger. *Horn*, It. *corno*, Sp. *cuerno*), which was used as a signalling instrument by ordinary foot-soldiers (the mounted nobles employed the trumpet for this purpose). Nevertheless, this great resonant metal instrument developed along similar lines to those of the buisine: to prevent the long unwieldy tube from warping, it was curved back on itself, this time in the form of a circle. Here England seems to have led the way for the rest of Europe. At all events, the oldest representation of a medieval circular horn is of English origin. It is carved on a choir-stall dating from the end of the fourteenth century in Worcester Cathedral, and represents a man blowing a horn with a funnel-shaped bell, the instrument being curled round his body. This important improvement seems to have met with prompt acceptance on the Continent; for in 1375 and 1385 the Duke of Burgundy sent to England for a number of horns, while in the sixteenth century the circular horn, which was also made with smaller coils, established itself throughout the rest of Europe. In France, particularly, it was received with the greatest favor.

Oliphant, Cornetto

The *oliphant*, that most costly and aristocratic, yet musically rather insignificant instrument, vanished completely during the Renaissance period. The small *cornettos*, on the other hand, were constantly used, but underwent no changes in their construction.

Organ

The construction of the *organ* made significant progress during the fourteenth and fifteenth centuries. In Rouen (Normandy) an organ was built in 1386 equipped with two manuals, each with about 40 keys. At approximately the same time in Germany or Flanders a keyboard for the feet was devised, known as a pedal. Its introduction was probably due to the fact that a particularly great effort was required to overcome the heavy air-pressure needed for the operation of the large pipes, an effort which was made more easily by the feet than by the hands. At this time, also, some churches found a single organ insufficient. Two organs, a larger and a smaller one, were placed in different parts of the building.

According to a report by the seventeenth-century musicologist and composer Michael Praetorius, the organ of the cathedral in Halberstadt, Germany, completed in 1361 and renovated in 1495 (Pl. XVIII), was equipped with as many as three manuals and one pedal. The pipes covered the complete chromatic scale. On the other hand, there were still quite a few organs in the fifteenth century with Bb, F#, and C# as the only chromatic notes.

Organs with well over 1,000 pipes were common during the Early Renaissance, and the organ of the cathedral in Amiens, France, built in 1429, is reported to have been equipped with no less than 2,500 pipes, receiving the necessary wind through bellows operated by the feet of men specially employed for the purpose. The use of such a large number of pipes, governed by individual keys, was made possible through the employment of register stops. These were sliders which enabled the player to connect to a keyboard at will a whole set of pipes, similar in construction and tone-colour, but different in size and pitch. The early Middle Ages had particularly favored the *mixtures*, or *furnitures*, in which every note was accompanied by fifths and octaves based upon it, so that the fundamental note sounded fuller and richer. This organum effect was unsuited, however, to the transparency of polyphonic music, as it stiffened and thickened the sound and resulted in undesirable dissonances. Thus, to the basic mixtures, from the end of the fourteenth century, a growing number of solo stops were added, with a single pipe to each note. It was gradually realized that the structure of the pipes had a great effect on their tone-color, and whole ranks of pipes were then built, some with a wider and some with a narrower bore, some conical, some inversely conical, or closed at the upper end ("stopped"). With the fifteenth century there began also the use of the sharper, shriller reed stops, which supplemented the traditional flue stops of the organ. In these reed stops the pitch was determined by the length, thickness and elasticity of a simple metal reed (cf. p. 293) and the tone-color by a short, primitive tube. Thus the organ of the Early Renaissance, with its many new stops, was ideally suited to bring to life the colorful music of the time. Flanders and Germany here showed the way, while England, and especially Italy, assumed a much more conservative attitude.

Portative

The tiny *portative* (in fourteenth-century Italy known also as the *organetto*) was employed primarily for music of a secular nature. It is significant that Raphael's St. Cecilia abandons her portative as the strains of heavenly music fall upon her ears. This tiny instrument had no register stops—the number of its pipes was equal to that of its keys—and it was not used to play harmonies, but only melodies. As all the pipes had the same width, irrespective of their length (Pls. XI, XIII, XVI), the timbre must have varied from note to note, which would have added an element of piquancy to the sound of the instrument. The portative was easy to play and so enjoyed great popularity among the musicians of the time.

Common as are the paintings and sculptures which contain representations of the portative, it might almost be said that no two of them show exactly the same instrument. There might be anything from six to thirty pipes, usually in two ranks, but sometimes in one rank, or in three. Press buttons (Pls. XI, XIII) or short levers in the modern sense served as keys. But the greatest differences lay in the gamut, which varied considerably from one instrument to another. Certain semitones were often missing and even notes of the diatonic scale were occasionally omitted. Since the number of pipes had to be as small as possible, to keep the instrument's weight down, it would seem that the maker of the portative consulted the performer—if they were not one and the same person—in each individual case. It is possible, too, that the pipes were changed for the performance of different compositions.

Compared with these individual variations, signs of the instrument's general development are slight. During the fifteenth century, which marked the portative's prime, the drones or bourdon pipes, conspicuous for their size and often separate from the rest of the pipes, were gradually discarded. At the same time portatives were built with keys in two rows instead of one; but this was done at first merely to save space, since the complete chromatic scale was hardly to be found in fifteenth-century portatives.

In addition to stringed and wind instruments quite a number of percussion instruments were used in Europe in the fourteenth and fifteenth centuries.

Carillon

A position of its own was held by the *carillon* (Fr.; Ger. *Glockenspiel*, It. *cariglione*), successor of the early medieval cymbala. It was in particular favor in Flanders, northern France and Holland during the fourteenth and fifteenth centuries. Large mechanical instruments, using sets of tuned bells, were placed in the towers of churches and city halls and connected with the clock. A rotating cylinder set with pins released hammers to play tunes at certain hours. Just as in Italy every city strove to outdo its neighbor in architectural masterpieces, so it was the ambition of the northern cities to possess an unusually perfect carillon, perfect both technically and tonally. To this end the number of bells was constantly increased. Instruments were built with more than 50 bells and with cylinders having many thousands of pins. At times even mechanical figures were added to increase the splendor of the show.

Kettledrum

In its original form, as introduced by the Saracens, the small, cauldron-shaped *kettledrum* had a stretched skin barely larger than the palm of the hand. It was always used in pairs, fastened to a strap slung round the performer's neck or attached to his belt (Pl. XIX). About the middle of the fifteenth century, however, this delicate instrument, which was suitable only for chamber music, was superseded by mighty war-drums, which spread from the east via Hungary and Poland, reaching first Germany and then western Europe. These instruments consisted of large, hemispherical, copper cauldrons over which a calf-skin was stretched. Thanks to their tremendous tone, these powerful drums quickly swept their smaller and older cousins from the field. Wherever the trumpet blared—at princely banquets, at tourneys, or in the field—there also the great kettledrums would roll. Strapped on the back of a horse, a pair of them accompanied nobles on the field of battle. Of course, there were those who opposed the all-too-noisy intruder. In 1511 we find Virdung writing of the "monstrous rumbling barrels [*Rumpelfessern*] which the Devil himself must have invented for the suppression of all sweet melodies and the whole art of music".

Snare Drum

As the kettledrum accompanied the trumpet, so the *snare drum*, with its cylindrical wooden body, was the chosen companion of the flute. The small, flat tabor was not the only form known to the fifteenth century. There was also an instrument with a deeper cylinder, spanned at each end with a skin held by thongs, and struck now with one drumstick, now with two. Across one of the skins a gut string, the "snare," was stretched, which caused a stridulant rattle when the instrument was played (Pl. XIX). The drum, which measured scarcely more than a foot in diameter, was still played in the oriental and early medieval manner—as a delicate rhythmic instrument, without any particular striving after loudness. A larger and noisier form of the drum will be discussed in the next chapter.

Tambourine

The *tambourine* was originally the· instrument of wandering musicians, showmen and jugglers, who inherited it from the Bacchus-cult of the Romans. The instrument was not only struck with the hand, but also thrown up into the air and caught again. In the late Middle Ages it was sometimes also given a part in art-music (Pls. XVI, XIX).

Jingle-Ring

Besides the tambourine there was the *jingle-ring* (Ger. *Schellenreif*), resembling it closely, but without the skin. This instrument, which was depicted by Raphael as well as other painters, consisted of a shallow wooden hoop with thin metal leaves, or jingles, let into the sides. It was held in one hand and struck with the other to make the jingles sound.

Triangle

The same tendency to supplement the natural tone of the percussion instrument with a rattling or jingling sound is evinced in the *triangle* (Pl. XIX). In the fifteenth century this instrument, consisting of a bent rod, was made in triangular form, or with four corners, roughly the shape of a trapeze (an early Italian name was *staffa* — stirrup). It was provided with several rings carried on the lower limb, which sounded when the triangle proper was struck. The clear-cut rhythms produced by the rod were thereby blurred, as in the tambourine.

Cymbals

Like the other percussion instruments of the time, the *cymbals* were not employed to produce a shattering noise. On the contrary, the two plates were brought together gently with no particular effort (Pls. XVI, XX), achieving a kind of ringing sound, fundamentally different from the sharp clash produced by the larger, later cymbals. Thus, generally speaking, one must think of most of the early percussion instruments as being delicate, weak in tone, and averse to any developments in the direction of extreme loudness.

IV

HIGH RENAISSANCE
(Sixteenth Century)

Clarity and balance were the main artistic aims at the beginning of the sixteenth century. The individual voices of a composition were considered to be of equal significance. Unlike medieval composers, who started with one voice and successively added the remaining parts, the composers of the High Renaissance created all the voices simultaneously and as an indissoluble unit. Each of these voices participated in the imitation of the thematic material. The melodic lines followed the inflections of the words; the texture of the compositions was solid and the harmonic language logical. While the traditional mixture of voices and instruments still persisted, the idea gained ground that the equally-treated voices of a composition should be entrusted to a single type of performer, thus achieving a perfect blend of sounds. If singers alone were used, pure *a cappella* music resulted. Conversely, pure instrumental music performed by instruments of the same kind (such as viols of different sizes) or, better still, by a single instrument on which a whole composition could be played (such as the lute or the harpsichord) fulfilled the artistic ideals of the time.

Isaac, Josquin
Leading composers in the first decades of the century were Josquin Desprez and Henricus Isaac, both born in the north around 1450, but spending a substantial part of their lives in Italy. They were contemporaries of the greatest painters of the High Renaissance. Isaac died in 1517, two years before Leonardo da Vinci; Josquin in 1521, one year after Raphael. Isaac's music at times reflects Gothic angularity and then again Renaissance elegance and smoothness. Josquin's compositions do not reveal

such duality, and the combination of individualism and imagination with strictness and self-discipline displayed in his church music and French chansons placed him in the forefront of Renaissance composers.

Willaert

Toward the middle of the century a highly significant contribution was made by Adriaen Willaert, who was born in Flanders and died in 1562 in Venice, where he had been active for more than three decades at St. Mark's church. Willaert brought northern and southern elements once more into a magnificent fusion. He combined Netherlandish polyphony with the Italian predilection for expressive harmonies and beauty of sound. In his *Psalmi spezzati* of 1550 he employed two choirs in alternation, introducing into music the spatial element so dear to the art of the later Renaissance and the Baroque.

Polychoral Technique

The *polychoral technique* originating in Venice gradually spread far beyond the confines of northern Italy and even of the Apennine peninsula. One of the finest examples of its use in sixteenth-century music is to be found on English soil. Thomas Tallis (d. 1585), organist at the Chapel Royal, a composer who never left England, contributed a Latin motet for no less than 40 voices divided into eight choirs.

Lasso, Palestrina

During the second half of the century music reached a climax in the compositions of Orlando di Lasso and Giovanni Pierluigi da Palestrina (both d. 1594). The tendency of the time towards harmonic clarity, lucid formal construction and expressive declamation of the text finds in their work the strongest realization. Lasso, a Franco-Flemish composer, spent his formative years in Italy and later entered the service of the Duke of Bavaria, whose chapel he directed for 38 years. Artistically, he was a most cosmopolitan composer, writing not only a large number of Latin masses and motets, but also Italian madrigals, French chansons and German polyphonic songs, which he performed with both singers and instrumentalists. Palestrina on the other hand, the first great native Italian composer in two centuries, spent his whole life in Rome and wrote almost exclusively for the Catholic church. His striving for tonal balance led Palestrina to forgo the participation of instruments and to compose pure *a cappella* music, for singers only.

German Protestant Chorale

Contributions of increasing significance were also made by adherents of the new Protestant creeds. Thus Martin Luther considered it to be important that the congregation actively participate in the service he established. He wanted the faithful to sing simple, easily-remembered and powerful tunes to texts in the vernacular. Some of these *Protestant chorales*, which were performed with instrumental accompaniment, were derived through German translations of Latin Catholic hymns; others borrowed their tunes from secular songs. Before long professional musicians also appropriated the new hymns, using them as a basis for elaborate polyphonic settings.

Huguenot Psalter, Anglican Chant

The attitude of the reformed churches of Zwingli and Calvin somewhat resembled that of the early Lutherans. They admitted into their services only compositions using the psalms in the vernacular. The tunes were borrowed from folk-songs and the congregation sang them in unison. Composers were encouraged, however, to give the psalms a more sophisticated and complex setting for use at home. In the Anglican service the tunes were presented in plain, four-part harmonization, closely following the meter of the English texts, a procedure partly taken over from French models.

Frottola, Villanella, Villotta, Balletto

Despite the religious fervor of the time, which witnessed both the Reformation and the Counter-reformation, secular music was by no means eclipsed. Worldly compositions, at times even with quite profane texts, played a big part during the Renaissance. In the early sixteenth century the *frottola*, which reflected the predilection of the time for straightforward and fetching music, enjoyed the greatest popularity in Italy. It was a simple three- or four-part song of lyrical character with the melody in the soprano and an unadorned chordal accompaniment. It could be performed by singers only or else by a singer accompanied by one or more instruments. Around the middle of the century the frottola was replaced by the *villanella* and the *villotta*. The former, a composition of Neapolitan origin, was rustic, humorous and sometimes satirical in character. It was written for three voices in a primitive style, spurning polyphonic or harmonic refinements. The *villotta*, on the other hand, was of north-Italian origin. It was a kind of folk-dance, written in four-part chords, preferably for a singer with instrumental accompaniment. Towards the end of the century the *balletto* came into fashion, which could be sung, played on instruments or danced. Italy showed the way and other countries, England in particular, enthusiastically followed suit.

Madrigal

On a much higher level was the *madrigal*, whose text dealt primarily with love or nature. This form of composition, in which each of the four or five voices was of equal significance, was meant primarily for competent amateurs. It could be executed by a mixed ensemble of vocalists and instrumentalists or by single singers performing each voice. The content of the madrigal was deepened by Willaert and his contemporaries, who imbued it with passionate feeling by making use of bold chromatic progressions. Luca Marenzio (d. 1599) employed clever tone-painting and subtly depicted the emotional content of the text. The fame of the new genre spread even as far as England, where under the leadership of such great composers as Thomas Morley (d. 1603?) and William Byrd (d. 1623) the madrigal was adapted to both the English language and the English mentality.

Polyphonic Chanson

In France the *polyphonic chanson* reached a climax in the works of Clement Jannequin (d. 1560?) and Claudin de Sermisy (d. 1562). It had a light, elegant, humorous, at times even frivolous character, distinguishing it from the more stately and sedate earlier Flemish chanson. This was entertaining chamber music for a vocal trio or quartet, or for a singer with instrumental accompaniment. Particularly popular were Jannequin's programmatic chansons describing the songs of the birds, the street cries of the vendors in Paris, or a hunting scene.

Ricercar, Canzona da Sonare, Toccata

While in sacred music of the Roman school, and frequently also in the secular madrigal and chanson, the traditional mixed ensembles were being replaced by singers only, the opposite process also went on during the High Renaissance. Pure instrumental compositions were written with increasing frequency, some of their forms being at first derived from music for earlier mixed or vocal ensembles. The imitative *ricercar*, introduced around the middle of the century, resembled a textless polyphonic motet. The *canzona da sonare*, on the other hand, appeared to be like the instrumental counterpart of the vocal French chanson. They were both written for instrumental ensembles or keyboard instruments, the ricercar also often for the lute alone. Before long idiomatic instrumental forms were also created without depending on former musical structures. The *toccata* for organ or harpsichord was a kind of technical study in which full chords and brilliant passages alternated. Eventually, imitative sections were inserted into the composition, thus endowing the form with greater solidity. The toccata was fully adapted to the character of keyboard instruments and was quite unsuitable for singers, as well as for most other instruments.

Variations

The *variation* technique offered instrumentalists an opportunity to ornament and paraphrase a simple tune in various ways. Instrumental ensembles, such as a "chest of viols" (see p. 100), but also solo instruments, such as the lute or the harpsichord, were well qualified to make use of it. A special kind of variation, the *basso ostinato* (Eng. *ground*), restated a bass line over and over again while the upper voices changed. Toward the middle of the century, variation technique was particularly practised in the Spanish *differencias*. Later it found a home in England, where the virginalists of the Elizabethan period, composers for the spinet and harpsichord, made significant contributions.

Dances

Instrumental dances assumed increasing significance during the sixteenth century. They were at first of a stately and sedate character. The *pavane* was a solemn dance in even time. It seems to have originated in Italy, where pavanes for the lute were first printed in 1508, but before long it appeared also in German and Spanish publications. The *saltarello* was a livelier dance in triple time. It often followed the pavane, appearing as the rhythmic transformation of its melodic and harmonic content. Toward the middle of the century the *galliarde*, a spirited dance in triple time of French or Italian origin, took the place of the saltarello.

Composers of Instrumental Music

Of the imposing array of composers who made important contributions to sixteenth-century instrumental music only a few can be mentioned here. In Venice, at St. Mark's church, not only Adriaen Willaert, but later also Andrea Gabrieli (d. 1586), Claudio Merulo (d. 1604), and Andrea's nephew, Giovanni Gabrieli (d. 1612 or 1613) were active, writing works which had the strongest impact on the music of the time. Through the blind organist Antonio de Cabezón (d. 1566), organ music in Spain reached a high level of artistry. He entered the service of King Philip II and travelled with him to London. His performances there might well have inspired the great English composers of keyboard music, such as William Byrd, Thomas Morley, and Orlando Gibbons (d. 1625).

Treatises

The strong interest in instrumental music manifested itself also in the publication of numerous theoretical monographs, describing the construction of specific instruments and serving as a guide for aspiring performers. Particularly significant contributions of this kind were made in Germany. Thus in 1511 Sebastian Virdung published a richly illustrated treatise describing the instruments known to him, and in the same year Arnold Schlick presented a monograph on organ construction and organ playing. The lute virtuoso Hans Judenkuning offered, at first in Latin and in 1523 in a German translation, a book on lutes and viols consisting of compositions for these instruments and instructions for their performance. Six years later Martin Agricola contributed a valuable treatise on all the instruments in simple German verses.

In Italy Silvestro Ganassi supplied manuals for playing the recorder and the viols (1535 and 1542/43), while in Spain Diego Ortiz provided a method of playing the viols (1553) and Tomas de Sancta Maria offered directions on how to perform on keyboard instruments and the vihuela (1565). The most extensive and valuable treatise describing the vast number of instruments built during the Renaissance was not published until the beginning of the seventeenth century. In 1618 Michael Praetorius, a German pupil of Giovanni Gabrieli, presented his *Organographia*, a most accurate and magnificently illustrated account of the multitude of instruments known at the time (cf. Pls. XVIII, XXVIII).

The Instruments

After 1500, the pictorial sources, which have been so important for information on earlier instruments, gradually dry up. They are more than adequately replaced, however, by the above-mentioned treatises. In addition, a not inconsiderable number of actual instruments built in the sixteenth century have been preserved. They have survived on account of their more solid construction and their exquisite workmanship, which made some of them seem like veritable collectors' pieces. The growing number of compositions specifically written for intruments also convey an insight into their resources.

On the basis of this significant new material it is clear that the early fifteen hundreds marked a decisive turning-point in the history of musical instruments. Those on which chords could be played, such as the lute and the harp, as well as the various keyboard instruments, now moved to the forefront of musical interest. But even instruments primarily meant to carry a melody were used to achieve harmonic effects. They were made in different sizes, so that a combination of like types could produce results similar to those obtained by a keyboard instrument. In England a whole "consort," a chamber-music ensemble of members of the same family of instruments, was particularly favored. Scarcely one of the single-voiced melody-instruments escaped the general tendency to form families. Toward the end of the century even those limited to a certain range by their particular nature were turned out with ruthless logic in several sizes. Today the giant *contrabass recorder*, reaching down to F, seems strange to us, just as strange as the tiny *soprano bassoon*, a twelfth higher than the parent instrument. The sixteenth century, however, needed different members of the same family to perform multi-voiced pieces; for the single instruments were no longer required to contrast sharply with each other, but, as far as possible, to blend harmonically. It is true that the combination of different types of instruments, with or without singers, still played an important part in the performance of polyphonic compositions. But the over-all variety of tonal colors was gradually reduced, the prevailing tendency being to achieve a monochrome rather than a polychrome effect.

The employment of musical instruments was also changed in another respect. The cheerful and eager generation of the fifteenth century was succeeded by a serious and dignified race of men whose strict code of propriety was laid down in Castiglione's classic *Il Cortegiano* (Venice, 1528). In painting the delicate and radiant colors of the fifteenth century gave way to deeper and richer tones. In music the gentle little portative, the thin rebec, the feeble mandola, the chirruping psaltery and the ethereal tromba marina all fell victim to this change in taste. They were utterly swept away, or, at the very least, forfeited the last shreds of their individuality. Other instruments were refashioned with the general aim of increasing their loudness and fullness of tone, as well as extending their range.

In one, not unimportant respect, however, a connection with the past was preserved. The sixteenth century, just as much as the preceding centuries, lacked the concept of gradual dynamic change, and, even up to the last third of the century, that of sudden alterations between *forte* and *piano*. The majority of the instruments in use were limited to their natural loudness and the performer had neither the desire nor the skill to vary the intensity of tone. One need only call to mind the medieval hurdy-gurdy or the Renaissance spinet to realize that dynamic contrasts were unattainable with them. During the last decades of the century echo-effects were not unknown in vocal music, but they do not seem to have been much used in instrumental compositions before Giovanni Gabrieli wrote his revolutionary *Sonata pian e forte* (1597) for two choirs of instruments (cornetto and three trombones in the first group, viola and three trombones in the second).

With its peculiar mixture of some conservative but many more progressive elements, this period is like the head of Janus looking simultaneously in opposite directions: to the future and to the past.

Vielle and Rebec

During the sixteenth century the *vielle* and the *rebec* had only one function: to give of their best, so that other instruments might evolve. Before long, they themselves were regarded as atavistic and excluded from the musical life of the day.

A different fate was meted out to their offspring. Though some of them, such as the lira da braccio and the lute-vielle, were eventually to fall by the wayside, others survived, and above all one of the most important instruments of modern times: the violin.

Lira da Braccio

The *lira da braccio* (Pl. XXII), which flourished in Italy in the first quarter of the century, represented an attempt to adapt the vielle to the demands of the new music while retaining its essential features. It preserved the fiddle's awkward position of the pegs, perpendicular to the table of the instrument, and was mostly content with a mere suggestion of the division of the body into two parts, an upper and a lower section, which in effect was hardly superior to the slightly waisted shape of the fifteenth century. The violin-like division of the body into three clearly-separated sections, upper, middle and lower, was rare. In principle the lira da braccio retained the five strings of the old vielle, although each of the two thick and slackly stretched lower strings had a companion string in the upper octave to lighten the tone. The seven-stringed instrument was frequently tuned d d^1 g g^1 d^1 a^1 d^2 (or e^2), with the two lowest strings lying alongside the finger-board as drones, in the medieval fashion. Even an early medieval name of the vielle, "lira" was retained, with "da braccio" added simply to distinguish it from a larger variant, of which we have yet to speak.

While the lira da braccio avoided the main stream of progressive development in all essential particulars, its makers expended the most loving care on all sorts of minor details. The noble curvature of the table and the back, as well as their slight projection over the side walls, was first seen in this instrument, and it was not long before these features were incorporated in the viola da braccio (cf. p. 101) and violin. It is also significant that the tuning of the upper five strings of the lira da braccio anticipated the tuning of the violin. For a short time this high-bred, if degenerate, offspring of the ancient vielle was held in the greatest esteem. In paintings of the early sixteenth century we see it again and again in the hands of angels; such specimens as have come down to us exhibit a rare beauty of workmanship, and in this connection it is of special significance that Raphael, in his fresco of Parnassus in the Vatican, defying all traditional representations, makes his Apollo play the contemporary bowed lira da braccio instead of the plucked lyre of antiquity. Even in a painting of the early seventeenth century a later form of the instrument can be seen (Pl. XXXIV).

Lira da Gamba

In spite of its conservative character, the lira da braccio did not wholly escape the general tendency of the sixteenth century towards the formation of families. Before the year 1600, at a time when the instrument had lost almost all its importance, a tenor type, the *lira da gamba*, was made, with two to four drones in addition to its nine to thirteen strings. This instrument, doomed in advance by the archaic arrangement of its strings, survived for a few decades only. The problem of constructing bowed instruments suitable for the new music was approached in a different way, and that proved to be highly successful.

Viola da Gamba

The early Middle Ages, as we have seen, had a form of vielle which was held in front of the body, and another, smaller form which was supported on the shoulder. The late Middle Ages showed a decided preference for the handier, smaller form; but with the beginning of the modern age, the taste for richer and more sombre coloring brought the larger form back into favor. True, this big vielle had to undergo a thorough transformation before it could become a really practical instrument. First, in order to counter the strong pull of the strings, it adopted the backward-slanting peg-box of the rebec. While this reform had occasionally been made in the small vielle of the fifteenth century, there is another which is entirely to the credit of the new age: the fundamental division of the body of the instrument into an upper portion (or "bouts"), a strongly waisted middle, and a lower bouts. The shallow waisting of the fifteenth century fiddle was no longer sufficient. To get at each string individually when

the instrument was held between the knees, a far more pronounced waist was necessary, and thus arose the semicircular
form of the middle bouts, with distinct corners; its clear demarcation from the upper and lower parts of the instrument was at the
same time consistent with the aesthetic sensibilities of the
Renaissance. To make playing with the left hand easy and to
avoid use of the higher positions, the vielle, following the model
of the lute, was given six strings, tuned in intervals of fourths with
a third in the middle. The gut frets, which gave the left hand a
better grip, were also taken over from the lute. Once the main
features were established, the further characteristics of the new
instrument emerged one by one. The flat back of the sounding-
box sloped in at the top, making the instrument easier to hold;
the shoulders met the neck at an acute angle; the peg-box was
crowned with a human or animal head; and the table was
pierced by the old C-shaped sound-holes of the fiddle. The bow
was held below the stick with palm upwards. Being gripped
between the legs, this new instrument, which was probably made
for the first time in Italy, was known as the *viola da gamba*, *gamba*
being the Italian word for leg. In Germany it was usually just
called *Gambe*, in France *viole*, and in England *viol*.

Before long a whole family of instruments was evolved on the
lines of the viola da gamba. The *bass viol* (Pls. XXXIV, XXXVI,
XXXVII, XL), tuned D G c e a d^1, was now the largest of the
group of three, which included an *alto-tenor* (tuned A d g b e^1 a^1)
and a smaller *treble* (tuned d g c^1 e^1 a^1 d^2). Viols steadily gained
in popularity owing to their light and silvery tone and their
suitability for the playing of chords. Eventually, the three main
types were considered to be insufficient and as many as six
different sizes were made, from the *descant*, some 28 inches in
length, to the *sub-bass*, whose length was as much as seven feet.
In England, which particularly favored the playing of viols, a
consort of at least half a dozen instruments of different sizes was
known as a "chest of viols", as it was customary to store them in a
specially built chest. All the viols were played vertically, mostly
supported by the leg or held between the knees of the sitting
player.

Lute-Vielle

The adoption by the viola da gamba of the stringing and frets of the lute had the advantageous result that lute-players found it easy to play the viol also. But while in this case the effect of the stimulus derived from the lute was entirely beneficial, the reverse must be said of a clumsy, unintelligent blending of vielle and lute which was used early in the century, above all in Germany. In the treatises of Virdung and Agricola we find representations of stringed instruments which show the division of the body into three parts and the curved rebec peg-box with almost exaggerated clarity; but in the same instrument we see the central rose of the lute, and instead of a bridge, there is the cross-bar of the lute, glued to the table to take the lower ends of the strings. Since the strings—of which, according to Virdung, there were no fewer than nine!—all lay in one plane, this *lute-vielle* (*Lauten-Fiedel*) was as good as unplayable. One would regard it as merely the invention of unpractical theorists, but for the fact that this queer instrument was occasionally also represented in works of art.

Viola da Braccio, Violin, Violoncello

While the large bass vielle, held in front of the body, was transformed into the bass viola da gamba, the small fiddle, held at the shoulder, was undergoing similar changes in accordance with modern ideas. Its body was likewise sharply divided into upper, middle and lower bouts; in addition, it was given the rebec's peg-box, crowned by a scroll. At first the new instrument had three strings, but after the middle of the century, four. Like the rebec, and partly also the vielle, it was tuned in fifths.

The slightly older sister-instrument, the lira da braccio, made two small, but none the less acoustically and aesthetically important contributions: the vaulting of the table and the back, and a slight projection of both back and belly over the ribs. Moreover, the shoulders of the two instruments did not slope, but met the neck at right angles. The bow was held above the stick with palm downward. A characteristic feature of the newcomer was its f-shaped sound-holes, the result of combining two c's facing in opposite directions (Pl. XX). The instrument had an alto-soprano range. It was supported on the arm and shoulder of the player and was accordingly called *viola da braccio*, or just *viola*, *braccio* being the Italian word for arm. In England it was usually known as *viola*, in France as *alto*, or, in accordance with its middle range, *taille*, in Germany as *Bratsche*.

Right from its inception the viola appeared with a descant instrument of similar construction, described in Italy by the diminutive *violino* (Eng. *violin*, Fr. *violon*, Ger. *Violine*; Pl. XX). We find this instrument for the first time around 1529, reproduced in a painting by Gaudenzio Ferrari. There it has only three strings, but a fourth was added before long. With the viola and violino appeared the *basso di viola da braccio*, later known as the *violoncello* ("The small violone," often called the *'cello*; see Pl. XX). Two further members were eventually added to the family: the *violino piccolo* (Ger. *Quart-Geige*) and a very rarely used *Gross-quintbass*. Thus was created the family of stringed instruments whose three original members were most significant for the future of music. Their tuning corresponded largely to that of the present day: for the violing, g d^1 a^1 e^2; for the viola, c g d^1 a^1; for the violoncello, C G d a or B♭ F c g. The violino piccolo was tuned a minor third or a fourth higher than the violin, while the Grossquintbass, in addition to the four strings of the violoncello, had a lower, fifth string in F$_1$.

The viola da braccio family seems to have originated in northern Italy. As early as the second half of the century, great instrument makers built various instruments of this type. Their warm, round and full tone won them friends and they quickly invaded the European musical scene. In view of their lively tone-quality they were particularly well suited for dance music, while high-class chamber ensembles were apt to give preference, at first, to the more reticent and sedate viole da gamba.

Hurdy-Gurdy

The *hurdy-gurdy*, with its bourdon strings and wooden wheel, lost all importance in an age which saw a tremendous development in bowed stringed instruments. Praetorius calls it "the peasants' and old wives' lyre," and scorns to treat it seriously. Brueghel has a painting of a group of blind beggars who, unaware of the danger, stumble into a river; one of them has a hurdy-gurdy, the badge, so to speak, of their forlornness. Throughout the sixteenth century the hurdy-gurdy remained the attribute of the blind beggar.

Tromba Marina

At the beginning of the sixteenth century the *tromba marina* took over from the lute the principle of constructing the body out of individual staves and from the rebec the lateral position of the pegs. But these improvements were of little help; the instrument had lost its appeal and was hardly used after 1550.

Cittern

The *cittern* in the new age also clung to its old, unwaisted shape derived from the medieval fiddle. Since it usually had five or six pairs of strings (and in exceptional cases considerably more), the originally narrow, elliptical body expanded until it was almost circular (Pl. XXI). The cittern of the Renaissance had a technically improved body, with flat back and table, and ribs which became shallower towards the base. The earlier frontal pegs were usually retained, but added to them was a set of pegs at an acute angle to them. This arrangement, which is not to be found on any other instrument of the time, might have hindered the widespread adoption of the cittern. Perhaps, on the other hand, it was this very unusualness of the instrument that caused it to be prized by the nobility and at times decorated in an exquisite and costly manner, as may be seen in the magnificent example by Girolamo de Virchis (Pl. XXI). The independence of the players manifested itself also in the fact that no specific tuning of the strings was generally adopted; on the contrary, a large number of rather unconventional tunings of the courses, such as G f# d a b, or b G d g d¹ e¹, or f# D A d a b, were in use.

Guitar

While most of Europe used the *guitar* (Pl. XXIII) sparingly, Spain took the *vihuela de mano*, as the instrument was called there, to its heart. A smaller type was used for folk-music, a larger, with 5–7 courses of strings (often tuned similarly to the lute, in G c f a d¹ g¹), for art-music. A substantial number of pieces for the vihuela de mano alone, or for two vihuelas, have survived. Among the great composers for the instrument, Luys Milán should be mentioned, as well as the virtuoso Miguel de Fuenllano, who arranged vocal works for the guitar and wrote numerous original compositions. It was only the growing interest in keyboard music which, towards the end of the century, checked the extreme popularity of the instrument.

Lute

By far the most important of the plucked instruments of the sixteenth century was the *lute* (Frontispiece, Pl. XX). In the music of Europe it played a part analogous to that of the piano in the nineteenth and early twentieth centuries. Again it was a valued participant in all chamber music, ideally suited to the accompaniment of singers, never absent from the larger ensembles, and very often used as a solo instrument. Various systems of notation for lute pieces, the so-called 'tablatures,' were devised in Germany, France, Italy and Spain. A large number of compositions in tablature have thus come down to us in both print and manuscript. The lute was often made of the most precious materials, such as ivory, ebony, or Brazil-wood, a practice followed only in the case of instruments which were highly prized. It is also significant that in France all makers of stringed instruments, whether plucked or bowed, are known as *luthiers* down to the present day.

The reason for the extraordinary regard enjoyed by the lute is easily found. It was the happy chance that an instrument which was already highly popular in the fifteenth century brought to the new age the very attribute that was desired above all, namely, handiness for the playing of chords. On the lute a melody can be performed and at the same time accompanied with chords.

From a technical point of view the sixteenth-century lute hardly differed from the fifteenth-century instrument. There were still five pairs of strings, and in addition a single string for the upper voice. Seven to eight frets were general, and so was the practice of playing with the bare fingers. The lute, however, did not escape the contemporary craze for forming families, and it was made in five, or even seven, different sizes, though the big, clumsy instruments, whose thick, slack strings produced a dull, muffled tone, can have had no more real importance than the impracticable miniature type. The parent instrument, the alto lute, with the tuning of which we are already familiar (cf. p. 72). was the instrument for which the overwhelming majority of compositions were intended.

Mandola

The *mandola* was almost wholly assimilated to the lute in the sixteenth century. The division of neck and body, which was of such importance structurally, was adopted, and the body itself was built up of many staves. The mandola was strung with four to five single or double strings. If it had not kept its distinctive peg-box, fixed to the neck at an obtuse angle or made in a curved form, and along with that its slender body, it would have been neither more nor less than a smaller lute. Owing to its weak tone, the mandola in the sixteenth century, far from enjoying the regard in which the lute was held, shared the fate of the hurdy-gurdy and became the instrument of beggars.

Harp

With the full-sounding *harp* the case was very different. Next to the lute it was the most favored plucked instrument of the day. Thanks to its versatility it satisfied the new requirements of the age, being admirably suited for chord playing, and could be left more or less unchanged. As the strings were increased in number the neck was lengthened in proportion to the sound-board and the pillar. Thus the slender shape of the fifteenth century gradually became fuller and heavier, approaching more closely— though on a larger scale, of course—the equilateral form of the Middle Ages. The stringing was at first always diatonic. It was only towards the close of the century that "chromatic harps" were built, with a separate string for each semitone.

Psaltery, Dulcimer

The *psaltery* led a rather precarious existence during the High Renaissance. It was used mainly as a Shrovetide instrument, although in the second half of the sixteenth century it is supposed to have enjoyed the special favor of German ladies. The *dulcimer*, known in France as *tympanon*, in Italy as *salterio tedesco*, in Germany as *Hackbrett*, fared even worse. It was characterized as an "instrumentum ignobile" (Luscinius, 1536) and a member of the "Musica irregularis" (Praetorius, 1618). No doubt their successful progeny, equipped with keyboards, were partly responsible for the low esteem in which the two instruments were held.

Clavichord

Although the *clavichord* originated during the Middle Ages, the instrument played no significant part in the history of music until the sixteenth century led to a strengthening of the harmonic sense. When this occurred, it brought the keyboard instruments to the foremost rank. The earlier clavichords, up to about 1530, had a maximum range of three and a half octaves (F – c³). Thereafter the instrument's compass was gradually extended downwards to C, which resulted in a peculiarity taken over from the organ. To effect a saving in the expensive material of the pipes, the older organs omitted the seldom-used notes C♯, D♯, F♯ and G♯ of the lowest octave; and since space was also a consideration, the keyboard was arranged in the following curious order:

D E B♭

C F G A B C

Clavichords, which were made by the men who also built organs, copied this strange arrangement, known as the "short octave," although a few keys and strings more or less could hardly have mattered. The earliest clavichord that has survived, an instrument built by Domenico da Pesaro in 1543, conforms to this arrangement.

Harpsichord, Clavicytherium

During the High Renaissance *harpsichords* were built mainly in Italy (Pl. XXV). Their range extended to approximately four octaves (C – c³ or d³). The instrument had richer powers of expression than the spinet, as it began to borrow from the organ the idea of register stops (cf. p.115). Harpsichords were at times equipped not just with one system of strings, but with two and in exceptional cases even three. These corresponded to a second or third row of jacks which, with the aid of register stops, could be engaged or cut out at will. Two of the registers were usually tuned at 8′ pitch; the third could be tuned an octave higher, at 4′ pitch. Towards the end of the century there were harpsichords with two keyboards, stepped one above and behind the other, each of which operated one part of the stops. By combining or opposing the voices it was thus possible to achieve certain tonal and dynamic contrasts.

The oldest dated cembalo is of Italian manufacture. It was completed in Rome in 1521 by Geronimo di Bologna, and is now in the Victoria and Albert Museum, London. The same collection includes the most valuable spinet in existence. It is encrusted with nearly 2,000 gems, and was built in 1577 by Annibale Rosso of Milan. In 1867 it was bought for £1,200.

The *clavicytherium* was very rare in the sixteenth century. The woodcut used by Virdung in 1511 shows the short strings on the left hand side, the long ones on the right hand side of the instrument and seems altogether not very reliable.

Spinet, Spinettino

During the sixteenth century *spinets* were built primarily in Italy and Flanders. The Italian instruments frequently had a six-sided, unsymmetrical form, with projecting keyboard and a range of up to four and a half octaves (C – f³, with "short octave"). The Flemish instruments, on the other hand, were rectangular, with built-in keyboard, and were apt to have a slightly larger range (C – a³, with "short octave").

Apart from the regular spinet a small-sized *spinettino* (Pl. XXIV) in the upper octave was in use. Moreover, instruments were occasionally built which combined the features of a spinet with those of a spinettino (Pl. XXXII). Such a "double spinet" or "double virginal" enabled the performer to play with one hand on an 8' register and with the other on a 4', as if he were using a harpsichord with two keyboards.

Wind Instruments

With the wind instruments, which in the nature of things have only single voices, and mostly a quite limited range, the formation of families played an even greater part than with the stringed instruments.

Recorder

The *recorder*, the most important member of the flute family at the time, was made in three different sizes by the beginning of the sixteenth century; a hundred years later, however, Praetorius, records as many as eight different sizes (Pl. XXVIII), all of them appearing also in slightly altered shape, tuned one tone lower to facilitate playing in different keys. The larger instruments (contrabasses were more than nine feet long!) had the double-winged key, covered with a fontanelle, instead of the duplicate lower finger-hole, and were blown through a brass S-tube for

greater ease in performance. Whether the thumb-hole at the
back of the instrument (Pl. XXVIII) was a sixteenth-century
innovation or not cannot be decided, since we have no medieval
recorders to refer to, and the pictorial representations of the
fifteenth century invariably show the front of the flute.

Pipe and Tabor

The combination of the one-handed *pipe* with the *tabor* was used
according to Virdung, by the French and the Netherlanders at
dances. Later, the English showed a particular predilection for
it, and one John Price is cited as a brilliant virtuoso at the end of
the sixteenth and the beginning of the seventeenth century.
Curiously enough, the one-handed flute was also made in two
(Pl. XXVIII) and sometimes even three sizes.

Double Recorder

The *double recorder* was by no means common in the sixteenth
century. Nevertheless, the instrument, consisting of two pipes,
usually alongside each other and cut from a single block, occurred
in two forms, one with the finger-holes pierced in different positions, the other with the finger-holes lying side by side. The
latter type, which had the advantage of being handier in performance, since the two adjacent finger-holes could always be
stopped by one finger, continued to be used in the Baroque
period, although it was never of any general importance.

Transverse Flute

During the sixteenth century the shrill Swiss pipe (Pl. XXVIII),
with its extremely narrow bore, was joined by a new kind of
transverse flute with a somewhat wider cylindrical bore, which
made the lower octave easier to blow and no longer limited the
instrument to the highest register. This new transverse flute was
made in several sizes (Pl. XXVIII), the larger ones being gradually
admitted to art-music (Frontispiece).

Dolzflöte

The *Dolzflöte* recorded by Praetorius (Pl. XXVIII) seems to have
been a recorder with the embouchure at the side, and was of no
practical importance.

Shawm, Pommer

The two sizes in which the *shawm* (known in France also as the *hautbois*, the "high wood") and the *pommer* (known in France also as the *grosbois*, or "big wood") were made at the close of the Middle Ages had increased by the beginning of the seventeenth century to no fewer than seven. The larger types (Pl. XXVI) were now so long that the fingers could not reach the lower finger-holes, and thus up to five long-levered keys, whose delicate mechanism was protected by a fontanelle, were added to the instrument. These keys still had two wings, so that the performer could use either the right hand or the left for the lower holes. Particularly interesting is the largest member of all, the huge *Gross-Bass-Pommer*, nearly ten feet in length, two specimens of which are extant. This monstrosity could be played only if the bell was supported, in church by a trestle, or in the open—as in processions—by the shoulder of a second man (Fig. 3).

FIG. 3. Players of a Gross-Bass-Pommer.
Drawing by R. Effenberger

Bagpipe

The lustre of the *bagpipe* paled in the sixteenth century. It was used only by shepherds, soldiers on the march, or dancing peasants. None of the older Brueghel's paintings of popular junketings would be complete without a bagpipe. Nevertheless the bagpipe also underwent the development common to all instruments in that age. It was made in no fewer than five different sizes, and technical improvements were added: it might have as many as three drones, and was sometimes even furnished with two chanters. Most important of all, however, was the radical transformation which occurred at the end of the century. In the Irish *Uilleann Pipes* (Elbow Pipes) or, as they are now called, Union Pipes, bellows operated by the arm were substituted for the mouth as source of wind, and this new form, which was taken up with particular enthusiasm in France, was to dominate the future.

Lastly, it must be noted that from the second half of the sixteenth century there was a new immigration of bagpipes from the east. Instruments of a Slavonic character made sporadic appearances in Germany, and in these not only the drones but also the chanters (the bells of which were animal horns) were cylindrical, and provided with a single reed of the clarinet type.

To join the few reed instruments known to the Middle Ages, a profusion of new ones appeared in the sixteenth century. The imagination of the age was at work, delighting in its powers of invention and seeking to discover ever new possibilities. But of all these forms only one, the first to be discussed below, proved to have a lasting value for the future.

Dulzian (Curtal)

In the second half of the sixteenth century a new kind of wood-wind instrument was constructed known as *Dulzian*, *Fagott*, *Kortholt* (Ger. for "short wood"), or *curtal* (Eng.). The instrument consisted of a billet of wood through which two channels were bored longitudinally, their lower ends being joined (Pl. XXVII). Together they thus formed a narrow conical bore, doubled back upon itself. The performer blew into the narrower end by means of an S-shaped brass tube, to which a double reed was attached. A small funnel—which in the *gedackt* or "stopped" dulzian was closed by a perforated cap, acting as a damper—represented the bell. About the end of the century the instrument was made in five sizes, from the descant to the double-bass, but the most important of all was the bass, the *fagotto chorista* or *Chorist-Fagott*, with a range $C - b^1$, which served as a substitute for the unwieldy larger pommers. The family as a whole was not very widely distributed before 1600.

Sordone

An extremely rare variant of the bassoon was the *sordone*. This consisted of a gracefully turned wooden billet bored with not just two but sometimes three parallel and connected cylindrical channels. It was made in five sizes from treble to double-bass.

Rackett

The *rackett* (also called in Germany *Wurstfagott,* "sausage bassoon," and similarly in France *cervelas*) shows a grotesque exaggeration of the bassoon principle. It was a small cylindrical box, $3\frac{1}{2}$ to 13 inches in height, which was bored with no less than nine connected cylindrical channels (Pl. XXX/1). The rackett was equipped with 10 to 13 finger-holes, which the performer covered not only with the tip but also with a joint of the finger. In Germany and France this curious, soft-sounding instrument enjoyed a certain vogue up to the end of the seventeenth century. It was made in four different sizes, with the great-bass extending down to D_1.

Tartölt

A variant of the rackett was the dragon-shaped, naturalistically painted *Tartölt*. A complete set of five different sizes is in the possession of the Vienna Kunsthistorisches Museum, the only ones of this kind to have survived.

Crumhorn, Schreierpfeifen, Bassanello, Cornamusa

Curious products of the sixteenth century were also several wind instruments in which the double reed was embedded in a wooden wind-chamber with a narrow slit to blow through. Here we have a development of the bagpipe and specifically of the early medieval *Platerspiel,* where neither personal expression nor variation of strength was desired. Overblowing was of course impossible. Since the instruments were so limited in range there was a special impetus toward the usual formation of families.

The commonest of these was the crumhorn (Fr. *cromorne, tournebout*; Ger. *Krummhorn*; It. *storto*), a mainly cylindrically-bored instrument shaped like a fishhook (Pl. XXIX). It was equipped with six finger-holes in front and a thumb-hole at the back. Crumhorns were made in five sizes, sometimes reaching a length of well over three feet. The two largest types used a key to cover the lowest hole. Far rarer were the *Schreierpfeifen* ("screech-ing pipes"; It. *schryari*), with a tapering bore narrowing towards the bell, and the *Rauschpfeifen* ("roar-pipes"), with the ordinary conical bore, constructed as sopranos, tenors and basses. Related to these instruments was the cylindrical *bassanello*, likewise made in three different sizes. Its invention was ascribed to the Bassani brothers, who were active as musicians at the English court in the second half of the sixteenth century. The *cornamusa* (from *corno muto*), made in five sizes, was likewise a straight, double-reed instrument with cylindrical bore. Its tube was closed at the end, and the air escaped through vents in the side. Modern performers of early music like to use reconstructions of these instruments.

Trumpet

By the beginning of the sixteenth century the small *trumpet* of the late Middle Ages, which was about as long as a man's arm, had vanished. The larger form, folded in such a way as to have three straight lengths of tube, parallel to each other and connected by small, U-shaped pieces of tube, needed no further improvement. The Early Renaissance had already found the classical form, which the new age would retain (Pl. XXXI). The instrument-makers of the sixteenth century were concerned less with the improvement of its tone than with the aesthetic appearance of the trumpet. It was often made of silver, occasionally also in fancy form and even gilded (cf. Pl. XXX/1). In Nuremberg and other German cities trumpet-making reached its culmination about this time, and the traditions of the craft were handed down from father to son, so that in a certain sense the German trumpet-makers were the counterpart of the classical violin-makers of Italy. At the same time the art of trumpet-playing made extraordinary progress. While compositions of the first half of the sixteenth century demand only a very modest degree of technical ability in the performer, later trumpet-playing had improved so much that "in the high register a good master may sound almost all the notes of the diatonic scale and even some semitones" (Praetorius). In fact, at this time certain performers could, without any special mechanical aid and solely by means of a highly developed control of the lips and the breath, blow the highest harmonics.

Trombone

After the disappearance of the small, arm-length instrument, the diminutives *tubecta* and *trombetta* were bestowed on the folded trumpet, since in the meantime a still larger variant had appeared. This was the *trombone*, from the Italian augmentative of *tromba*. In Germany it was known as the *busune* (the augmentative of *busine*) or *Posaune*; in Spain as the *sacabuche* (from *sacar*, to withdraw or pull out, and *buche*, inside); in France as the *saquebute*; and in England as the *sackbut* (Pl. XXVI). This instrument, already known at the end of the Early Renaissance, first attained importance in the sixteenth century. In the slide-trumpet we saw an early attempt to make the trumpet capable of diatonic playing at the lower end of its range, where the overtones lie far apart. But this form had the disadvantage that the whole instrument had to be pushed and pulled to and from the performer, to the peril of pure intonation. Another solution was now discovered. In the folded trumpet the U-shaped connecting tube between the first two parallel tubes was not fixed to them, but fitted over them as a movable sleeve, reaching almost to the mouthpiece. If this connecting-piece, the slide, was worked to and fro over the main tubes, the effective length of the instrument as a whole was altered, and with it the complete series of natural tones. The farther away the slide was pushed, the deeper became the fundamental note and the series of harmonics based upon it (cf. p. 295f). Diatonic as well as chromatic progressions could be played on the instrument, and so, in later years it needed no appreciable improvement. Its tone must always have been characterized by the same nobility, power and solemnity that we admire to this day, although the thicker walls and the narrower bell of the early trombone softened the sound, enabling it to be used with singers or string players.

The High Renaissance at once set to work to make trombones of various sizes; of these, the alto, the tenor and the bass achieved importance.

Cornetto

During the sixteenth century the trumpet and the trombone completely overshadowed the single-coil circular horn, which was used primarily by hunters. On the other hand, the small, finger-hole horn of the Middle Ages, called in Italy *cornetto*, in

Germany *Zink*, in France *cornet à bouquin*, enjoyed an increased popularity. Since the trumpeters formed a highly privileged guild, which only with great reluctance played with other instrumentalists, and since the tiny treble trombone was more or less useless, the trombone choir lacked a treble voice, and this lacuna was best filled by the cornetto. Provided with a very narrow mouthpiece, a thumb-hole at the back and six finger-holes in front, the instrument was very well suited for the playing of melodies. A certain irregularity of tone, which was a feature of the finger-hole horns, was readily overlooked, since the instrument made it possible to get over the difficulty of collaboration with the trumpeters.

The cornetto was usually made of wood, more rarely of ivory (Pl. XXX/1). In its straight form, with round tube, it was the *cornetto muto* (Ger. *stiller Zink* or *gerader Zink*); in its curved form, with octagonal tube, it was the *cornetto torto* (Ger. *krummer Zink*). The curved instrument, when fashioned from two separate pieces of wood, was provided with a black leather casing. The cornetto had a basic range of two octaves $(a - a^2)$, which good players were able to exceed. Its technical flexibility induced many composers to write sonatas for violin or cornetto. The inevitable attempt to create a family of cornetti resulted in the construction of a small *cornettino* (Ger. *Kleinzink*), pitched a fifth higher, and of a large S-shaped bass, known as the *cornone* in Italy and *Grosszink* in Germany. It was equipped with one key and tuned a fifth lower than the standard instrument.

Serpent

In Italy and France there was also a great double-bass cornetto, fashioned in the shape of a double S, to bring the six finger-holes within the player's reach. This bore the descriptive name of *serpent* (Pl. LIX/1). Like the cornetto torto, the instrument was made of individual pieces of wood and covered with leather. It had a strongly conical bore and was played with a cup mouthpiece. In the sixteenth century serpents were mainly employed in churches to reinforce male voices.

Alphorn

In the mountainous regions of Europe, trumpets and horns, which might be either straight or coiled, were made for the benefit of herdsmen. These were built up from long staves of wood, and in order to make them air-tight they were closely bound with bast; the distinctive result was known as the *Alphorn*, a type of instrument that probably had its origin in the very distant past. It is celebrated in many folk-songs, and down to the present day it is inextricably associated with romantic Alpine impressions.

Church Organ

During the High Renaissance the growing interest in polyphonic music led to a steady increase in the number of register stops provided for the larger *church organ*. Players wanted to give the individual voices different tone-colors. They aimed at achieving a balance between the heavy mixtures of the Middle Ages and the contrasting sonorities produced by individual stops. Thus in sixteenth-century organs we find a substantial number of different registers, from the mighty 32' (32 foot) stops to tiny 2' and even 1 stops. The all-important terms, 32', 2' and 1' stops, which are used here, need some explanation. If, with a register of flue-pipes, depressing the C key causes a pipe of approximately 8 feet in length to sound C, while the D key produces the note D, and so on, it is said that the whole register is an 8' stop, sounding "normal". But if, with another register, depressing the C key causes a pipe of double the length to sound C_1, depressing the D key, D_1, each key producing a note an octave deeper than in the 8' stop, then the whole register is known as a 16' stop. Similarly, in a 32' register the pipes sound two octaves lower than normal; with the 4' stop, on the other hand, they sound an octave higher, with the 2' stop two octaves higher, with the $5\frac{1}{3}'$ stop a fifth higher, and so on.

The most important register of the organ was the *Open Diapason*, known in Germany as the *Prinzipal*, a powerful, medium-bore, metal flue-pipe, generally in 8' length. In great favor also were the 8' and 16' "stopped" registers, closed at the top; the pipes of these, being only half as long as open ones of the same pitch, saved both space and material. Their tone, however, lacked brilliance. The "half-stopped" pipes were equipped with a narrow little chimney in the upper end to let the wind out (e.g. the metal *Rohrflöte*); other pipes had an inverted conical bore, i.e. tapering towards the top (e.g. the wooden *Gemshorn*). There were also several reed stops, in which the tone was produced by a vibrating metal tongue (cf. p. 293). This group includes the powerful 16' *trombones*, operated by the pedal, the 8' *trumpets* with inverted conical tops, and the 4' *shawm*, or *hautbois*. In addition, sixteenth-century organs used various mixture stops, known already to the Middle Ages; in these fifth and octave; third, fifth and octave; twelfth and double-octave; or pipes tuned to other intervals taken from the series of harmonics, were made to sound together. These are only a few of the numerous register stops already known at the end of the sixteenth century and widely used by organists of the time. Hand in hand with the increase in the number of registers went a further increase in the number of pipes included in a given stop, and therefore in the range of the keyboards. As early as 1519 Anthony Duddington mentions an English organ with a range of four octaves; and similarly Pietro Aron in his *Toscanello*, which appeared in Venice in 1523, speaks in a perfectly matter-of-course way of the range C – c³. As a rule the so-called short octave, which has already been mentioned in our account of the clavichord, was used for the lowest notes.

While in Italy great pains were taken with the development of the manuals, the pedal lagged behind, and the only Italian author of the sixteenth century to mention the pedal at all— Vincenzo Galilei—speaks of it in a somewhat disparaging manner. In Germany, on the other hand, the pedal was zealously employed in the sixteenth century as a means to the richer development of polyphony. In Kleber's *Tabulaturbuch*, as well as in the *Fundamentum* of Hans Buchner—two important works containing organ music of the first half of the sixteenth century— the direction *pedaliter* is expressly given.

Portative
The *portative* occurred only during the early years of the sixteenth century. It was now invariably provided with a regular keyboard, furnished with two ranks of pipes and producing all the notes of the chromatic scale. Despite this progress, the instrument was rapidly losing ground. It was too small, too gentle, too feeble in tone; and since it was played only with one hand, its technical potentialities were too limited.

Positive

In addition to the tiny portative and the huge church organ, there was a medium-sized instrument known usually as the *positive* (Pl. XXXIII). Having more than one register, and being played with both hands, it was far better able to satisfy the musical requirements of the age. Yet because a second person was required, to work the bellows, and because it had neither the portability of the portative nor the fullness of tone and rich possibilities of the church organ, its use was rather limited. It was employed mainly as a house organ, although some churches kept the small positives they had previously acquired for use in addition to their large organ.

Regal

While the positive was equipped as a rule with flue-pipes only, the *regal*, which made a first appearance during the early Renaissance, was a kind of miniature organ provided with metal reeds. In the second half of the sixteenth century Georg Voll of Nuremberg hit on the idea of giving the instrument the form of a folio volume, and this proved very popular. The twin bellows were made to look like the covers of a book (Pl. XXX/2), and the keyboard could be taken off, folded up and packed into the "book". Thus the closed instrument looked for all the world like a venerable old family Bible. This was particularly satisfying to an age with such a highly developed taste for mechanical surprises.

Carillon

Since the beginning of the sixteenth century it had become possible to play the *carillon* not only mechanically, but also by means of a keyboard. As larger bells and hammers were produced by the end of the Renaissance period, a pedal-board was added to the manual for the deeper notes. In its final form the instrument became more and more frequent in central and western Europe, including England. In these areas, however, it never attained anything like the same popularity as in its true home, Flanders, northern France and Holland.

Kettledrum

Among the membranous instruments the great military *kettledrum*

(It. *timpano*, Fr. *timbale*, Sp. *timbal*, Ger. *Pauke*), the faithful companion of the trumpet, held the highest rank from a social point of view. The true home of this instrument of eastern origin was now Germany. Duke Philip the Bold of Burgundy dispatched a kettledrummer, with other musicians, "pour aller en Allemagne aux escoles de leur métier." Similarly, James Turner wrote in 1683: "The Germans . . . permit none under a baron to have them (i.e. kettledrums) unless they are taken in battle from an enemy."

The construction of the instruments, which were used mainly in pairs, was simple and efficient. The metal cauldrons were covered by skins held in place by hoops; from the end of the sixteenth century, screws were generally employed to regulate the tension of the membrane.

Snare Drum
Besides the tabor, the companion of the one-handed pipe, and the small snare drum, the new age also used a larger form of the *snare drum*. Instruments with two membranes, standing some two feet in height and twenty inches in diameter, were preferred. They were played with two sticks, their ribs were of wood, or occasionally of metal, and the membranes were stretched with the aid of hoops and cords. A snare was drawn across one of the heads. While the kettledrum was the knightly instrument, the double-headed drum was the pacemaker of the infantry. It was especially favored by the Swiss mercenaries, who used it with the fife. Thus the instrument came to be known as the Swiss drum, the French calling it *tambourin de Suisse* or *tambour de lansquenet*, the Germans *Schweizer Trommel*, and the Scotch *swesch*.

Tambourine, Triangle, Cymbals
The *tambourine*, the stock-in-trade of the medieval jugglers, had lost all its importance by the beginning of the new age, as the strolling players who favored it receded increasingly into the background. Likewise, the High Renaissance rarely used the *triangle* and the *cymbals* (Pl. XX).

Xylophone
One of the latest immigrants from the east was the *xylophone*,

known in the sixteenth century in Germany as the *Strohfidel* or *Hölzernes Gelächter*, in France as the *claquebois* or *patouille*; later in Italy as the *timpano*. It consisted of tuned wooden rods or bars, at first cylindrical but later prismatic in shape. These rods rested on rolls of straw and were struck with hammers. The instrument, which achieved a moderate distribution only in eastern and central Europe, hardly developed at all, since no place was found for it in serious music. The twenty-five rods which Martin Agricola attributed to the xylophone, in 1528 (three years after the earliest trace of the instrument, in Holbein's "Dance of Death"), were not increased for a long time.

V

THE BAROQUE ERA
(1600–1750)

Instrumental music came into its own in the period from 1600 to 1750, which we may designate in the widest sense as the Baroque era. Pure, vocal *a cappella* music practically ceased to exist and vocal music required the accompaniment of instruments. On the other hand, pure instrumental music, without the participation of human voices, gained in significance. Much of this music was idiomatic, intended for a specific group of instruments, or even for an individual instrument. Even in compositions for voices and instruments concern for problems of orchestration was apparent.

The great innovation of the time was the general acceptance of the *thoroughbass* or *continuo*, as it was usually called. This started out as a kind of musical shorthand in which only the melody and the bass were fully notated, while the filling notes of the middle parts were implied with the help of figures. The "realization" of the middle parts was left to the discretion of the performers. This system proved so useful that it was kept in force—though with many modifications—throughout the Baroque period.

The early Baroque took as its maxim "Speech must dominate in vocal music". This age-old idea was propagated with new vigor around the year 1600 and led to monumental developments, which influenced even instrumental music: Three new genres were created: opera, cantata, and oratorio. They originated in Italy, which during the Baroque period assumed a leading position in the history of music.

Italian Opera

Opera started out as an attempt to revive the ancient Greek

drama. The earliest scores preserved—compositions on the Orpheus myth by J. Peri and G. Caccini—are based on plain recitatives in which the vocal melody closely follows the meter and the natural inflections of speech. The vocal lines were accompanied by a thoroughbass in long notes, which was probably realized mainly by plucked stringed instruments. Quite different was the opera *Orfeo*, which the great Claudio Monteverdi (1567–1643) wrote in 1607 for Mantua. Though he still made use of the recitative style, a substantial number of arias, duets, and choral sections were inserted into his score. Above all, he was not satisfied with the tiny group of players used in the earlier operas. Monteverdi dipped into the large reservoir of instruments provided by the Renaissance. His *Orfeo* prescribed a small recorder, 4 trumpets, 2 cornets, 4 trombones and 17 bowed instruments of various sizes; in addition, 2 cembali, 2 positive organs, 1 regal and 5 plucked instruments were stipulated in turns for the realization of the continuo. No less than 26 numbers for instruments alone are to be found in this score.

However, Italian opera did not continue along these lines. It gradually turned into a vehicle for the singers to display beauty of tone and technical skill, while the stage architect provided a sumptuous display of machinery, decorations and costumes. Dramatic truth and a clear enunciation of the text were eventually held to be of little importance. The singers were not only permitted, but expected, richly to ornament the melodic lines of their arias. The orchestra was not supposed to compete with these predominant forces. It was relegated to the background and used only a minimum of wind instruments. With its neutral, monochrome tone, provided by the strings, it offered the unassuming support desired by vocal virtuosi.

In the works for the stage by Alessandro Scarlatti (1660–1725), the leading opera composer at the turn of the century, the orchestra is by and large assigned a minor role. Nevertheless, we owe to him the establishment of one of the most important forms of instrumental music. As an introduction to his operas he used an orchestral three-movement *sinfonia*, consisting of a fast, a slow, and a second fast section. This type of overture remained in general use in Italian opera for a long time, but it achieved even greater significance as the basis of the future orchestral symphony.

During the Baroque era Italian opera dominated the European

stage. In particular Austria, Germany and England served as enthusiastic host countries. England, in the opera *Dido and Aeneas* by H. Purcell (1659–1695), produced an immortal master-work. Hamburg developed a native German opera (its chief composer, R. Keiser, 1674–1739, was among the most gifted orchestrators of the time), but neither was able to stem the tidal-wave advance of the Italian opera.

French Opera

The only country that was able to offer successful resistance to the Italian influence was France. Characteristically enough it was a native of Italy, subsequently a naturalized Frenchman, who succeeded in creating a typically French genre of dramatic music. J. B. Lully (1632–1687) wrote heroic operas in which the vocal melodies do not obscure the text, but rather support it, in a manner he had learned from the great actors of his time.

Ballets, so dear to the French public, played a large part in French opera, and chorus and orchestra were likewise assigned important tasks. The orchestra consisted basically of 24 bowed instruments divided into five parts—six instruments each for the dominating soprano and bass lines and four for each of the three middle parts. Keyboard or plucked instruments and bassoons were used for the realization of the basso continuo. For special effects flutes, oboes, horns, trumpets and timpani could be added to the basic orchestra of strings. Lully established a form of opera prelude consisting of a solemn introduction in dotted rhythms followed by a somewhat faster-moving fugal section, while the end might return to the mood of the beginning. This French *ouverture*, like the Italian sinfonia, played an important part in the development of instrumental music. Lully's ideas dominated the French opera for a long time. His greatest successor, J. P. Rameau (1683–1764), continued along similar lines, but used, among other innovations, more sophisticated orchestral effects.

Oratorio, Passion

The *oratorio* might be regarded as a kind of contemplative or religious counterpart to the opera. It is as old as the opera and was originally presented in the prayer room, the *oratorio*, of Italian monasteries. In performance the oratorio usually has the character of a concert; scenery, costumes and acting have to be provided by the imagination of the audience. A narrator, the *testo* or *historicus*, often tells the story, and the chorus participates vigorously in the action. G. F. Handel (1685–1759), 'the greatest oratorio composer of the Baroque period, was also a superb orchestrator. In his Italian operas written for British audiences he had to limit the size of his orchestra on account of the smallness of the orchestra pits in the London theatres. But even there, for special effects he used four horns (*Giulio Cesare*) or four trumpets (*Rinaldo*). He was in a better position when he performed oratorios on the concert stage. Here his basic string orchestra consisted of up to 15 violins, 5 violas, 3 violoncellos and 3 basses, as well as 2 harpsichords. The strings were at times subdivided; pizzicato and mutes might be prescribed for special results. Vocal solos were accompanied as a rule, by a part of the strings and one harpsichord only. On the other hand, in purely orchestral sections and as an accompaniment to the chorus, both harpsichords and the full complement of strings were used. For special occasions certain wind, percussion and plucked stringed instruments joined Handel's orchestra. These included flutes, oboes and bassoons; trumpets, horns and trombones; kettledrums and carillon; harp, lute and theorbo; occasionally an organ replaced the harpsichords.

Related to the oratorio is the *Passion*, for performance during Holy Week. Its text is based on a narration of the suffering and death of Christ according to the Gospels. J. S. Bach (1685–1750) contributed the two supreme masterworks in this field: the *St. John Passion* and the *St. Matthew Passion*. In the latter Bach used a sound-producing body whose size and composition seems to have been inspired by the polychoral style of the past. He employed two choruses and two orchestras of stringed and wind instruments, each with its own organ for the continuo. A third organ, placed high up on the altar wall of his church, originally added a chorale tune to the heaving masses of sound. On the other hand, the two Passions also offer examples of a delicate and intimate kind of scoring. In one number a lute and two viole d'amore play a prominent part. The composer used and combined, moreover, viola da gamba, oboe d'amore, and oboe da caccia; solo violin, solo flute, and solo oboe, with an unerring feeling for the expressive potentialities of these instruments.

Sacred Concerto, Church Cantata

The *sacred concerto* was of particular importance for the religious music of the seventeenth century. The term "concerto" refers here to the collaboration and competition of groups of sound, which the age found so fascinating. Composers never tired of exploring the contest between various human voices, between soloists and chorus, between vocalists and instrumentalists. Protestant Germany took the lead in this field, with H. Schütz (1585–1672) as its greatest representative.

In the later part of the Baroque period the *church cantata*, which had its roots in the sacred concerto, assumed a central position in the Lutheran service. In the cantata the individual sections were sharply separated and significant features were taken over from the contemporary opera. It was Bach again who carried the new form, which owed so much to a secular model, to its highest development. He used not only solo voices and chorus in his cantatas, but almost every instrument known in his time. The old concerto spirit is still much in evidence. For instance, Bach liked to combine the solo voice in an aria with an instrument of the same range, thus achieving fascinating exchanges between the dissimilar pair.

Motet

The polyphonic and polychoral style of the sixteenth-century *motet* survived during the Baroque period. Although the motet had no separate instrumental sections, it was not performed *a cappella*. The human voices were accompanied at least by an organ or harpsichord and complete sets of instrumental parts, reinforcing each of the vocal lines, have been preserved.

Anthem

In England, the *anthem* emerged as counterpart to the motet and church cantata. In the works of Purcell, and especially of Handel, it was a multi-sectional composition using two choruses and luxurious orchestral sounds.

Mass

The *mass* during the seventeenth century appeared both in a progressive and in a conservative form. The polychoral style remained in use, and at the consecration of Salzburg cathedral, in 1628, a mass for no less than twelve different-sized choruses was performed. There were 16 vocal and 34 instrumental parts, including strings, flutes, oboes, trumpets, cornettos, trombones and two organs. On the other hand, in Mantua as early as 1607, the Franciscan monk L. da Viadana offered a mass for solo voices and continuo only. This form remained in use during the following decades, though the size of the vocal and instrumental apparatus was gradually increased. Starting with A. Scarlatti, Italian composers introduced operatic elements into the mass. The text was subdivided into individual numbers, which assumed at times the form of the operatic aria. Bach's gigantic B Minor Mass marks one of the highpoints of this development. It consists of no less than twenty-five numbers: arias, duets, four-part, five-part, and eight-part choruses, with changing orchestral accompaniments. Bach's coloristic ingenuity manifests itself, for instance, at the end of the *Quoniam* (No. 11). It is scored for bass solo, French horn, 2 bassoons and continuo, and this extremely dark coloring is succeeded, without pause, by the luminous orchestral setting of 2 flutes, 2 oboes, 3 trumpets and timpani; a contrast of overwhelming impact used in the *Cum sancto Spiritu*.

Instrumental Music for Keyboard Instruments

Most of the instrumental forms of the sixteenth century lived on during the Baroque period, although some basic features, and with them the name of the genre, might change. The *ricercar* and the somewhat livelier *canzona* for keyboard instruments consisted of chains of sections, each of which developed a new theme in imitative style. A later version used a single theme only, which was rhythmically and melodically modified in each successive section. A third method was to employ a single theme without alterations, but to add changing counter-melodies. Before the middle of the seventeenth century the German term *Fuge* (Eng. *fugue*) was introduced for such polyphonic keyboard compositions, and it eventually found general acceptance.

Fugal sections were also inserted into the *toccata*, thus modifying its basic improvisatory character. The combination of a homophonic piece with a strictly polyphonic one led eventually to the creation of the important double form: *prelude and fugue*.

Experimentation with the keyboard fugue was carried on

throughout the Baroque period by many composers. They worked towards the monothematic fugue, which did away with variations of the main theme and also with changing counter-melodies. Variety was achieved henceforth by introducing modulations into the central section of the fugue. The basis of this important transformation was the gradual emergence of *equal temperament*, which began to replace the earlier mean-tone temperament. This new system of tuning divided the octave into twelve equal semitones. Not a single interval—except the octave—is completely correct acoustically, but not one of them, on the other hand, sounds offensively bad. Performers on keyboard instruments were gradually enabled to modulate freely, even to distant keys. Equal temperament did not find very wide distribution before 1800, but all through the Baroque period composers were striving towards its realization, and the modulating fugues bear witness to this movement.

Chorale Prelude

During the seventeenth century the dividing line between music for stringed keyboard instruments and music for the organ was not always easy to draw. Among the limited number of compositions obviously intended for the organ, arrangements of Lutheran chorale melodies played an important part, as the congregation enjoyed hearing the familiar tunes newly interpreted. At first the variation form, dear to the seventeenth century, was used for the ever-changing presentation of chorale melodies. Later the *chorale prelude*, an arrangement of the hymn tune in a single movement, became predominant. In this the chorale melody was often presented in one voice in long extended notes, or surrounded by melodic ornaments, while the remaining voices supplied an elaborate accompaniment. Increasingly, the meaning of the text found programmatic expression in the setting provided by the composer.

Not only in the development of the chorale prelude, but in every phase of organ music, Protestant Germany gradually took the lead during the Baroque era. This was due partly to the strong interest of the Germans in polyphonic music, and partly to the important role which the Lutheran church assigned to independent organ music. It is not surprising, therefore, that a German Lutheran organist should have become the greatest organ composer of all times. J. S. Bach brought composition for the "king of instruments" to its uncontested culmination.

The Well-tempered Clavier

But Bach was almost equally great as a composer for the stringed keyboard instruments: harpsichord and clavichord. In the fugues of *The Well-tempered Clavier* (1722) the composer not only used modulations within the individual pieces; he presented in addition compositions written in each of the twelve major and twelve minor keys. Clearly, this work was meant primarily for stringed keyboard instruments. Compositions for the organ at that time rarely had more than four sharps or four flats. The progressive method of tuning was obviously adopted more slowly by the huge, cumbersome organs with their countless pipes, than by the comparatively small-sized claviers.

Clavier Suite

France, which had always shown a special fondness for the ballet, took the lead in the development of dance music for the clavier. It was no longer meant for the stage or ball-room, but for intimate domestic entertainment. The composers arranged some twenty dances of about a dozen different types, all in the same key, into an *ordre*. It was up to the performer to select a combination of these pieces. The great French masters of the *clavecin*, especially François Couperin (1668–1733), known as *le Grand*, were fond of this informal arrangement. The orderly German mind, on the other hand, created well-rounded short *suites* combining four dances of different national origin: *allemande* (German), *courante* (French), *sarabande* (Spanish), *gigue* (English). This basic pattern was often enlarged in the eighteenth century. Following Italian models a prelude, not of a dance character, might introduce the suite, and some French court-dances, such as *menuet*, *gavotte*, or *bourrée*, might be inserted next to the *sarabande*. Bach's great sets of clavier suites follow this enlarged pattern.

Clavier Sonata

The *clavier sonata*, to which the future was to belong, was created in the seventeenth century. J. Kuhnau (1660–1722) was one of the first to use this form. His "Biblical Sonatas" for stringed keyboard instruments offer entertaining examples of early program music. Domenico Scarlatti (1685–1757), the son of Alessandro, cultivated the single-movement form of the sonata. He left close on 500 sonatas which ingeniously explore the technical possibilities of the clavier.

In conclusion it must be stated that it was quite rare for Baroque composers to indicate the nature of the stringed clavier instrument for which individual pieces were intended. The performer is lucky if he can deduce from the nature of the music whether the author had a harpsichord, a spinet, or possibly a clavichord in mind. As mentioned above, even the choice between organ and clavier was quite often left to the performer, especially in earlier music.

Trio-Sonata, Solo-Sonata

It is characteristic of the artistic trends at the beginning of the seventeenth century that new instrumental ensembles were created·through a process of elimination and reduction rather than through augmentation and enlargement. The earlier combination of three melody instruments accompanied by a bass was reduced in 1607 by S. Rossi in Mantua to two solo instruments with continuo, and in 1617 by the violinist B. Marini in Venice to a single instrument with bass.

Thus two new ensembles were created which were of decisive significance for Baroque music: the trio-sonata and the solo-sonata.

In the *trio-sonata* two violins or violin and cornetto, or two cornettos, or violin and oboe, etc., competed with each other, while the bass offered the supporting third voice. The list of composers who contributed trio-sonatas is very long. It includes, among many others, the great Italian violinist A. Corelli (1653–1713), the French ballet composer and violinist J. M. Leclair (1697–1764), and in England, Purcell and Handel. Their works were mostly performed by four instruments: two violins (or violin and oboe, etc.) accompanied by a harpsichord and a bass viol or violoncello. Some composers, however, foremost among them Bach, reduced the number of executants to two and even one. A single part was entrusted in the traditional manner to a melody instrument, the second part was given to the right hand of the harpsichordist, and the bass to his left. In organ sonatas the composer even went a step further, by having the two melodic lines performed by the two hands of the player and the bass by his feet on the pedal. In both cases the partial or complete neglect of the filling chords points towards future developments.

In the *solo-sonata*, usually a single violin was combined with a continuo accompaniment. It is typical of the dominant position of the brilliant, technically often very demanding violin part in the solo-sonata that the designation of the genre did not take into account the essential collaboration of the continuo. Like the trio-sonata, the solo violin sonata spread from Italy all over Europe. A large number of composers, among them numerous violin virtuosi, cultivated the genre; thus G. Tartini (1692–1770), the famous performer and theoretician, has left us close on 200 works of this kind. A group of composers, largely of German origin, dropped the supporting thoroughbass and produced works for an unaccompanied solo instrument. The greatest composer of such works was again Bach, who in typically Baroque manner created the illusion of a polyphonic texture through instruments (violin, violoncello, flute) whose very nature seems to exclude such devices.

Trios and solos assumed various musical forms, most frequently those of the *sonata da chiesa* and the *sonata da camera*. The *sonata da chiesa* (church sonata, originally intended for use in a religious service) consisted usually of four movements with the tempos slow —fast—slow—fast. The *sonata da camera* comprised primarily dance movements. It appeared also under the designation "partita" or "suite", while the term *sonata da chiesa* was abbreviated into "sonata". Both suites and sonatas were—as stated above—also used in clavier music.

Orchestral Suite

The orchestral music of the time also showed a leaning toward the suite of dances. The early seventeenth century witnessed the appearance in Austria and Germany of "variation suites," chains of dances of different character which were, however, all in the same key and appeared like a theme and its variations. Later German composers used a chain of independent dances which were introduced by a French "ouverture" of the Lully type.

Concerto

The competition between individual sound-groups so dear to the time found significant application in pure instrumental music. From about 1620 soloistic episodes for two or three violins were used with increasing frequency in large-scale compositions. A systematic use of the concerto principle was initiated in the last third of the seventeenth century. Three different types gradually emerged. At first a form was created which in our time is designated as a *concerto symphony* or *orchestral concerto*, although the term was unknown in the Baroque period. In this groups of instruments competed with each other, but no sharp distinction was made yet between soloists and accompanists. The *concerto grosso*, which was developed next, used a small group of three or four solo instruments, the "concertino", accompanied by a string orchestra, the "ripieni," in a contest with the full body of performers known as "tutti". The form of the concerto best known today was the last to be developed. The *solo concerto* used only a single solo instrument, such as the violin, oboe, or trumpet, accompanied by a string orchestra.

A large number of Baroque composers cultivated the various types of instrumental concerto. Of particular importance, on account also of his great influence on Bach, was A. Vivaldi (c. 1678–1741). The composer wrote close on 450 concertos, most of them for violin, but also works for recorder, transverse flute, clarinet, oboe, bassoon, trumpet, viola d'amore and mandoline. To Bach we owe the short-lived genre of the concerto for one, two, three or four harpsichords, accompanied by string orchestra. The method he employed was as simple as it was effective. He usually entrusted the solo part of a violin or woodwind concerto to the right hand of the cembalist, while the left hand played the bass part of the composition. So his cembalo concertos were as a rule arrangements of his own concertos for violin, oboe or oboe d'amore; but he also transformed a concerto for four violins by Vivaldi into a concerto for four cembalos.

The Instruments
When in 1618 Michael Praetorius was describing the host of late-Renaissance musical instruments (whose numbers even the nineteenth century hardly surpassed), the days of this gigantic instrumental array were all but past. Large orchestras were still used, but composers employed only a fraction of the different types of instruments the sixteenth century had so lavishly pro-

vided. A radical change in artistic outlook had taken place and it resulted in a decisive alteration of the musical scene. In Italy the aesthetic ideal was no longer dignity and rigid majesty, but emotion and the genuine language of the heart. All instruments that could not sing were now relegated to the middle and lower registers, to supply the dark, uniform ground-colors which were exacted by the musical contemporaries of a Caravaggio.

The Baroque preference for extreme contrasts had a decisive influence on the range of musical instruments. On the one hand, there were determined efforts to provide ever deeper basses. Harpsichord and organ extended their range downwards; bass strings were added to the lute, and the lute family was enlarged by the addition of new and bigger members. In addition, powerful wind instruments, such as the double bassoon and the contrabass trombone, were now constructed. On the other hand, the highest value was set on those instruments that were best equipped for producing a singing tone, and thus for competing with the human voice in tenderness, mellowness and emotional expressiveness. This tendency is very clearly seen in the case of the stringed instruments. The inexpressive plucked instruments yielded pride of place to the bowed instruments, with their power of communicating every shade of feeling. The violin became the queen of instruments, outstripping her elder sister, the heavy viola. The fame of the violin was carried by virtuosi throughout the length and breadth of Europe, and violin-making soared to heights barely attained before in any branch of instrument-making. The cooler, more reserved members of the viola da gamba family were left behind, and even in ensemble playing leadership passed to instruments of the violin type. As early as the first half of the seventeenth century there were pure string ensembles in Italy composed of members of the violin family, which were to form the nucleus of all later orchestras.

The same tendency towards expressiveness and tenderness had its effect on the wind instruments. The rigid double reeds enclosed in a wind-chamber, with their inability to register any dynamic shades, disappeared without leaving a trace. Only the bassoon and the shawm, reborn as the oboe, survived, instruments whose reeds were unconfined and were now held between the performer's lips in order to soften their tone. At the close of the seventeenth century the wind band was augmented by its two noblest singers, the darlings of the later Romantic period, the clarinet and the French horn.

The Baroque period displayed an increased interest not only in the use of tone-color in music, in contrasts between light and dark, high and low, thunderous threat and tender animation, but also in dynamic contrasts. The alternation of forte and piano was now widely used as an aid to expression. New, graduated dynamics, dependent not merely on the actual nature of the instrument, but also on the personal control of the performer, won increasing favor, and the instrument-makers took this tendency into account. During the first half of the eighteenth century the striving towards individual expression assumed even larger proportions. The softer, the more tender its tone, the more highly an instrument was cherished. The new and gentler sister of the vigorous oboe was known as the "oboe d'amore", and a stringed instrument provided with sympathetic resonance-strings was called the "viola d'amore". Even the long-forgotten tromba marina was resurrected, since its harmonics appealed to the sensibilities of the tender age.

The pastoral poetry of the eighteenth-century Rococo period also left its traces on musical instruments. The nation that produced a Watteau and a Lancret sought for means to express the new pastoral mood in music, and found it in the hurdy-gurdy and the bagpipe. The principle of the constantly-sounding bass drone, the very thing for which these instruments had been discarded by the Renaissance, rendered them particularly suitable for the expression of pastoral sentiment.

Let us now turn to a discussion of the individual members of the Baroque instrumental family.

Viola da Gamba

As already mentioned, the silvery, and slightly nasal tone of the *viola da gamba* family (Pls. XXXIV, XXXVII) told against it in the contest with the violin and its relatives. Not only in tone quality, but also in sheer volume of tone the instruments were at a disadvantage, as the right hand of the player had to exercise care in guiding the bow over the strings, to avoid producing an unwanted note on one of the close-lying adjacent strings.

After the middle of the seventeenth century the only member of the family to retain any real importance was the prototype, the bass viola da gamba (Pls. XXXVI, XL, XLIII), while the higher and lower members suffered a decline. In England this bass-viol was made in two sizes, as the regular "consort viol" and the somewhat smaller and handier "division viol," used to play improvised figurations on a given tune. In Germany, and above all France, the bass-viol was cultivated by the virtuosi, who, among other things, had a seventh string added at the lower end of the range, and for greater ease of playing procured a flatter neck. These small improvements, however, were not sufficient to preserve the instrument from decline. Although French ladies in the eighteenth century sometimes used a smaller type, the *pardessus de viole* (tuned in g c^1 e^1 a^1 d^2), the bass-viol itself became increasingly rare; and when the viol virtuoso Carl Friedrich Abel died in 1787, the viola da gamba, in the words of Gerber, the great eighteenth-century lexicographer, was buried with him.

Viola Bastarda (Lyra-Viol)

A variant of the bass-viol was the *viola bastarda*, which in addition to the longitudinal sound-holes of the viol had the rose of the plucked instruments. According to tradition this instrument, known in England as the *lyra-viol*, was provided by Daniel Farrant, at the beginning of the seventeenth century, with a feature of oriental, and particularly of Indian stringed instruments: resonance-strings of fine wire, which were stretched beneath the finger-board, where they sounded sympathetically as soon as a note was produced by the bow on the regular strings. This delicate, ethereal accompaniment lent a peculiar charm to the tone of the instrument.

Though the resonance-strings of the viola bastarda were soon discarded, they were more successfully adopted by two other related instruments.

Baryton

The *baryton*, or *viola di bordone* (Pl. L), was a seventeenth- and eighteenth-century form of the viola bastarda, tuned in A, d, f, a, d^1, f^1. It was made in a heavy, guitar-like shape and equipped with the two kinds of sound-hole of its prototype. The baryton's neck was gouged out at the back, so that not only did the wire strings (tuned at semitone intervals) sound in sympathy in the usual way, but they could also be plucked by the thumb of the performer's left hand. Thus *pizzicato* and *arco* had to be played simultaneously, which did not improve the grip of the left hand. The extreme difficulty in playing which resulted was enough to prevent any very wide distribution of the instrument.

Viola d'Amore

The alto of the viola bastarda was the *viola d'amore* (Pl. XLII), invented, according to tradition, in England in the middle of the seventeenth century. This instrument was made in the shape of a viol, or with a highly fantastic outline, and held like a violin. It had six or seven gut strings, frequently tuned in A d a f¹ a¹ d² or A d a f♯¹ a¹ d², and an equal or larger number of diatonically- or chromatically-tuned resonance-strings made of wire. The soft vibrations of the sympathetic strings gave a peculiarly affecting quality to the tone, which made the instrument a special favorite during the eighteenth century. Vivaldi wrote a concerto for it, Bach employed it several times in his works, and even in Mozart's day there was still a celebrated viola d'amore virtuoso in the person of Karl Stamitz, who died in 1801.

Violin (Viola da Braccio) Family

The members of the *violin family* were among the most successful instruments of the Baroque period. In small and large ensembles, in every type of instrumental music, in opera, oratorio, and cantata they played a most significant part. The lead within the group was assumed by the *violin* itself, whose warm and rich sound, as well as its aptitude for dramatic effects made it ideally suited for the most varied purposes. Basically the Baroque violin resembled the modern instrument. However, its neck and finger-board were somewhat wider and also shorter, as performers usually played in the first five positions, hardly ever going beyond the seventh. The bridge was lower, flatter and thicker, which facilitated the production of chords while making it difficult to play forcefully on a single string. Inside the instrument the bass-bar, glued to the table beneath the lowest string, was probably thinner and shorter, and similarly the sound-post, connecting table and back, had a smaller diameter, since a comparatively feeble tone met the demands of the time. The bow (Fr. *archet*, Ger. *Bogen*, It. *archetto*), too, was shorter than it is to-day, and its stick was slightly convex (outward-curved). At first the hair was simply attached to the upper end of the stick; the ribbon of hair was considerably narrower than in the modern bow and no provision was made for changing its tension mechanically. As the artistic demands made on the violin gradually increased the construction of the bow had to be altered. By the first half of the eighteenth century the bow had been lengthened, straightened, and made from finer and more flexible wood. It was often equipped with a screw-knob which enabled the player to move the "nut" or "frog"—the block at the lower end to which the hair is attached—and thus tighten or loosen the hair at will. Moreover a "head," a hatchet-shaped wooden block, gradually came to be inserted at the upper end of the bow between stick and hair, thus increasing its effective length. Italy, which—as we shall see presently—was leading in the construction of stringed instruments, showed the way here, with countries north of the Alps gradually following suit.

The slightly larger *viola* (Pl. XXXVIII) resembled the violin in its principal features. For the convenience of performers— players often alternated in using violin and viola—the instrument was usually made on too small a scale, with the result that its tone lacked the violin's lustre. The viola was essential, however, for use as a filling, middle part in ensemble music. In particular five-part instrumental compositions, which were frequently written in the seventeenth century, depended on violas for the realization of the alto and tenor voices. It is characteristic that Bach liked to play the viola in ensemble music, as from this central location he could best observe the unfolding of the whole. work. In his sixth Brandenburg Concerto he also wrote very effective solo parts for the instrument.

The *violoncello* was at first only a clumsy instrument, meant to reinforce the bass line. In the second half of the seventeenth century, however, it assumed a more elegant, smaller and slimmer shape, and in 1689 the first solo compositions for violoncello were written in Italy. Also around that time, perhaps, players changed the position of their right hand. They no longer held it palm upwards, as viola da gamba players did, but palm downwards, which made possible a better control of the bow and a stronger tone. Henceforth the potentialities of this sonorous instrument were increasingly explored, Bach's suites for unaccompanied violoncello, written around 1720, and the concertos for violoncello and strings composed by Leonardo Leo in 1737–38, being milestones in this development.

The *double-bass* (Fr. *contrebasse*, It. *contrabasso* or *violone*, Ger. *Kontrabass*) appeared in various shapes. Italian instruments showed features of the violin family, while outside the peninsula, especially in Germany, it assumed certain characteristics of the viola da gamba, such as a flat back sloping in at the top, and shoulders that met the neck at an acute angle. There was as little uniformity in the stringing. Five strings (tuned e.g. F_1 C G d a or D_1 E_1 A_1 D G) were the rule, but there were also instruments with six, more often with four, and sometimes even with three strings.

In addition to the main instruments which were in general use, the Baroque period also employed some short-lived members of the violin family which were of limited importance only.

The tiny *violino piccolo* was occasionally used by Bach. With improved playing in the high positions on the violin the need for this inefficient instrument, with its feeble tone, disappeared. In 1756 Leopold Mozart in his *Violinschule* stated that the instrument was out-dated.

In France, during the eighteenth century, an instrument called the *quinton* was made, a five-stringed violin, tuned g, d^1, a^1, d^2, g^2.

At about the same time there appeared in Germany a tenor instrument called the *viola pomposa*, some 30 to 32 inches in length and usually tuned d, g, d^1, g^1, c^2. In performance it was held neither under the chin, like the violin and viola, nor between the legs like the 'cello, but leaning against the left upper arm.

A smaller form of the violoncello, the *violoncello piccolo*, was likewise used in the first half of the eighteenth century. It was equipped with four strings, tuned like those of a violoncello, to which at times a fifth string in e^1 was added. Bach's sixth Suite for Violoncello was written for this five-stringed instrument.

Makers of Stringed Instruments

During the sixteenth century the main types of bowed instrument had attained their final classic shape. As their form met every need, the development of details could begin. The makers of the period strove to augment the tonal and aesthetic beauty of the various instruments by the selection of woods and varnishes, and by minute readjustments of the proportions, of a nature perceptible only to experts.

Italy, which had first developed the modern forms of the stringed instruments, remained their center of production. In consequence of an unbroken workshop tradition, and favored by a lively demand—especially from France—certain towns of Italy and the neighboring Tirol achieved supremacy in this field. Although stringed instruments of every type were made, the main object of the master-craftsmen was the improvement and refinement of the "queen of instruments," the violin. The first important center of violin-making was Brescia; its oldest eminent master was Gasparo da Salò (1540–1609). The very few examples of his work that have come down to us are still somewhat old-fashioned in detail, but they none the less show the typical shape, which was later to become the norm. Gasparo's pupil was Giovanni Paolo Maggini (1580–1632), in whose person the Brescia school reached its zenith. Following at first in the footsteps of his master, he eventually made his own richly ornamented model, notable for its low ribs and lightly waisted middle bout. Maggini's instruments are distinguished by a mild, yet sonorous tone-quality.

After the middle of the seventeenth century the leadership passed from Brescia to Cremona. The founder of the Cremona school was Andrea Amati (1535 to after 1611), the first of the celebrated family. He left his workshop to his two sons, Antonio and Girolamo, and these were followed by Nicola (1596–1684), Girolamo's son, the most eminent member of the family. The violins of the Amatis have a highly-vaulted table and a varnish of singular perfection. Their tone is distinguished by sweetness and softness. The beauty of their sound was regarded as unsurpassable in the seventeenth and eighteenth centuries, and it was not until the nineteenth century that a preference was shown for the more powerful instruments of Nicola's greatest pupil, Antonio Stradivari (1644–1737). This "master of all masters", after decades of research, constructed a larger, flatter model, which, although it is not inferior to the violins of the Amatis in tenderness, far exceeds them in volume and fullness of tone. The precise and careful workmanship of these violins is no less remarkable than their musical qualities; Stradivari instruments remain to this day the utterly unrivalled ideals of tonal and aesthetic perfection. The third master of the Cremona school, and again the most important member of a large family of violin-makers, was Giuseppe Guarneri (1698–1744), called *del Gesù*, after the holy monogram, IHS, with which he marked his violins. His instruments are less regularly constructed, but the tone is always beautiful. The greatness of this artist, round whose life a host of legends have been woven, was not recognized until long after his death, and then by the daemonic Paganini, a congenial spirit. Under Stradivari's pupils and successors the significance of Cremona as a violin-making center gradually declined.

The only non-Italian school which was able to rival the Italians, at least for a time, was situated in the neighboring Tirol. It owed its fame to the work of the gifted Jacob Stainer (1617–1683), who spent a substantial part of his life in Absam near Innsbruck. His instruments had a highly-vaulted table, and their tone was unusually tender and flute-like. During the seventeenth and eighteenth centuries they enjoyed a quite extraordinary vogue, and amateurs paid even higher prices for them than for those of Amati. Bach owned a Stainer violin and so did Mozart's father, the great violin teacher Leopold Mozart.

After these leading makers of stringed instruments there came a whole series of German, French, English and American workshops, which were all more or less dependent on the traditions of the great Italian schools, but never equalled their models.

Pochette or Kit

In the Baroque period the members of the violin and viola da gamba families assumed a position of such prominence that earlier bowed instruments were eliminated or thrust into the background. Only the rebec, although not used in serious music, was still able to play a certain part. In a small, club-shaped form (Pls. XXXIV, XLI/1), and sometimes, in the eighteenth century, in the shape of a miniature violin, with three to four strings tuned to (c^1), g^1, d^2, a^2, it was used by dancing-masters to indicate rhythm and melody to their pupils. Goethe tells us, in his *Dichtung und Wahrheit*, that as a young student in Strasbourg, he learned to dance the minuet to the strains of this little instrument. Accordingly the rebec was known at this time as *Tanzmeistergeige* ("dancing-master's fiddle"), or, since it was preferably carried in the pocket, as *poche* or *pochette*. The English name, *kit*, was possibly derived from "Kithara." It was at times made of precious materials, such as rosewood, ivory or tortoise-shell, and decorated with gems and pearls. In the Rococo period the pochette was occasionally constructed so whimsically that the bow could be tucked away inside the instrument, and not only the bow, but even a fan or a powder-puff.

Hurdy-Gurdy

In the Rococo period, as mentioned above, the *hurdy-gurdy* (Fr. *vielle à roue*, It. *lira*, Ger. *Radleier*) was the subject of a certain revival. In France (Pl. XLIV/2) it was usually equipped with two melody strings, both tuned to g^1, and four drones, tuned G g d^1 g^1, or c g c^1 with one drone suppressed. Sympathetic strings and a drone that ran over a bridge, one leg of which drummed on the table of the instrument, were occasionally used. The eighteenth-century hurdy-gurdy had 23 keys and a compass of two octaves. It was the favorite instrument of the French nobility, which indulged in the sentimental dream of leading a pastoral life.

Tromba Marina

Yet another stringed instrument which had enjoyed the esteem of the Middle Ages was granted a temporary popularity during the Baroque period. This was the *tromba marina*, which was now made in a larger and heavier form, so that it could no longer be held in the air, but had to be set on the ground (Pl. XLI/2). Its body was built up from several staves, and its peg-box was similar to that of a double-bass. In order to enhance the ethereal effect of its harmonics, this instrument too was sometimes provided with up to 50 sympathetic strings, which were fitted inside the body. The tromba marina was particularly popular in France, where it was considered to be a nautical instrument. The great theorist Marin Mersenne claimed in his *Harmonie universelle* (1636–37) that it was invented by sailors, and J. B. Lully wrote in 1660 a *Divertissement pour les matelots* (for sailors) scored for a tromba marina and strings. After the middle of the following century interest in this curious instrument rapidly decreased.

The widely-read musical author J. S. Petri stated in 1767 that the tromba marina was employed only "in nunneries, where they had no trumpets", and before long even this limited use was discontinued.

Cittern
As with the bowed progeny of the fiddle, so with its plucked offspring, the *cittern*, the more efficient peg-box of the violins was finally victorious in the seventeenth century, while the peculiar mixed position of the pegs used during the sixteenth century disappeared. In addition to the parent instrument (Pl. XXXIX), which usually employed five or six courses of wire strings of different pitch, there were several variants.

Citrinchen
As early as 1618 Praetorius recorded: "About three years ago an Englishman came to Germany with a very small cittern in which the lower part of the back was left half open." This little *Englisches Citrinchen*, as it was called in Germany (It. *citarino*), had eight strings in four courses and was often tuned in f^2 a^1 d^2 g^2. In its native land, as well as in France, it was primarily used in barbers' shops. In Germany too, around that time, a special type of cittern was evolved. This was the Hamburg Citrinchen, with a bell-shaped outline and ten strings in five courses. J. S. Bach was probably referring to this instrument when he said that his ancestor Veit Bach liked to while away the time by playing the "cythringen".

Bass Citterns
In addition to these small citterns the Baroque period, in its love of extremes, and stimulated by the need for low bass instruments capable of sounding chords, produced various *bass citterns*. The four-foot high *bandora* or *pandora*, with seven courses of metal strings reaching down to G_1, was probably invented in England. The slightly shorter *orpharion*, or *orpheoreon*, was equipped with eight courses of strings, the lowest of which was tuned in C. In the eighteenth century France and Italy produced archcitterns, using gut strings instead of the former wire strings. About half of them were "off-boards" (bass strings not running over the finger-board), which had their own peg-box placed above the

peg-box of the regular strings. In these archcitterns, as in most citterns, the number of strings and the tuning were subject to great variation.

Lute

The *lute* of the seventeenth and eighteenth centuries gradually lost the high esteem it enjoyed during the Renaissance. In order to adapt the instrument to the requirements of the Baroque period the six main pairs of strings were supplemented by a varying number of additional strings in the bass; yet even these did not enable the lute to hold its own, since it had to compete with the growing popularity of the harpsichord. As a solo instrument the lute had a late flowering in France in the works of Denis Gaultier (d. 1672), but he had no successor of equal stature, though his works influenced the development of the French clavier style. In the eighteenth century progressive musicians made fun of the large number of strings used on the lute. Thus in 1713 the famous musical author Mattheson wrote in his *Neu-Eröffnetes Orchester:* "If a lutenist reaches the age of eighty he has assuredly tuned his lute for sixty years . . . and yet now there is trouble with the strings, now with the frets, now with the pegs, so that I have been told that in Paris it costs as much to keep a lute as to keep a horse." Shortly after these words had been written the lute became a thing of the past; and it speaks well for its former importance that even in its last years it found a biographer. In 1727 appeared E. G. Baron's *Untersuchung des Instruments der Lauten* ("Treatise on the Lute"), a work which endeavoured to plead the cause of the lute, but was really no more than its obituary.

Archlutes

The bigger types of lute, the great *archlutes*, which were made as early as the sixteenth century (though it was only in the seventeenth that they won a position of importance), satisfied the demand of the Baroque era for instruments capable of providing an effective continuo accompaniment. These archlutes, which occurred in various forms, always possessed—like the bass citterns—in addition to the ordinary peg-box for the finger-board strings, a second peg-box for the bourdon strings which ran beside the finger-board. For the lower notes longer strings were used, and there was no need to stretch them as slackly as in the lute, so that the tone of the instrument was improved. Several different types of archlute were employed.

The *theorbo lute* or *theorboed lute* retained the lute's body, neck and reverted peg-box. The second peg-box, however, was in the same plane as the neck, which it seemed to continue; the two peg-boxes were thus at right angles to each other (Pls. XXXVIII, XXXIX). Various methods of tuning the instrument were used.

In the *theorbo*, the main peg-box seemed to be an extension of the instrument's neck. The second peg-box ran approximately parallel to it and was joined to the first by a short S-shaped connecting-piece. The theorbo had a length of approximately five feet. In the seventeenth century its strings were usually single (tuned F_1 G_1 A_1 B_1 C D E F/G c f a d g); in the eighteenth they were usually paired (tuned: F_1 F G_1 G A_1 A B_1 B C c D d/E e F F A A d d f f a a d^1 f^1).

The *chitarrone* (Pl. XLV/1) resembled the theorbo, but it had a smaller body, while the length of the connecting-piece between the two peg-boxes was considerably increased; thus the total length of the instrument could be as great as six feet. According to Praetorius it was tuned F_1 G_1 A_1 B_1 C D E F/G c d f g a. Monteverdi was one of the first composers to prescribe, in 1619, "*chitarone o spineta*" as continuo instruments.

The *angelica* was of lesser importance. It was a kind of theorbo without frets, whose sixteen strings were diatonically tuned, as is the harp, which made it easier for amateurs to play.

Mandola

The *mandola* (Pl. XXXIV), which seems very small compared with the preceding giants of the instrumental world, was known in the seventeenth century by all sorts of diminutive names: *pandurina, mandurina, mandürchen,* etc. It was made with the characteristic reverted or gently backward-curving head, and had at first four or five pairs of strings tuned, according to Praetorious, in c g c^1 g^1 c^2. Later, single strings were preferred.

Mandolin

The *mandolin* (Fr. *mandoline*, Ger. *Mandoline*, It. *mandolino*) is a small, lute-like instrument with a deeply-vaulted back, fashioned from individual staves, and a table sloping at the lower end.

Wire strings are carried over a low bridge and fastened to the rib. The instrument is equipped with a peg-board and the pegs are at right angles to the plane of the table. The neck is fretted and the mandolin is played, in the ancient oriental manner, with a plectrum, to which a constant vibratory movement is imparted.

The mandolin may well be an ancient Italian folk-instrument, but it became generally known only in the later part of the seventeenth century. It was fitted, in different parts of Italy, with four, five or even six courses of strings. In the eighteenth century the Neapolitan mandolin came to the fore; with its four pairs of strings, tuned as in the violin, it was capable of performing music written for the highly-esteemed bowed instrument. Outside Italy the mandolin was hardly ever met with until after the middle of the eighteenth century.

Colascione

Italy was also the home of the *colascione*, a lute of Asiatic origin, with a small body, a very long neck equipped with gut frets, a reverted head and two or three gut or wire strings tuned— according to Mersenne—in (E) A d. Later five and even six strings, tuned D G c f a (d^1), were employed. This instrument had its period of popularity in the seventeenth century. In the eighteenth it was discarded by serious musicians in its native Italy, though in northern countries it was still occasionally used as a bass instrument to reinforce the continuo.

Guitar, Chitarra Battente

Throughout the Baroque period most *guitars* (Pls. XXXVI, XXXVIII) were equipped with five pairs of gut strings, tuned A, d, g, b, e^1. The shape of the instrument's body had not been altered since the sixteenth century, but the position of its pegs underwent a curious change. While the other stringed instruments adopted the more efficient peg-box with lateral pegs, the guitar, which had used lateral pegs from the beginning, changed over in the seventeenth century to a board in which the pegs were arranged at right angles to the table. This alteration might have been due to the influence of a close relative of the guitar, which first made its appearance in the early eighteenth century, though some of its features were surprisingly primitive for that period. This instrument, which was known in Italy as the *chitarra battente* and in Spain as the *vihuela de peñola*, reveals a close relationship to the medieval fiddle. The chitarra battente retained the vaulted back of the vielle, which it combined with the straight ribs of the ordinary guitar (Pl. XLIV/1). The strings were led over the whole length of the table to the lower edge of the body, and the pegs were at right angles to the plane of the table. This table sloped away slightly at its lower end, and there were five courses of strings, plucked in the medieval fashion with a plectrum (Sp. *peñola*).

As the Baroque lute was equipped with an increasing number of strings it became unwieldy and harder to play. The guitar, on the other hand, gradually adopted single strings and with its conveniently flattened back it turned into the natural substitute for the complex and out-moded lute. Thus the first half of the eighteenth century witnessed throughout Europe, and particularly in France, a growing interest in the guitar, and it became the favorite instrument of musical amateurs.

Harp

It was one of the main aims of Baroque instrument-makers to provide the *harp* with the chromatic semitones which had long been available to the other stringed instruments. The seventeenth century experimented further with the *chromatic harp*, which had a separate string for each note of the chromatic scale; these were often arranged in two rows. Praetorius mentions an instrument so constructed, and there were attempts to perfect the system even in the nineteenth century, though the great number of strings required made such harps very cumbersome. More successful than the chromatic harp was the *hook harp* (Ger. *Hakenharfe*, Fr. *harpe à crochets*, It. *arpa a nottolini*; Pl. XLV/2), invented in the Tirol in the second half of the seventeenth century. A varying number of pivoted hooks were attached to the neck of a diatonically-tuned harp; pressed against the strings, these shortened them sufficiently to raise the pitch by a semitone. As a popular instrument the hooked harp is still in use today— notably in Czechoslovakia.

The disadvantage of the system, that the harpist, in order to alter the pitch, had to stop playing with one hand, was overcome by the invention in southern Germany in about 1720 of the *pedal harp*. In this instrument all the hooks for raising the pitch of each like note in the different octaves were attached to a common mechanism, actuated by the player's feet. With the help of seven pedals, which could be fixed in the depressed position, it was now possible to raise all the notes of the diatonic scale by a semitone.

Like the Renaissance, the Baroque period set its own aesthetic stamp on the harp. The front pillar took the form of a classical column, supporting a heavy volute which constituted the end of the neck. The harp, which was often gilt, appeared more massive and imposing.

Psaltery

In the seventeenth and eighteenth centuries, the *psaltery*, which was plucked with the fingers, made its appearance in a more efficient variant, known as the *pointed harp* (It. *arpanetta*, Fr. *arpanette*, Ger. *Spitzharfe*). This instrument, used in the popular music of the time, was shaped like a wing and had a sound-box placed between two ranks of strings. On one side of it were the high strings of steel, and on the other the low strings of brass. The player stood the pointed harp on a table or rested it on his knees. He played the melody with one hand on the front of the instrument and the accompaniment with the other on the opposite side.

Dulcimer

The *dulcimer*, in which the strings were struck with light hammers (Pl. XLI/1), was often encountered in the Baroque period. Each course of this instrument consisted of two, three, four or even more strings. These were usually divided by a bridge in the ratio of two to three, thus producing notes a fifth apart. Around the year 1700 the dulcimer was improved by the dancing-master Pantaleon Hebenstreit, who constructed a larger and more sonorous instrument with strings of metal-covered gut and steel, having a range of from four to six octaves. This was known as the *pantaleon* or *pantalon*. Even Hebenstreit's improvement, however, could not raise the instrument to a position of real significance. Apart from other defects, the prolonged reverberation of the strings made the execution of rapid passages impossible; also, in such a comparatively lightly-built instrument, it was difficult to keep the very

large number of strings (there might be over 100) correctly
tuned.

Folk Zither
Popular forms of psaltery and dulcimer occurred in the Alpine
regions of central Europe and also in Scandinavia. The local
form was known in Germany as *Scheitholt* and later simply as
Zither, in Sweden as *hummel*, in Norway as *langleih,* and in Denmark
as *humle*. As a rule each consisted of a straight and narrow, or
sometimes curved, body over which strings were stretched. The
instruments were frequently placed on a table; their strings were
shortened by the fingers of the left hand, occasionally with the
help of a little stick; and they were plucked with the fingers of the
right hand or with a plectrum. During the Baroque period these
popular instruments were gradually enlarged and equipped
with an increasing number of strings. They became more
efficient and in the Alpine regions of central Europe music and
dancing were unthinkable without the accompaniment of a
zither.

Of the psaltery-like instruments, those provided with a keyboard enjoyed the highest esteem in the seventeenth century and
in the first half of the eighteenth.

Clavichord
The *clavichord* was essentially an instrument for the home. It was
the solo instrument for small rooms, and it was also the instrument which gave the player the most immediate control over the
tone. Technically, the clavichord underwent a trifling yet
characteristic change towards the end of the seventeenth century.
In view of the ever-increasing musical demands it was desirable
that the chromatic semitones should be available even in the
lowest octave, but many performers were unwilling to relinquish
the familiar device of the "short octave," so the F♯ and G♯ keys
in the lowest octave were "broken," as in the organ. Their upper
(longer) halves now gave F♯ and G♯, their lower (shorter) halves
D and E as before (Pl. XLVI/1). Not until the eighteenth century
was this curious expedient of the "short" and "broken" octave
finally discontinued.

In the early eighteenth century the clavichord underwent a
second and much more important change. The system of the

"fretted" (*gebundenes*) clavichord made it impossible in many cases for notes lying close together to be played simultaneously, yet the new developments in harmony called for an end to this limitation, so the "fret-free" (*bundfreies*) clavichord was constructed, in which every key had its own course of strings. Its compass was usually four octaves $(C - c^3)$ and a stand was always needed to support the heavier and larger case. Many performers, however, continued to use the small, light and more easily tuned older instrument, so that the new improvement was not universally adopted.

Harpsichord

The *harpsichord* (Pls. XXXIV, XLVIII) offers the strongest contrast to the clavichord. Its more brilliant and powerful tone made it the instrument for large music-rooms and the theatre. It was very important for the execution of a figured bass, and indispensable for the performance of orchestral music. The composers of the Baroque period liked to conduct large-scale secular works from the harpsichord.

It is true that the tone of the instrument was not flexible and capable of variation, like that of the clavichord. The direct transmission of emotion through the keys to the strings was impossible in the harpsichord; on the other hand, thanks to its high technical development, it was capable of producing a number of dynamic and even tonal contrasts.

The harpsichord of the Baroque period was larger and had a robuster tone than the Renaissance instrument; it had a greater compass, and sometimes also a greater number of stops or registers. Besides the four-foot, it had one or two eight-foot stops, and sometimes a lute register (in which felt or leather dampers were pressed against the strings, so that the tone was muted and resembled that of a lute). Occasionally also a separate set of jacks plucked the strings close to the end of their vibrating length, thus producing a strongly nasal sound; and in German instruments a 16-foot register is also sometimes found. These stops could be employed singly or combined at will. Moreover, with the two-manual instrument, one keyboard could operate the high stops, and the other the low; one could produce loud notes, the other soft, so that the musician had a number of dynamic and coloristic gradations at his command.

It should be borne in mind that on the Baroque harpsichord the registers were as a rule operated by hand. The player established the desired registration at the beginning of a piece and could change it in the course of his performance only if the music provided a long enough rest for one hand. So present-day harpsichordists, who operate the register stops on modern instruments with the help of pedals, ought to refrain from excessive changes in registration, which were impossible on harpsichords before 1750.

Italy, where the bowed instruments were brought to a climax of perfection during the Baroque period, was less interested in making the comparatively stiff and unyielding cembalo. After the end of the sixteenth century the center of harpsichord construction moved further north, to Flanders, where the members of the Ruckers family of Antwerp, in particular, acquired fame as makers of these instruments. Their cembalos, distinguished by beauty of workmanship and tone, were in great demand throughout Europe and particularly in England.

Clavicytherium

The space-saving *clavicytherium* (Pl. XXXV) was usually equipped with two eight-foot registers and occasionally also with an added four-foot stop. Very few specimens have survived, possibly because eighteenth- and nineteenth-century makers liked to transform clavicytheriums into upright pianofortes with hammer action.

Spinet

The *spinet* (Pls. XXXVII, XXXVIII, XL) may be likened to a small, compact and delicate harpsichord. However, it had only one eight-foot register and one manual. As compared with the harpsichord, the spinet had the advantages of being cheaper to produce and easier to move about. At the same time, it was louder than the clavichord, so that it could be employed not only as a solo instrument, but also in chamber music. However, the growing demand for subjectivity of expression and dynamic contrasts gradually made these advantages seem less important. During the seventeenth century the spinet began to lose ground throughout Europe. Only in England was it widely used in the eighteenth century. There, a larger, wing-shaped instrument with an eight-foot register was known as a "leg of mutton." Its tuning-pins were placed behind the nameboard, like those of a harpsichord, and it was supported by a solid stand.

Wind Instruments; Recorder

In the middle of the seventeenth century French instrument-makers rebuilt the *recorder*. They constructed the instrument, which had hitherto consisted of a single staff, in three sections, thus making it much easier to tune; at the same time they considerably increased the taper of the bore. The unpractical double finger-hole (the lowest hole) in the smaller forms was replaced by a single, movable hole; the bottom section of the tube was made to rotate, so that the performer could shift the little finger-hole to a position convenient to him.

In addition, a conspicuous aesthetic transformation of the instrument took place. The earlier recorder had the shape of a smooth staff, as befitted the restrained, simple taste of the Renaissance. But around 1650 it assumed a shape which was obviously determined by Baroque canons of form (Pl. XLVII/2). The tube left the lathe with various dilations, so that its form was made more imposing and assumed a gracefully curved profile.

That the recorder did not undergo any further technical development may be attributed to the fact that it gradually went out of favor. Of the eight sizes mentioned by Praetorius in 1618, only three were still in use a century later: a descant, with a range f^1–f^3, an alto-tenor, with a range c^1–c^3, and a bass, with a range f–f^2. Mattheson was not alone in feeling—as he wrote in 1713— that one "could easily grow out of conceit" with the instrument "on account of its gentle and ingratiating character"; for the soft, equable tone of the recorder could not satisfy the growing demand for subjective expression, for dynamic and tonal contrasts. Little by little the "flauto" or "flute," as the instrument was called at that time, was ousted from its position during the first half of the eighteenth century and replaced by the transverse flute.

Flageolet

A variant of the recorder was the (French) *flageolet*, which owed its employment to the Baroque delight in extremely high notes. This instrument, which is said to have been invented by Juvigny

in Paris at the close of the sixteenth century, was remarkable for
the unusual position of its finger-holes, four being in the front
and two in the back of the pipe. The compass of the instrument
was g²–a⁴, and as a rule its parts were written a twelfth lower than
they actually sounded. Under the name of *flauto piccolo* Handel
used the instrument in *Rinaldo* and in *Acis and Galatea*, and
Bach introduced it into his sacred cantatas Nos. 96 and 103.

Transverse Flute

In the *transverse flute* (It. *flauto traverso*, Fr. *flûte traversière*, Ger.
Querflöte), the act of blowing is less mechanical than in the
recorder; overblowing is easier and the instrument offers oppor-
tunities for greater dynamic and tonal variety. Of course the
simple transverse flute of the Renaissance was far from adequate,
and extensive modifications were necessary before it could play
its part in serious music. It was again in France, where there
was a particular interest in wind instruments, that the transformation was effected (Pl. XLIII). In the second half of the
seventeenth century the parent instrument—the soprano of the
Renaissance period—was divided like the recorder into three
parts: the head with the mouth-hole, the middle joint and the
foot. The head was still cylindrical in bore, but in the middle
joint and the foot the bore tapered towards the open end. In
addition to the six finger-holes there was a closed key (D♯) for
the little finger. In the first half of the eighteenth century the
middle joint itself was divided in order to facilitate the correction
of defects of intonation. After 1720 the foot was also divided and
two further keys were added.

In 1677 Lully introduced the improved transverse flute into
the orchestra of the opera, and in 1707 the French flute virtuoso
and composer Jacques Hotteterre investigated the potentialities
of the instrument in his *Principes de la Flûte Traversière*. Soon after-
wards Mattheson described it as "an instrument worthy of high
esteem," and in 1717 Bach used the *flauto traverso* for the first time.
It also says much for the rising reputation of the instrument that
a king, Frederick the Great of Prussia, was one of its most
enthusiastic amateurs.

Oboe

Among the wind instruments of the Baroque period the *oboe* (from the French *hautbois*, high or loud "wood") played an especially important part. It came into being during the second half of the seventeenth century—above all, in France—as an improvement of the shawm (Pl. XXXIV). While the shawm was a crudely-made double-reed instrument with a wide, conical bore and was fashioned from a single piece of wood, the oboe was much more carefully constructed; it consisted of three sections and its bore was narrower. The oboe had not the shrill, bleating tone of the older instrument; its sound was softer and more delicate, which was partly due to the fact that the *pirouette*, the old cup-shaped connection between the mouthpiece and the instrument, was discarded around the middle of the seventeenth century; now the reed was no longer taken right into the mouth, but held between the lips. The player was therefore able to exert a certain control over the strength and quality of the tone, and overblowing became possible.

The oldest oboe was provided with only six finger-holes, of which two were doubled; two small finger-holes were placed on the same level and close together, so that the player could cover one or both with the same finger. They were intended to produce the semitones f^1 or $f\sharp^1$ and g^1 or $g\sharp^1$, respectively. The instrument also had three keys; of these one was provided with double wings ("swallow-tail"), while the other two were situated opposite each other, so that they could be used by either the right or the left hand, for it was still a matter of choice which of the player's hands was the lower. The "swallow-tail" key closed an otherwise open hole, thus lengthening the tube and producing the lowest note c^1, while the doubled key opened holes for the note $e\flat^1$. The new instrument, which had a compass of two octaves, c^1–c^3, quickly became popular. In 1671 Robert Cambert prescribed its use in his opera *Pomone*, and before long it was the favorite wind instrument of the Baroque period. It was played in conjunction with the violin or as a solo instrument, and hardly any other wind instrument was more frequently employed.

Oboe d'Amore

A typical creation of the late Baroque's emotionalism was the *oboe d'amore* (Fr. *hautbois d'amour*, Ger. *Liebesoboe*), which appeared during the first half of the eighteenth century. It was somewhat larger than the oboe and pitched a third lower (compass a–a²). German instruments had a bulb-shaped bell, instead of the ordinary funnel-shape, and this added to the instrument's soft and mellow tone. The oboe d'amore was first prescribed by J. S. Bach in 1723, and thereafter it was among the favorite instruments of Thomas Cantor, who liked to employ it on account of its warm and intimate sound.

Alto Oboe, Oboe da Caccia, English Horn

As the oboe originated in the shawm, so in the Baroque period the alto pommer, by a process of refinement, became the *alto oboe* (Fr. *taille de hautbois*, or just *taille*; Pl. XLVI/2). In the first half of the eighteenth century this instrument, which was pitched a fifth below the regular oboe, was often given the bulb-shaped bell of the oboe d'amore. The result was an instrument with a warm, full tone which was also known by the not very suitable name of *oboe da caccia* (hunting oboe; Pl. XLVI/2). According to Zedler's *Universal-Lexikon* (1735), it was actually employed in the chase. But this use of the instrument cannot have been very frequent, for its tone was peaceful and anything but loud; indeed, Bach employed it for especially tender passages.

As the finger-holes of the oboe da caccia, which was 30 inches long, were a considerable distance apart, the device was often adopted of curving the instrument like a sickle (Pl. XLVI/2), or making it in two parts, joined together at an obtuse angle. A leather casing was fitted over the parts to make the joint air-tight. This new form, developed before the middle of the eighteenth century, was also given a pear-shaped or spherical bell. Perhaps because the deeper-toned oboes were particularly valued in England (Henry Purcell, in 1690, prescribed the use of a "tenner haut-boy" in his *Dioclesian*), it gradually became the custom to describe this new form as the *English horn* (Fr. *cor anglais*, Ger. *Englischhorn*, It. *corno inglese*, Sp. *cuerno inglés*). The curved shape of the instrument might have been responsible for its designation as a "horn."

Musette

The great interest taken by France in the oboe was extended to the *bagpipe*; in about 1610 a new variety was evolved there. Its chanter was a gentle-sounding oboe, but with a narrow, cylindrical bore, while the drone was a kind of rackett about six and a half inches in height, in which the bore ran up and down twelve times or more. The length and therefore the pitch of this drone could be altered. About the middle of the seventeenth century the famous virtuoso and maker of flutes and oboes, Jean Hotte-terre, added a second, straight chanter for the highest notes, thus giving the instrument a range of almost two octaves (f^1–d^3). Since wind was supplied by bellows which were compressed under the left arm, the *musette*—as the instrument was called in France—had considerable possibilities. Lully did not hesitate to employ it in the operatic orchestra. And when the Rococo passion for pastoral poetry was at its height, the musette became a fashionable instrument. Equipped with ivory pipes and decorated with tasteful magnificence, it turned into a favorite instrument of aristocratic amateurs.

Bassoon

In the first half of the seventeenth century the Chorist-Fagott was transformed in France into the *basson* (Eng. *bassoon*, Ger. *Fagott*, It. *fagotto*). This double-reed instrument consisted of two conical tubes which were fixed into and connected by a small block of wood, the "butt." The bassoon had a tube-length of eight and a half feet and a range of almost three octaves (Bb_1–g^1). It was fitted with three keys, to which a fourth was added in the first half of the eighteenth century.

Together with the oboe, the bassoon was admitted to the orchestra in 1671 in the production of Cambert's opera *Pomone*. As the bass of the woodwind, and also for reinforcing the bass strings, the instrument achieved a position of increasing im-portance. Among the first composers to employ the bassoon as a solo instrument was Handel, who in 1738, in his *Saul*, prescribed two bassoons, in order to symbolize the appearance of Samuel's ghost by their dull, hollow sound.

Double Bassoon

In its preference for sombre tones, the Baroque period created a *double bassoon* (Pl. XLVII/1), an octave below the ordinary bassoon. According to Praetorius, this was first made around 1620 by Hans Schreiber in Berlin. The new instrument was troublesome to construct on account of its great size. In addition, its intonation was extremely unsatisfactory, as the finger-holes were necessarily too small in proportion to the bore of the instrument. So it failed to achieve any importance in practical music.

Clarinet

The great wave of refinement, having dealt with the double-reed instruments, finally reached those with single reeds. In this group, the musical sounds are produced by the vibrations of only one piece of cane-reed (cf. p. 292).

A primitive woodwind instrument with cylindrical bore and equipped with a single reed had been known in Europe from the earliest times. It was usually called a *chalumeau*, or in Italy *zampogna*. In Germany someone hit on the idea of adding the chalumeau, with its single reed, to the number of serious musical instruments, as a rival to the double-reed pipe, the shawm, which the French had improved. The transformation was mainly the work of the Denners, a Nuremberg family of instrument-makers. After 1700, Johann Christoph Denner provided his carefully-constructed instrument with two keys. His son added a third key, and in particular a little hole near the mouthpiece, which facilitated overblowing. The new instrument was still called the chalumeau, but on account of a certain tonal affinity with the highest register of the trumpet (see below), it was known also as the little clarino or *clarinetto*. It seems to have been employed first in Germany, especially in Hamburg. In 1710 Reinhard Keiser prescribed it in his opera *Croesus*, in 1713 it was mentioned by Mattheson and by 1720 it had reached Antwerp. But the triumphant progress of the clarinet did not begin until the middle of the century was passed.

Trumpet

During the seventeenth century and the first half of the eighteenth, the art of the trumpeter remained on the same high level as that of which Praetorius spoke. Trumpet parts which go up to d^3, e^3, and f^3 occur in the compositions of the period, and Altenburg, who in 1795 wrote a history of the trumpet, declared that on a C-trumpet even g^3, which is the 24th harmonic, could be sounded. However, the trumpeters of those days appear to have set certain limits to their competence, which resulted in a division of labor. The "clarino" player, who used a comparatively shallow mouthpiece, played the highest parts and rarely descended into the lower register. The parts below the highest were taken by the "principal" trumpeter, who used a rather deeper mouthpiece, and only by exception ventured into the higher register. The extraordinary accomplishment of the trumpeters, and above all of the "clarino" player, made any special technical improvements of the instrument superfluous.

The performers of the Baroque period preferred to play in the key of D major, which could best be produced on trumpets with the fundamental note D, the so-called D-trumpets, which had a sounding length of over seven feet. However, the need gradually arose for instruments that could play other keys also. A trumpet in C was constructed, which had a length of eight feet, as well as shorter trumpets in E♭, F, etc. Sometimes the pitch of a trumpet was simply lowered by one or more semitones through the use of "crooks," short loops of extra tubing inserted between the mouthpiece and the main tube.

The trumpet maintained its inherited pride of place throughout the Baroque era. It was always employed for special effects, on solemn and stately occasions, and on festive days. Whenever it appeared, it played a leading role as a matter of course. A "clarino" part written as an accompaniment was hardly conceivable. After the middle of the seventeenth century the trumpet assumed increasing significance in art-music and it was also admitted as a solo instrument in opera. Thus Cavalli in an aria of his *Artemisia* (1656) had two trumpets compete with the human voice.

It should be borne in mind, however, that the large trumpets of the Baroque era, with their narrow bell, had a rounder, warmer and softer tone than the much shorter trumpets (with a considerably higher fundamental note) used in our time. It is characteristic that Bach in his second Brandenburg Concerto lets the trumpet compete with as delicate an instrument as the recorder.

Slide Trumpet

The *tromba da tirarsi*, or *slide trumpet*, and the *corno da tirarsi*, or *slide horn*, were sometimes prescribed in Bach's scores. The composer employed them in the accompaniment of chorales when tones and semitones were to be played in the deeper octave (c^1–c^2), where the natural notes of the instrument lay far apart. The Baroque slide trumpet resembled the ordinary folded trumpet of the time, except that its mouthpiece was attached to a tube which the player could push into the body of the instrument. With the help of this device every natural note could be lowered by a semitone, a whole tone, or a tone and a half, so that it was possible to play the chromatic scale even between c^1 and c^2. What the precise difference was between the tromba da tirarsi and the corno da tirarsi is not certain. In the score of his Cantata No. 46 Bach prescribes "tromba o corno da tirarsi." This may well imply that the terms were interchangeable; quite possibly they both referred to the slide trumpet, as a real slide horn does not seem to have existed.

Trombone

As with the trumpet, so in the case of the *trombone* family the Baroque period found it unnecessary to make any essential changes. At the beginning of the seventeenth century, to meet the need of the period for dark tone-colors, a contrabass twice as long as the tenor, and therefore an octave lower, was added to the family. Its invention—according to Praetorius—was due to Hans Schreiber, the Berlin town-musician, who was also the first to build a double-bassoon. Neither the large contrabass nor the little descant survived in the general practice of the time. In the popular reinforcement of vocal choirs by means of trombones, the alto trombone went with the contralto voice, the tenor trombone with the tenor voice, and the bass trombone (Pl. XXXIV) with the bass voice, while the vocal descant was reinforced, not by a trombone, but by a cornetto.

During the Baroque period trombones were usually tuned in F or E♭ (alto and bass) and in B♭ (tenor and double-bass). Crooks served to lower these tunings by any interval from a semi-tone to a fourth.

Horn

The Renaissance and the Early Baroque knew the circular horn mainly as an instrument of the hunt (Ger. *Jagdhorn*, It. ˉ*corno da caccia*, Fr. *cor de chasse*, Sp. *corneta de cazador*). In the second half of the seventeenth century the potentialities of the instrument for wider use were discovered. It seems that the French were mainly responsible for propagating the horn, but we know that

before the close of the century horns were also being made in
Germany and England. In 1705 R. Keiser employed the instrument in Hamburg (in *Octavia*), in 1715 A. Scarlatti used it in
Naples (in *Tigrane*), in 1717 Handel introduced it into his *Water
Musick*, and Bach prescribed it in many of his scores. Naturally
such a widely-used instrument was also improved technically
and adapted to the aesthetic demands of the time. Gradually the
tube of the horn was lengthened; it was given a slender, mostly
cylindrical, trumpet-like body, a funnel-shaped mouthpiece and a
wide bell. Although horns were made in various sizes, the one in
F was employed most and crooks to change the tuning found
increasing use. The new instrument, known in England as the
French horn and in Germany as *Waldhorn* (Fr. *cor d'harmonie*, It.
corno, Sp. *cuerno*), was capable of sounding as many as sixteen to
twenty partials (Pl. IL). Its tone was warm and tender in the
piano passages, while the forte had a brilliant, pealing quality,
attributes that before long were to secure for the horn a highly
significant position in the orchestra.

Cornetto

The *cornetto* retained its Renaissance form during the Baroque
period. Mersenne, writing in 1636, compared its sound to "a
ray of sunshine piercing the darkness." But later generations had
very little use for the instrument, which performers found
extremely hard to play, while to listeners its tone seemed dry
and lusterless. Early eighteenth-century church music occasionally
used it still, particularly as the treble of the trombone choir and
as reinforcement for children's voices (Bach prescribed it in
eleven cantatas!), but it was banished from all forms of secular
music.

Serpent

The *serpent* (Pl. LIX/1), like the cornetto, underwent no technical
transformation during the Baroque period. Contrary to the
parent instrument, however, it did not have to suffer a decline
in prestige. By overblowing and with the help of six finger-holes
a range of two and a half octaves and more ($D–b^1$ or even $A_1–d^2$)
could be covered; besides, the instrument was surprisingly
versatile. According to Mersenne, its tone equalled the power of
twenty of the loudest singers, and yet it could be employed in

the softest chamber music. The instrument was widely used in western Europe. It was indispensable for the church music of France and Belgium. Handel, who first came across the serpent in England, employed it in his *Water Musick* (1717) and his *Fireworks Musick* (1749) to provide a substantial bass for these outdoor compositions. In Germany the instrument was hardly used during the Baroque period, but even there it was to come into its own again at a later date.

Church Organ

The *church organ* of the seventeenth century reached a high standard of technical efficiency. This was largely due to two improvements in its construction that had been made at a somewhat earlier time but only came to full fruition during the early Baroque period. They concerned the bellows and the soundboard.

In place of the older bellows, with their many folds of leather, a new type was introduced made of wood and containing only a single fold. The simpler and stronger construction of these bellows made it possible to provide a more regular supply of wind, and so produce a more uniform tone. Of course, the wind still reached the interior of the organ in puffs. This defect was remedied when the air drawn in by the bellows was stored in a reservoir, and only then conveyed to the pipes. Canon Galpin first noted such a reservoir in an English organ built in 1629. The control of the organ's wind supply was further improved through the invention of the "wind gauge" by the German organ-builder Christian Förner in 1667. This is a manometer-like device which makes it possible to measure the pressure of the air inside the organ.

The second important improvement in organ construction was the ever-increasing use of the more reliable "slider" soundboard as against the all-too-sensitive "spring" sound-board. As these were two forms of one of the fundamental components of the organ, their function will be (briefly) explained.

The air pumped by the bellows passed through conduits into the undivided wind-chest and from this to the sound-board, which contained a number of separate channels, the "grooves." In the old "spring" sound-board a special valve, whose function was to admit or exclude the wind, was fitted in the grooves for each individual pipe; but the arrangement was complicated and costly. In the new "slider" sound-board, in which each groove ran under all the pipes of a given note on the keyboard, the "sliders" (strips of wood suitably pierced working across the grooves) admitted the wind to the pipes or cut it off. If a stop or register was to be cut out the solid parts of the sliders closed the respective pipes. When the register in question was to be included again, the slider was pulled out until the holes were under the feet of the pipes, so that the wind could enter them freely when the key was depressed. This arrangement was less expensive and less likely to break down than the old form of spring sound-board, and during the Baroque period it was universally adopted.

As regards its musical capabilities, until the first decade of the seventeenth century the organ had been adapted above all else to polyphonic music. Its individual registers were clearly distinguishable; they did not merge or melt into one another. Dynamic contrasts could be achieved only within certain restricted limits. The organ could speak neither in tones of thunder nor in ethereal whispers, and any sort of crescendo or decrescendo was impossible. Its tone was light and transparently clear, as the wind pressure was low and there were almost twice as many four-foot as eight-foot stops.

In the course of the seventeenth century and the first half of the eighteenth this type of organ was modified in the direction of subjective expression and a more flexible and variable tone. Even the Thirty Years War in Germany and the Civil Wars in England were unable to check this significant development.

The "tremulant," a rotating device, usually operating in the wind channel, which produced pulsating notes of a plaintive character, was increasingly employed. Possibly the *Bebung* of the clavichord and the vibrato of stringed instruments induced organists to make use of a similar effect. The great interest taken in the stringed instruments during the seventeenth century led to the introduction of string registers. The color of the narrow flue-pipes was denoted by such descriptive names as "viola da gamba" or "violin." Indeed, the organ even paid its tribute to the Baroque enthusiasm for the beauty of the human voice, for it introduced the "vox humana," a reed-pipe which attempted to copy the tones of the human larynx. The Italians, who had always aimed at coloristic effects in organ music, now took the initiative by devising registers which were no longer clearly contrasted with each other but became harmoniously interfused; the other musical countries of Europe readily followed their example.

The employment of "couplers," devices for connecting the individual keyboards, together with the pipes controlled by them, became more general. Sometimes, also, with the help of "transmissions," the pipes controlled by one manual could be brought into play by another. The combination of stops so obtained led to the increasing production of new tonal colors which did not differ from each other very greatly. The rigidity of tone that had characterized the organ at the beginning of the seventeenth century was to a great extent submerged a century later by the wealth of these interpenetrating nuances. Moreover, devices were introduced which made it possible to produce a dynamic crescendo and diminuendo. Individual registers were enclosed in an echo-chamber, in which their tones were effectively damped, in order to produce the greatly appreciated echo effects. In 1712 the organ-builder Abraham Jordan, in London, devised a pedal attachment by which the front wall of the echo-chamber could be opened or closed while the organ was playing. With the help of such a "swell" box a crescendo or diminuendo effect could be obtained.

Organs were usually equipped with two or three manuals and a pedal, each with its own set of pipes. The pedal and the first manual, known as the "Great Organ," sounded the strongest and most majestic registers, the second manual or "Choir Organ," the sharper and more pungent stops. If a third manual was provided it frequently activated warm, singing registers.

Positive

The more imposing the dimensions of the great church organs became, the more marked was the difference between them and the smaller type of fixed *positive* organ (Pls. XXXIII, XXXVI, XXXVII), designed for use in a chapel or music-room, or in ordinary living-rooms. It was generally built with only one manual, and without a pedal; the pipes were usually flue-pipes in four-foot and two-foot, or sometimes even in one-foot tone, while reed-pipes were rare. With its tender, gentle tone the instrument proved useful for accompaniment rather than as a solo instrument. So, in contrast to its limited use in the sixteenth century, it achieved wide distribution in the Baroque period, primarily as a continuo instrument.

Regal

Likewise the *regal*, which was usually constructed with only a single eight-foot register of reed-pipes (Pl. XXX/2), was employed in the seventeenth century chiefly as an instrument for the realization of a thoroughbass. It was particularly suitable for accompanying a choir of trombones, on account of its powerful, snarling tone. The instrument was put to this classic use as early as 1609 in Monteverdi's *Orfeo*. But the sentimental eighteenth century took exception to the harsh and unaccommodating tone of the instrument, which Mattheson described, with characteristic bluntness, as "extremely unpleasant." It did not survive beyond the middle of the eighteenth century.

Kettledrum

The *kettledrum*, which in the first half of the seventeenth century was still predominantly the military instrument of the German princes, began to make its way into the orchestra. It was placed on a metal tripod and played with short sticks ending in little discs. Lully had used the kettledrum in France by 1670, and it often appeared in the scores of Bach and Handel. In such music the kettledrum was usually employed in the company of trumpets. It was used in pairs, which were tuned to an interval of a fourth or a fifth. One was tuned to the tonic and the other to the dominant, and since the tuning-screws did not allow a rapid change of pitch, this was usually left unaltered during the performance of a piece of music. Handel, in his *Fireworks Musick*, was one of the first composers to use three kettledrums.

The social status of the kettledrum, as the companion of the trumpet, was still high during the Baroque period. Silver kettledrums were not unknown, and they were sometimes hung with costly embroideries. Of course, it must not be overlooked that from the second half of the seventeenth century, quite apart from the use of the kettledrum in serious music, there were also performers who handled the instrument in a playful and humorous manner. Such players tossed the sticks into the air and deftly caught them again, accompanying their performance with acrobatic contortions of the body; in France and Germany, moreover, negro performers on the kettledrum appear to have been all the rage. This may be regarded, perhaps, as a revival of the medieval connection between the musician and the acrobat or juggler.

Snare Drum

The *drum* of the seventeenth century resembled that of the Renaissance. Not until the eighteenth century was the height of the instrument somewhat reduced. At the same time the wooden body was gradually replaced by a more durable brass shell, though this innovation did not become general until the middle of the century. Nor was the drum immediately able to break away from its purely military use and obtain a firm footing in orchestral music.

Tambourine, Triangle

The *tambourine* was regarded as an instrument of the gypsies, and was of no importance in the Baroque era. Similarly, the *triangle*, according to Mersenne, was used only by beggars.

Castanets

Castanets (Sp. *castañetas*, "little chestnuts", Fr. *castagnettes*, Ger. *Kastagnetten*, It. *castagnette*) are pairs of small, shell-shaped clappers made of hard wood, or sometimes ivory, connected by a loop at the upper end. The player's thumb holds one half of the instrument, while the fingers strike the other half against it in short, dry, subtly-rhythmical beats. Two pairs of castanets are usually employed together, a larger and a smaller one, for the player's two hands. The instrument is of oriental origin, and to be found on Greek vases. At a very early date it made its way into Spain and the culturally related regions of southern Italy. Before long the Iberian peninsula had promoted the castanets to the rank of its national instrument of the dance. Together with Spanish dancers it travelled into all parts of Europe. By 1600, Richelieu, castanets in hand, had danced the saraband before Anne of Austria, and a century later a German dancing-master (Tauber's *Rechtschaffener Tanzmeister*, 1717) made the castanets the subject of an exhaustive analysis.

Carillon, Glockenspiel

The *carillon*, consisting of a set of bells, reached its culmination in the seventeenth century. Hardly any technical improvements were considered necessary after the Renaissance. In the Netherlands, where the carillon thrived, the need was also felt for a smaller, less unwieldy practice instrument. Acquaintance with the Javanese *saron*, consisting of a set of tuned slabs of bronze which the Dutch found in newly-conquered Indonesia, may have led to the construction of such a substitute. It was described by Brossard (1703) as "An instrument that uses a row of metal plates arranged like a keyboard. These plates are struck with two little rods which have a ball at one end; a tone is produced thereby, resembling that of bells." Although Brossard called this instrument a carillon, a designation used also by Handel in his *Saul* for a set of tuned metal plates, we shall refer to it by its German name, *Glockenspiel*, to avoid confusion with the earlier, large instrument. At times the Baroque glockenspiel was also equipped with a manual, and even with a pedal.

Xylophone

It was probably in Holland, the land of the glockenspiel and the carillon, that the notion was first conceived of providing the *xylophone* with a keyboard. However, the weak and inexpressive tone of the instrument by no means justified the expense of this technical improvement, so the innovation never achieved wider distribution.

On the whole it may be said that the Baroque era, in its striving after emotional expression, treated the so-called instruments of percussion—whether their sonorous elements consisted of parchment, metal or wood—with a certain reserve, to be explained by the inflexible character of their tone.

VI

THE CLASSICAL PERIOD

(1750–1810)

Classical music went through two preparatory stages before it reached its full development. Even before the death of Bach there was a movement afoot to replace majestic splendour by graceful delicacy. The buskins of Baroque pomposity were exchanged for the dancing slippers of the *style galant*. It did not take long, however, for a reaction to set in against such superficial levity. "Back to nature" was the new slogan, originating with J. J. Rousseau. It implied a return to subjectivity and the outpouring of feeling. German literature and music accepted it eagerly and *Empfindsamkeit* (affected sentimentalism), with its unrestrained emotionalism, became the fashion. Finally, in the seventeen-eighties, the spirit of these earlier phases, along with the strictness of Baroque polyphony, were fused together, and a unique balance of form and content was achieved, a complete blend of inspiration and intellect. J. Haydn (1732–1809) and W. A. Mozart (1756–1791) provided in their masterworks the finest examples of this fully developed *classical style*. L. van Beethoven (1770–1827), with his forceful, virile approach, continued where they left off, giving the style new meaning. The highly individual, at times problematic, character of his later works led to a new phase in the history of music, which will be discussed in the next chapter.

The expression of personal feeling and of strong emotions was of paramount concern to the leading composers, swayed by the tenets of *Empfindsamkeit*. As a first step in this direction the rigidity of earlier dynamic patterns had to be broken. The stratified dynamics of the Baroque period, with their sharp distinction between pianissimo, piano, and forte, seemed insufficient. Transitions between these clearly separated steps had to be achieved; it should be possible to increase the intensity of sound, in a kind of dynamic glissando, from the weakest to the strongest level or, on the other hand, to have loud music gradually fade out. Thus *crescendo* and *diminuendo* were introduced. Whole orchestras proudly displayed their skill in producing a crescendo, and a newly developed instrument, the pianoforte, owed much of its general success to its dynamic flexibility. It was able not only to sound softly and loudly, but also to produce gradual transitions between dynamic steps.

Opera

In the field of *opera* the classical period witnessed the same striving toward clarity and simplicity of expression, the voicing of true feeling and strong passion, which leading spirits postulated in some of the other arts. A famous formulation of these ideas was put forward by C. W. v. Gluck (1714–1787) in the preface to his opera *Alceste*; and practical applications of the concepts were offered by the composer in a number of Italian and French serious operas, which revolutionized the character of the music-drama. In the field of comic opera—the Italian *opera buffa*, the French *opéra comique*, and the German *Singspiel*—no reform movement was required, as these forms, created for the most part during the eighteenth century, were from the outset based on the principle of unaffected simplicity. Here, on the contrary, the classical period had to provide greater solidity of plot; at times even serious elements were introduced, a trend which witnessed its greatest manifestation in Mozart's *Don Giovanni*, with its perfect balance between comedy and tragedy.

In these various operatic forms the instruments not only provided background and atmosphere; they also commented on the action and supplied the necessary local color. Since the voices had to renounce the superiority they had so often usurped in earlier operas, the instruments moved into an important, though never dominant position. Gluck and his followers also upgraded the instrumental prelude to the opera. The overture, hitherto a neutral introduction which could be used one day for this, the next day for another work, now assumed a programmatic character, anticipating the mood of the first scene or, more often, portraying in pure sound the whole of the drama that was going to unfold. Practically every great composer of the time made significant contributions to this genre; in fact, in some cases the colorful instrumental introduction is today much better known than the drama itself.

Oratorio

In the field of *oratorio* composition the first decades after the death of Handel were completely overshadowed by the composer's powerful artistic personality. While no work of comparable significance was produced, English music-lovers conceived the idea of celebrating the approaching centenary of Handel's birth with commemorative concerts. In 1784 two performances of *The Messiah* took place in London's Westminster Abbey, which demonstrated also the penchant of the time for the use of huge groups of performers: in this case 274 voices and 252 instruments (157 strings, 89 wind instruments, 4 kettledrums and 2 organs). The celebration was so successful that it was repeated in several of the following years, for the last time in 1791, when—according to an eye-witness—"the band was a thousand strong." The accuracy of this number may well be doubted, but we know for certain that the performance was attended by Haydn, at that time a visitor in the English capital. It may well be that the impressions he gathered at this memorable concert inspired Haydn to embark on the composition of his own two great oratorios, which in a way continue the tradition of Handel's works in this genre. At all events, when Haydn's oratorio *The Creation* was performed for the first time in Vienna, in 1798, as many performers as could possibly be accommodated were crowded into the ballroom of the Princely palace, which had opened its doors for this unique event.

Church Music

During the classical period leading composers, most of all Haydn, Mozart and Beethoven, made outstanding contributions to Catholic *church music*, while Protestant religious music lost much of its former significance. The output of the leading Catholic artists was remarkable, not only as to quality, but also as to quantity and variety. A breathtaking number of Graduals, Offertories, Motets, Antiphons, Te Deums, Masses and Requiems were produced. Some of these pieces telescoped individual sections of the text into each other so as to be almost shockingly brief, while others were extended to such length that they could no longer be fitted into the liturgical framework. The accompanying instruments consisted at times of two violins and bass only, but more often than not of good-sized orchestras. Trumpets and kettledrums were occasionally employed; trombones frequently reinforced the voice parts, and occasionally four horns replaced the customary pair. The woodwind section was apt to include flutes and/or oboes, as well as bassoons, and in later scores also clarinets. For special effects English horns and basset-horns were introduced, besides an organ, used not only for accompaniments, but as a leading solo instrument.

Clavier Music

The *clavier* played as big a part in the classical era as the violin did during the Baroque period. Practically every composer of the time wrote works for a stringed keyboard instrument, and there was an incessant demand on the part of musical amateurs for pleasant, technically not too demanding compositions which could be performed by a single person.

Players had not just one, but four different types of clavier at their disposal. Up to the late 'sixties the harpsichord, the spinet, and the clavichord were generally accepted as the domestic instruments of the keyboard player. Between 1770 and 1775, however, they were gradually replaced by the new pianoforte, which combined the clavichord's flexibility of tone with the stronger sound of the harpsichord, thus making the earlier instruments appear obsolete. Germany alone, and in particular northern Germany, where the affected sentimentalism of *Empfindsamkeit* kept a strong hold on the minds of music-lovers, resisted the intrusion of the newcomer. C. P. E. Bach (1714–1788), Sebastian's second son, who lived in Berlin and later in Hamburg, and excelled as a clavier composer, had not much use for the pianoforte, but preferred the intimate and expressive clavichord for his solo compositions. As late as 1785 the poet and composer D. Schubart still rhapsodized: "He whose heart is often fain to find relief in tender sentiment—he passes by the harpsichord and piano, and chooses the clavichord."

In other countries, however, the painoforte—or piano, as it is conveniently called—took the unchallenged lead. In London J. Christian Bach, the Thomas Cantor's youngest son gave the first recital on the new instrument in 1768. Stylistic features indicate that the sonatas Haydn wrote after 1770 were intended for the piano, while Mozart and Beethoven never employed any other type of clavier.

The option *pour le Clavecin ou Pianoforte*, which we find indicated in late eighteenth-century and even in early nineteenth-century editions must not mislead us. It was a venerable tradition to offer performers the choice between different modes of execution. The Renaissance had its "to be sung or played," the seventeenth century presented as alternatives "Clavier or Organ," and the early eighteenth century "Violin or Flute." So the century's third quarter developed the formula "pour le Clavecin ou Pianoforte" which was unthinkingly repeated long after it had lost its meaning. Similarly the designation *Hammerklavier*, which appears on the title-page of Beethoven's last sonata, should not be interpreted as a reference to a technical innovation. Beethoven, who increasingly employed German headings in his later works, preferred to use the German word Hammerklavier instead of the less accurate Italian pianoforte; but even his early sonatas, op. 2, were intended for a stringed keyboard instrument equipped with hammers.

The new instrument which attracted such strong interest had of necessity to undergo changes. The tinkling, flat tone-quality which had discouraged earlier composers had been overcome by the time Haydn and Mozart turned to it. Their piano was well suited for the performance of delicate cantilenas and pearly passages, but lacked strength and resonance. Beethoven's instrument had remarkable, new sound-qualities which were largely the result of recent technical improvements. They will be discussed in connection with Romantic clavier music.

Chamber Music

The two main types of Baroque *chamber music*—"trio"-sonata and "solo"-sonata—were carried over into the first decades of the new era. The ascendancy of these forms came to an end, however, as soon as the piano was generally accepted. The reason for this lay in the tone-quality of the new instrument. The sound of the harpsichord had blended smoothly with that of stringed or wind instruments and it was therefore well suited to accompany them. The piano, on the other hand, had a tonal quality of its very own, which was noticeable in any ensemble and unsuitable for the modest supporting role accorded to the keyboard instrument in these genres from the past. Moreover, the arrival of the piano coincided with the demise of the thoroughbass, and these two factors led to a complete reorientation of chamber music. Different attempts were made to cope with the new situation and they resulted in several successful solutions of the problem. In the early "solo"-sonata the violin had been the leader and the harpsichord the accompanist. A violoncello occasionally reinforced the bass line. In the middle of the eighteenth century these roles were partly reversed: the piano became the soloist, while the violin, and the optional violoncello, assumed unimportant accompanying parts and could even be omitted without materially endangering the composition. A main function of the stringed instruments in these sonatas and trios was to reinforce the weak tone of the early pianos; as soon as claviers capable of producing more substantial sounds were available, the genre—to which even Haydn made sizeable contributions—disappeared. In the later duos and trios the stringed instruments were no longer relegated to a menial supporting role, but were considered as partners with equal rights. The Baroque idea of the *stile concertato* was now applied to two or three instruments which in their tone-quality offered the most effective contrast. Numerous works contributed by Mozart and Beethoven in this field showed the way to later composers.

Another group of works took the "trio"-sonata as its point of departure. Here the cembalo was simply omitted, and the gap between the range of the violoncello and that of the two violins was closed through the insertion of a filling viola. The result was the completely homogeneous genre of the string quartet, for two violins, viola and violoncello, the noblest product of classical chamber music. For composers and performers, amateurs and professional musicians, this ensemble of four—now blending, now clearly contrasting—instruments offered a challenge and a powerful stimulation. All three of the great Viennese composers were inspired to their loftiest achievements in this genre.

Apart from the main combinations of instruments mentioned here, various chamber music ensembles of less significance were used. They consisted of strings only, or wind instruments only, or combinations of both; and the collaboration of a piano was often enlisted. The number of movements also varied greatly. Three or four were most common, but there were compositions with two only, and others with as many as ten or twelve. Early chamber music works were apt to bear titles like "Partita," "Divertimento," or "Cassazione." In these, a gay, playful or tender character was often stressed. Minuets and marches were frequently included and especially sets of variations, in which, in each successive section, the lead was entrusted to a different member of the ensemble.

Orchestral Music—The Symphony

In 1637 the first public opera house was opened in Venice. Hitherto opera performances had been staged only for special occasions, in the palaces of the nobility; this new venture, on the other hand, made them available to anyone who bought a ticket. Before the end of the century a similar process of democratization had been applied to concert life. A violinist in London sold tickets for concerts to be given in his home, and the audience was invited to choose the program. In eighteenth-century London the concerts of the Academy of Ancient Music flourished; later the Bach-Abel concerts were added, arranged by Sebastian's youngest son and a successful gambist. Paris had the famous *Concerts spirituels*, as well as the *Concerts des amateurs*. In German cities with a wealthy middle class, such as Berlin, Frankfurt, Hamburg or Leipzig, public concerts were offered regularly.

A new kind of music was required to satisfy the demands of the audiences for interesting and novel artistic fare. The spirited young *symphony*, which began to flower around the middle of the eighteenth century, met these needs to perfection. The concert symphony—usually known in the classical period as a *sinfonia* or *ouverture*—was a descendant of the Italian opera prelude, which by now had completely freed itself from all operatic connotations. To the three movements, fast-slow-fast, of the original sinfonia was added before long a middle movement in the form of a minuet, which proved surprisingly resistant to change and was only dislodged, after a reign of half a century, by Beethoven's hard-driving, jocular *scherzo*. Other significant features resulted from the interplay of various instruments and the exploration of their technical and coloristic potentialities.

Not only the number of movements increased, but also the size of individual pieces. In particular the initial movement, which had started out from the concise binary form of Baroque dances, was gradually enlarged into a substantial ternary form consisting of an "exposition," displaying the thematic material, a "development," treating it in varied ways and modulating to distant keys, and a "recapitulation," making a slightly modified restatement of the first section. This so-called "sonata form" was applied to every type of instrumental music, but it was of particular importance for the symphony. In the development section the musical ideas, presented in their entirety or broken up into brief motives, were offered not only in different keys but also in constantly changing coloristic garb. Instruments of different ranges—wind instruments as well as strings—were called upon to participate in the musical elaboration. Similarly, long-drawn-out melodies were often entrusted not just to one instrument; composers liked to break them up into smaller units, which they assigned in quick succession to various instruments. The masterworks of the classical period seemed to abolish the musical class-system of the Baroque period, with its dominant soloists and subservient accompanists, and to aim at a more democratic method of orchestration, with equal rights and equal responsibilities for all the musicians.

The growing attendance at orchestral concerts necessitated the construction of bigger concert halls. This in turn, together with the era's predilection for powerful sounds, led to a constant enlargement of the size of the orchestra. In the middle of the century small groups of players—mostly strings—were still frequent. Before long two oboes and two horns were added, and then gradually bassoons, flutes, trumpets, timpani and two additional horns. Somewhat later clarinets were incorporated into the orchestra, and for special effects trombones, double-bassoon, piccolo flute, English horn, basset horn and the "Janissary" instruments, triangle, cymbals, large drum, etc. The spectacular increase in the size of orchestras may be illustrated by the following numbers. In 1766 Haydn, *Kapellmeister* to Prince Esterházy, had 17 players at his disposal (6 for violin and viola, 1 violoncello, 1 double-bass, 1 flute, 2 oboes, 2 bassoons, and 4 horns). In 1795, the orchestra which was assembled for him in London was more than three times as large. It consisted of close on 40 string players, two performers on each woodwind part, one on each horn and trumpet part, and one on the timpani. Beethoven was still satisfied with an orchestra of approximately the same size, although in his lifetime even larger orchestras made an appearance.

Haydn liked to conduct his symphonies from the harpsichord. He may have done so even during his stay in England, long after the cembalo had lost its preeminence. Other orchestras of the time were mostly conducted by the concert-master (the first violinist), who vigorously wielded his bow. After 1800, the job was often done by artists specially trained as conductors. They used, at first, a paper or leather roll, later a stubby baton held in the middle.

It is hard to overestimate the gigantic consumption of symphonies during the classical era. It has been said that more than 7,000 works of this genre, written before 1810, have been preserved. We may safely assume that the output was in fact much larger and that an equal number of symphonies did not survive.

The Concerto

The Baroque *concerto* lived on during the classical era with some of its basic features changed. Its structure was remodeled under the influence of the all-pervading sonata form. Moreover, the role of the soloists was drastically altered and their relationship to the orchestra revised. The earlier concerto primarily explored the coloristic contrast between one or several soloists and a larger group of accompanying strings. Excessive technical difficulties were usually absent from the solo parts. The classical concerto, on the other hand, was written for virtuosi who wanted to display their mastery of the instrument. The scores even allotted space for cadenzas, in which the soloists were free to interpolate brilliant passages. But the composers did not neglect the orchestra either. In the fully-grown classical concerto the soloists quite often developed ideas jointly with members of the orchestra; not infrequently they merely accompanied while the lead was given to the orchestra; and, above all, there were always long stretches in which the orchestra was on its own while the soloists had rests. The result was the kind of well-balanced work of art which the classical era particularly appreciated.

Concerti grossi, with four or more soloists, were well known in the second half of the century. However, in these *symphonies concertantes*, as they were commonly called, the numerous soloists were apt to interfere with each other and unduly extend the length of individual movements. Thus the symphonie concertante enjoyed only a marginal success, while the solo concerto was one of the favorites of the time.

Concerti were written for practically all the instruments that played a role in the instrumental music of the classical era. The harpsichord concerto lived on from the Baroque period into the century's third quarter. Thus C. P. E. Bach, between 1733 and 1778, contributed no less than 50 works of this genre. In 1788, the year of his death, the old composer made a rather curious concession to the taste of the younger generation. He wrote a *Concerto doppio a Cembalo concertato (e) Fortepiano concertato*. By this time, of course, the piano had already become the generally acknowledged favorite as a solo instrument. With its vast musical and technical capacities, and its tone well set off against the sound of the orchestra, it was an ideal solo instrument in a concerto. Mozart followed the general trend in writing close on two dozen concertos for one, two, and three pianos. The violin's popularity as a solo instrument nearly matched that of the piano; Italy made particularly significant contributions in this field. Concerti for solo flute and for solo violoncello were not infrequently written, and similar compositions for almost every instrument of the orchestra were produced at one time or another. Altogether the rich harvest of classical concerti reflects the enthusiasm of the period for instrumental brilliance, which to some extent replaced the infatuation of the Baroque period with vocal prowess.

Treatises

It is an indication of the revolutionary changes that took place in music around the middle of the century that three highly respected musicians of the time felt the need to offer *treatises* explaining in detail the rules governing instrumental performance. These men sensed the confusion in the minds of the younger generation, which was not sure yet of the way it was to take, and they set out to establish firm guide-lines for the instruction of students. In 1752 the flute virtuoso and instructor of King Frederick the Great of Prussia, J. J. ·Quantz, offered his *Versuch einer Anweisung die Flöte traversiere zu spielen* ("Essay on playing the transverse flute"). It was followed by C. P. E. Bach's *Versuch über die wahre Art das Clavier zu spielen* ("Essay on the true art of playing keyboard instruments"; Part I, 1753, Part II, 1762) and L. Mozart's *Versuch einer gründlichen Violinschule* ("Essay on a thorough method of playing the violin"; 1756, the year his son Wolfgang was born). All three "Essays" supplied the performer with basic technical instruction concerning the handling of his instrument. But in addition they are mines of information about the performing practice and stylistic problems of the time, questions relating to the execution of accompaniments, grace notes, the correct tempo, the organization of ensembles, etc. The close interrelation between instrumental technique and musical interpretation found its clearest expression in these knowledgeable works by creative artists.

The Instruments
Compared with the wealth of instruments at the musician's command in earlier centuries, the classical period had at its disposal an instrumental array of only modest dimensions. The increasing subjectivity of the musical idiom in the previous two centuries had resulted in a process of strict selection, so that the composers of the period 1750–1810 employed less than a dozen instruments for the great majority of their works. This was in accordance with the sense of economy and the striving for lucidity and precision which characterized the classical period.

The composers of the time regarded each instrument as an individual entity, and in their compositions they endeavoured to bring out its particular qualities as clearly as possible. It would not be easy to transfer a string quartet by Haydn, a horn concerto by Mozart, or a piano sonata by Beethoven to other instruments. In such music each participant makes use of an idiom that no other instrument can master. During the second half of the eighteenth century, the striving after tonal color increasingly engaged the composers' interest and naturally stimulated the technical development of the musical instruments. The tremendous improvement in the construction of instruments which occurred in the course of the nineteenth century had its beginnings in the classical period.

The conscious economy of means must not be confused with puritanical austerity. In order to obtain special results, instruments outside the ordinary orchestral body were unhesitatingly included, and their effectiveness was enhanced by the prudent and sparing use that was made of them. In the course of this chapter various examples of this practice will be given.

Violin Family

The steady disappearance of musical instruments after the middle of the eighteenth century is particularly evident in the case of the bowed strings. Of the many types which have been mentioned in the preceding chapters the only ones to attain importance were the members of the violin family—the *violin*, the *viola*, and the *violoncello*, together with the *double-bass*, which stood midway between the viola da gamba and the viola da braccio. They formed the basis of the orchestra for secular and ecclesiastical purposes, and they played an essential part in chamber music and as solo instruments in concerti. Even the ponderous double-bass (which was generally tuned, from the end of the eighteenth century, in E_1, A_1, D, G) was not excluded as a solo instrument. Haydn, Dittersdorf, Vanhal and C. Stamitz wrote concertos for it with orchestral accompaniment.

The extension of the fingering of the left hand to higher and higher positions enlarged the upward range of all the members of the violin family. This process was most strikingly evident in the case of the violoncello. J. L. Duport in his *Essai sur le doigter du Violoncelle* . . . (1770) placed the technique of the instrument on a new basis, and introduced the use of the thumb in playing the higher notes. Voltaire complimented him by declaring: "Sir, you know how to turn an ox into a nightingale."

To meet the increasing demands on their efficiency, changes obviously had to be made in the construction of the violin and its relatives. Around the year 1800 the finger-board and neck were lengthened, in accordance with the tendency to explore the higher positions. The bridge was raised and more strongly curved, to enable the performer to play more forcefully on each string. Consequently the neck had to be tilted backwards slightly, so that the finger-board could remain parallel with the strings, the finger-board itself being more cambered and broadened at its lower end. Thinner strings were used and the lowest overspun with silver wire. As the pitch was raised and the volume of sound increased, the bass-bar and sound-post in the interior of the instrument had to be more solidly constructed. As a result the majority of all earlier instruments were rebuilt at this time.

The *bow* of the stringed instruments reached its classical perfection in the same era through the efforts of F. Tourte (1747–
1835) in Paris. He established the standard length of 29½ inches for
the violin bow, the viola and 'cello bows being somewhat shorter.
For the stick he used the extremely hard and resilient Pernambuco
(Brazil) wood which, under heat, was bent inward, thus achieving
a concave shape of maximum elasticity. He widened the ribbon
of hair and improved its attachment to the movable "frog." In
typically classical manner none of the features of his bow were
newly invented, but Tourte established their perfect combination,
in exquisite workmanship, which has remained unsurpassed up
to the present.

Baryton

The *baryton* achieved a certain importance during the second
half of the eighteenth century, thanks to the music-loving Prince
Nicholas Esterházy, who was himself a performer on this instrument. At the Prince's court the violinist Luigi Tomasini, and
above all Joseph Haydn, wrote duets and trios, and other pieces
of chamber music, in which the baryton played a decisive part
(Pl. L). Although it was not widely distributed, this instrument
held its own with great tenacity.   When the nineteenth century
was well advanced, S. L. Friedel, of Berlin, was still able to win
success as a baryton player.

Hurdy-Gurdy

The reputation which the *hurdy-gurdy* enjoyed during the Rococo
period survived into the second half of the eighteenth century.
No lesser composers than Mozart and Haydn wrote music for
this instrument, although Haydn's *lira organizzata* was not the
simple hurdy-gurdy with strings alone, but the more ingenious
variant with an enclosed organ attachment. The keys of Haydn's
instrument not only shortened the strings, but could at the same
time admit wind to the tiny pipes, while the wheel, besides acting
as a bow, served also to work some bellows.   Haydn's patron was
the King of Naples, who delighted in playing the lira organizzata
himself. The numerous nocturnes and concertos which the master
composed for this instrument so gratified the sovereign that he
tried to induce the composer to settle down in Naples. Haydn,
however, preferred to accept Salomon's invitation to come to

PLATE XXXIII

Positive organ with four registers, around 1600. Berlin, Musikinstrumenten-Museum des Staatlichen Instituts für Musikforschung, Preussischer Kulturbesitz.

PLATE XXXIV

Allegory of Hearing. Among the numerous instruments represented are (from l. to r.): harpsichord, trombone, kettledrum, 3 viole da gamba of different sizes, mandola, pochette, shawm, lira da braccio, lute played by woman, various kinds of horn. In the background l., a group of musicians; on the wall r., a painting showing Orpheus surrounded by animals. Jan Brueghel, A.D. 1618. Madrid, Prado.

PLATE XXXV

Clavicytherium with two 8′ registers. The folding doors are painted with religious and musical subjects. Italy, 17th century. New York, Metropolitan Museum of Art, the Crosby Brown Collection of Musical Instruments, 1889.

PLATE XXXVI

The Family of Jacques van Eyck. Represented are bass viola da gamba, positive, and guitar. Gonzales Coques (1614–1684). Budapest, Museum of Fine Arts.

London. Had he gone to Naples the history of music might well have followed a very different course.

Guitar

The number of plucked stringed instruments was as greatly diminished as that of the bowed ones. The leading instrument of the Renaissance and the Baroque periods, the lute, with its larger variants, the different archlutes, almost disappeared. The fashionable instrument of the day was the *guitar*, which spread into the rest of Europe from Spain and played an important part in France, England and Germany. In place of the inconvenient double strings it now had single strings, increased in number from five to six, and tuned to E, A, d, g, b, e^1. In point of tone the new instrument was even less satisfactory than the lute, but it was easily tuned, and with the help of the fixed metallic frets on the finger-board it was easily played. J. S. Otto, one of the leading German guitar-makers of the day, justly wrote of this instrument: "The guitar very quickly won general favour, since for anyone who loves singing it provided the pleasantest and easiest accompaniment, and moreover it is readily carried about. Everywhere one saw guitars in the hands of the most respected ladies and gentlemen." To this one may add that one of the advantages of the instrument was its simplicity and cheapness, so that it was not merely the instrument of aristocratic amateurs, but a genuinely popular instrument. It even became the practice to convert the valuable old lutes into guitars, often in a most barbarous and primitive fashion.

Lyre-Guitar

A typical product of the French Empire period was the *lyre-guitar* (Pl. LIV/3), equipped with the guitar's six strings, in customary tuning, but provided with two lateral arms which created the shape of an ancient lyre. It may be regarded as an expression of the contemporary effort to resuscitate classical antiquity. Simon Molitor, a Viennese composer and guitarist, wrote of this instrument in 1806: "The new lyre (guitar) which appeared in France only a few years ago . . . is a welcome sight to lovers of the beautiful forms of antiquity. Its tone—though stronger than that of the guitar, on account of the larger body— is nevertheless dull and as though held back within the instrument."

In addition, the two arms of the lyre-guitar hindered the player, so it was never of any practical importance. This fashionable instrument, which owed its ephemeral success mainly to its adoption by the fair sex, barely survived the first quarter of the nineteenth century.

Cittern

Among the many members of the *cittern* family, whose strings in the classical period varied in number from 6 to 14, was an instrument with slightly inward-curved sides which took its name from the fashionable instrument of the day and was known as the *English guitar*. In later specimens the strings were not tuned with pegs, but were attached to little metal hooks, which could be tightened by means of screws. Tuning of the two single and four double strings (in c, e, g, c^1, e^1, g^1) was effected with a spanner of the watch-key type. In order to spare the fingers of fair musicians, Christian Klauss, a German living in London, conceived the idea in 1783 of constructing a "keyed English guitar," in which the strings were struck by means of keys and hammers, as in a piano. But in spite of all these improvements, by the first decade of the nineteenth century, the cittern had been thrust into the background by the guitar.

Mandolin

During the classical period the small Neapolitan *mandolin*, with its four double-strings tuned as in the violin, became extremely popular. In the various music-loving countries of Europe it was now employed, with guitar accompaniment, as a popular substitute for the violin. It was even admitted on occasion to the ranks of the serious musical instruments. In 1764 Arne employed it in his *Almena*, and Grétry, in 1778, in *l'Amant jaloux*. Mozart immortalized it by his serenade in *Don Giovanni*, and Beethoven composed a sonatina and an adagio for mandolin and clavier.

Harp

The *harp* was particularly valued at this time in France; it was there that the final steps were taken towards its technical perfection, which gave it a place among the instruments of the orchestra. On the pedal harp the pitch of each string could be raised by a semitone; however, certain intervals, such as a and b♭ (a♯) or d and e♭ (d♯), could not be played simultaneously because in each case only one string was available for the two notes. An improvement was sought and finally achieved, but it took up to the second decade of the nineteenth century for an instrument to be built that satisfied the highest requirements. The improved harp will be described in the next chapter.

Aeolian Harp

The *Aeolian harp* (Fr. *harpe d'Eole*, Ger. *Äolsharfe*, It. *arpa d'Eolo*) owed its popularity to the affected sentimentalism of the eighteenth century and the romantic movement of the nineteenth. The construction of the instrument is of the simplest. It consists of an ordinary rectangular box, over the top of which are stretched a variable number of strings of different thicknesses, but all tuned to the same note. The instrument is placed where the wind can blow on it, and sometimes a special device is employed to ensure that the wind strikes the strings at the right place. The strings begin at first to sound in unison, but if the wind rises the overtones are brought out, producing harmonies of a strangely ethereal nature.

The history of the Aeolian harp goes back into the remote past; the fascinating sound of strings vibrating in the wind attracted the attention of the ancients. It was recorded of King David's harp that it began to sound at midnight, when the north wind passed through its strings. St. Dunstan, who lived in the tenth century A.D., was regarded as a magician because he made a harp which played by itself when he placed it in a draught. Father Athanasius Kircher (d. 1680) was the first to build Aeolian harps of the modern type, and the poet Alexander Pope introduced them into England in the first half of the eighteenth century. Since then the Aeolian harp has played an increasing part in poetical literature, its gently nostalgic, mysteriously ethereal strains having often been celebrated by the romantic poets.

Clavichord, Spinet, Harpsichord

As mentioned above, the stringed keyboard instruments of the Baroque era survived during part of the classical period. The little "fretted" (*gebundenes*) *clavichord*, which was so easily tuned (since one pair of strings always served to produce several notes), so inexpensive to make, and so portable, was built in unaltered form until far into the second half of the eighteenth century. The "fret-free" (*bundfreies*) clavichord, however, was more widely distributed, and it was now increased in size, in order to satisfy the universal demand for greater volume of tone. For the same reason the larger types of *spinet* were built in England, in an attempt to rival the harpsichord in strength of tone. The *harpsichord* itself was provided in 1769 by Burkat Shudi in London with the "Venetian Swell," a device intended to take the wind out of the sails of the newly-invented piano. Fixed above the strings was a system of shutters (borrowed from the organ), which were operated by a pedal (Pl. LI). If the shutters were open while the instrument was being played the tone was forte; if closed, the tone was piano. But that was not all; the new device also made it possible to achieve some kind of dynamic transition. If the shutters were gradually opened while the instrument was being played a sort of crescendo was obtained; if they were slowly closed, a decrescendo.

There is no doubt that the great composers of the classical period were quite familiar with these different clavier instruments from the past. However, in the course of time, their interest centered entirely on the new piano.

Piano

The origin of the *piano* (its full name in Eng., Fr. and It. is *pianoforte* or *fortepiano*; in Ger. it is sometimes called *Hammerklavier*) dates far back into the period dealt with in the last chapter, but as it had not then come into general use, the description of its first beginnings has been reserved for this chapter. The invention was already in the air at the beginning of the eighteenth century. How otherwise can we explain the fact that it was made about the same time in three different countries—in France, Germany, and Italy? In 1716 the French clavichord-maker Marius exhibited models of a *clavecin à maillets*—a hammer harpsichord— while between 1717 and 1721 the German organ-builder G. Schröter constructed a hammer action which by his own admission was suggested by the hammers of the pantaleon. But earlier still, in 1709, Bartolomeo Cristofori, a Florentine builder of harpsichords, had built a hammer-clavier whose mechanism was so ingenious that one is tempted to regard it as the result of prolonged research. In 1711 Scipione Maffei discussed the invention exhaustively in the *Giornale dei letterati d'Italia*; moreover, two of Cristofori's instruments have survived to this day. One of these, built in 1720, and now in the Metropolitan Museum, New York, does not, unfortunately, contain the action in its original form. The other, dating from 1726, which is in the Leipzig collection of musical instruments, is substantially unaltered, so that its mechanism may be taken as the pattern of Cristofori's invention. Figure 4 shows it in diagrammatic form. When the player depresses the front part of the key, *k*, the back part, and with it the *linguetta mobile*, as Cristofori called it (the

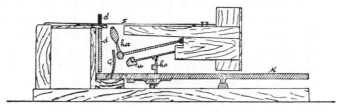

Fig. 4. Cristofori's action in a pianoforte of the
Universitäts Museum, Leipzig

"hopper" *ho*), moves upwards. This actuates an under-hammer *u*, which in turn throws the hammer *ha* against the string *s*. This device ensures that the hammer falls back immediately after the blow, whether the key is released or held down, so that the string is free to vibrate. The recoiling hammer is caught by the spring *g*. A damper, *d*, attached to the far end of the key, springs upwards and frees the string directly the key is depressed. It falls back against the string when the key is released.

The next chapter in the history of the piano was enacted not on Italian, but on German soil. The organ-builder G. Silbermann had won such a reputation as a maker of harpsichords that he was actually credited with the invention of the new instrument. Silbermann showed his Hammerklavier, which was based on Cristofori's invention, to J. S. Bach, who praised its tone but complained that too much strength was needed to depress the keys, and that the volume of sound was insufficient. Silbermann continued to work at the instrument, improving it until Bach was able to praise it unreservedly. But the time was not yet ripe for the Hammerklavier. Bach was too steeped in the tradition of the old keyboard instruments to acquire a pianoforte for his own use, or write music for it.

Before long the instruments built by Cristofori and Silbermann were further developed. German piano-makers who had emigrated to England on account of the Seven Years' War helped to found an important school of clavier-building there. The leading firm to emerge in the field of English piano-manufacture was that of Burkat Shudi and John Broadwood, who also made important contributions to the evolution of the special type of mechanism known as the *English action*. This device shows a certain resemblance to the old Cristofori action. As in that, the end of the hammer is attached to a lever which is independent of the key, and the hammer-head points to the back, away from the player. A pusher connected to the end of the key drives the hammer against the string and moves out of the way directly the note is sounded, so that the hammer can fall back into the resting position. In contrast to this device is the *German action*, invented about the middle of the eighteenth century and known also as the *Viennese action*, since Vienna became the principal center of German piano-manufacture. Here the hammer, which is attached directly to the farther end of the key, points toward the player (Pl. LII/1). When the end of the key rises, the hammer, pivoting against an escapement just beyond the key, strikes the string. Thereupon the escapement releases the hammer so that it falls back into the resting position.

The invention of the German action has often been attributed to Johann Andreas Stein of Augsburg, a pupil of Silbermann's. Mozart visited him in 1777, and in a letter to his father spoke of Stein's instruments (Pl. LIII/1) in terms of the highest praise. Stein's action, which was made in an especially perfect form by his son-in-law, Andreas Streicher, who was a friend of the poet Schiller and worked in Vienna, is distinguished by its light touch and the small movement of the keys. It favored a brilliant, "pearling" technique, such as is required by Weber's compositions for the piano. Hummel said of the Viennese action: "It readily responds to the most delicate touch. It allows the performer to obtain every possible *nuance* in his interpretation; it speaks clearly and promptly, has a flute-like tone, and does not hamper fluency by requiring an excessive effort." Despite these advantages, the Viennese action was inferior in fullness and beauty of tone to the English. In the classical period the two actions ranked equally; but the Romantic movement, which called for greater volume of tone, awarded victory to the English action.

The original form of the hammerklavier was the grand piano shaped like a harpsichord (Pl. LIII/1). The piano was its direct offspring, and in the eighteenth century many instruments which were originally built as harpsichords were transformed into hammerklaviers by changing the action. There were even instruments of the "grand" form which used both jacks and hammers together. After 1750 the small rectangular *square piano* (Fr. *piano carré*, Ger. *Tafelklavier*, It. *pianoforte da tavola*) appeared, in which the strings were parallel with the front of the keyboard (Pl. L). This was equipped with tiny hammers, which seem very primitive when compared with the ingenious action of Cristofori's first instruments; but they fulfilled their purpose perfectly, and the instrument was played only with the delicate, careful touch used for the clavichord.

The small, hard heads of the hammers, which were covered with thin leather, produced a rather light, flat and unchanging tone. In order to enrich the musical possibilities of the piano, it was soon provided with different stops, which slightly modified the quality of the tone. The stop that lifted all the dampers at the same time produced a *forte*. On the other hand, if the hammers were moved a little to one side, so as to strike one string only, instead of two, the result was the softer *una corda* register. Strips of leather or silk, which were slipped between the hammers and the strings, produced a *piano* or *pianissimo* effect. A brush, which was applied to the strings from above, and made the instrument sound as though the strings were being plucked, was known as the *harp* register, while a padded slat, which was pressed against the strings from below, gave the *lute* register. Sometimes there was a shutter swell, as in the organ and the harpsichord, in order to produce crescendo and decrescendo effects. The enthusiasm of Mozart's contemporaries for Turkish music even led to the introduction of a sort of drum attachment—a mallet which struck against the sound-board.

At first the stops for including or cutting out the registers were fitted above the keys, as in the harpsichord. But this arrangement had the obvious disadvantage that the player had to use his hands to operate them, and so was forced to interrupt his performance; before long, therefore, this job was given to the musician's legs. The registers were now changed by the knees; but as this method of operating the stops often shook the lightly-built instrument, pedals were installed. As yet, these pedals were without the wooden, lyre-shaped support which they were after-wards given in the grand piano, and they were not very robustly constructed.

After the middle of the eighteenth century the grand piano and the square piano had a rival in the upright piano. In 1745 Christian Ernst Friederici, of Gera, built a "pyramid" piano after the pattern of the clavicytherium; and fifty years later William Stodart, in London, patented a piano in the form of a bookcase. Before long there were "giraffe" pianos (Pl. LIII/2) and "lyre" pianos, as the instruments were called, in accordance with their outward form. But all these types had the disadvantage of a certain dullness of tone, and they were not very strongly constructed. So the problem was attacked from another side. Whereas in all types of upright hitherto constructed the narrow end of the piano was at the top and the wrest-plank at the bottom, the narrow end was now made to rest on the floor, and the wrest-plank was moved to the upper edge of the sounding-board. This new type, known as "pianino," or "piano droit" substantially reduced the instrument's height. It was first built about 1800. By that time Germany, Austria and England were not the only countries engaged in the manufacture of pianos. In Paris the inventive S. Érard was active and in Philadelphia J. I. Hawkins, who strengthened the method of construction by using a metal frame and metal braces. The stage was set for the piano's magnificent development during the Romantic period.

Wind Instruments

As regards the *wind instruments* the classical period was no more consistent than in the case of the stringed instruments. Certain instruments underwent the most dramatic transformation while others remained almost unchanged.

Transverse Flute

The changes which accompanied the transition from the Baroque to the classical period may be observed cleary in the flutes. Whereas in connection with Bach's and Handel's music "flauto" or "flute" usually meant recorder, after the middle of the eighteenth century it implied the use of the *transverse flute*. No one would ever think of employing recorders for the flute parts of a symphony by Mozart or Haydn. The clear, more expressive, more powerful tone of the transverse flute was victorious over the tender and rather monotonous recorder.

Until late in the second half of the eighteenth century the transverse flute retained the form which it had assumed in the Baroque period. Only after 1775—that is, about the time when the classical style was approaching its culmination—was its improvement seriously taken in hand. Since only the notes of the scale of D major were really true, keyed holes were made for such other notes as were frequently required. To the already existing key for $d\sharp^1$ others were added for $g\sharp^1$, $b\flat^1$ and then f^1. Moreover, Richard Potter, a London maker, increased the length of the instrument and gave it, below the fundamental note d^1, a $c\sharp^1$ and a c^1, which were controlled by two further keys. About 1800 this instrument, with its six keys, was widely distributed. At the beginning of the nineteenth century a key for c^2 was added, and a second key for f^1, which facilitated the fingering.

So the one-keyed flute, of which Burney had written in 1772 that it was "natural to those instruments to be out of tune", evolved in the course of a few decades into a highly developed instrument with eight keys. But with this the transformation of the flute was by no means complete; indeed—as we shall see in the next chapter—it had really only now begun.

Although the descant or treble flute in the fundamental key of D major was in general use, it was by no means the only type which existed in the classical period. In military bands, from the close of the eighteenth century, instruments a semi-tone or a minor third higher were employed, as they were louder and shriller than the ordinary flute. On the other hand, just as there was an oboe d'amore, so there was a *flûte d'amour* (Fr.), a minor third lower than the ordinary flute. Equally rare was the bass flute, an octave lower than the descant flute, which was made more manageable by bending back part of the tube through an angle of 180°, so that it lay beside the main tube.

Piccolo

The smallest flute, known as the piccolo flute, or just *piccolo*, (Eng.

and Fr.; Ger. *Piccoloflöte*, It. *ottavino*) is of more importance than the larger types just mentioned. It is an octave higher than the ordinary flute and reaches almost to the upper limit of recognizable pitch. Of course, the highest notes of the piccolo, in the fourth octave above middle C, were hardly ever employed, owing to their shrillness. The piccolo came into use towards the end of the eighteenth century, and its history since then has been that of the large flute. Apart from the absence of the keys for the deep c$\sharp^2$ and c^2, which are superfluous in an instrument whose higher notes are its chief recommendation, the arrangement of the keys is essentially the same as in the ordinary flute. The piccolo flute, on account of its sharp, powerful tone, was especially valued in military bands, but it also found its way more and more rapidly into the opera and symphony orchestras. Gluck, in his *Iphigénie en Tauride*, and Beethoven, in his Pastoral Symphony, used its sharp tones in passages descriptive of a storm.

English Flageolet

While the long reign of the soprano recorder came to an end about the middle of the century, a smaller type, the *English flageolet*, continued to play a certain part in England, France and Belgium as a dilettante instrument, at dances and convivial gatherings. This instrument had the finger-holes of the large recorders and was equipped with two or more keys. It had a narrow mouthpiece of ivory or horn, and its upper section included a pear-shaped distension which contained a sponge, intended to catch the moisture. Small ivory studs were often fixed between the holes, to guide the performer's fingers to their proper places.

Double Flageolet

Between 1800 and 1820 *double flageolets* were made in England. On the whole they were constructed like the ordinary English flageolet. The left-hand instrument usually had seven finger-holes and a thumb-hole, and the right-hand one four, and these were so placed that the instrument on the right usually sounded a third lower than that on the left. The two flutes could also be played separately. The popularity of this type is shown by the comparatively large number of specimens preserved in collections. However, the mechanical quality of its tone, and its modest compass of less than an octave (it was often d^2–c^3 or $b\flat^1$–a^2), prevented its admission to the orchestra.

Oboe

The *oboe* no longer had such a privileged position among the wood-wind instruments as in the Baroque period. At first the transverse flute, and later the clarinet also, disputed the lead. It is characteristic that Mozart rescored his great Symphony in G minor, already completed, in order to include clarinet parts, largely at the cost of the oboes. The development of the oboe during the eighteenth century was correspondingly modest. *The Complete Tutor*, in 1808, dealt with practically the same instrument as that used by Hotteterre in 1708. The oboe of the classical period was usually made of boxwood, more rarely of ebony or ivory. The three keys of the Rococo period were reduced to two, as it became the rule in the second half of the century that the player's right hand was the lower (cf. p. 151). It might appear that the instrument had regressed by surrendering one of its three keys, but actually there was no real change.

English Horn

In exceptional cases the *English horn*, standing a fifth lower than the oboe, was employed by the classical composers. Jommelli used it in 1741, Haydn in two early divertimentos (Hob. II/16 and 24), and Gluck in his *Alceste* of 1767. But the peculiarly melancholic and pastoral effect of the instrument was not fully exploited until the Romantic period.

Clarinet

Among the wind instruments of the classical period the *clarinet* was particularly successful. Its warm, vital tones, full and luscious in the lower register and becoming shrill only in the highest notes, won it an increasing number of friends. In 1749 Rameau employed it in his *Zoroastre* and in the second half of the century the instrument gradually found wider use. While at first the clarinet was usually played by oboists or flutists, later, separate clarinet players were seen with increasing frequency in the various orchestras. Mozart became intimately acquainted with the instrument in 1777, in Mannheim, and promptly conceived a strong affection for it. In addition to using it in the orchestra, he wrote chamber compositions with clarinet parts (trio and quintet), as well as a clarinet concerto. Weber, too, was among the special admirers of this instrument.

The clarinet, by reason of its predominantly cylindrical bore, behaves, in an acoustic sense, like a stopped pipe (cf. p. 289). In its voice the even-numbered harmonics are only faintly represented, and they cannot be produced by over-blowing. The finger-holes and keys must therefore cover not merely an octave— as in the oboe, for example—but the twelfth lying between the fundamental note and the third partial. Performers could therefore play on the clarinet, in the classical era, only in keys closely related to its fundamental set of harmonics. Because of this, the instrument had to be made in various sizes (cf. p. 297). The principal instruments were the sopranos, in C, Bb and A, the fundamental keys of which were C major, B flat major, and A major. The last two were the most frequently employed. For keys prescribing flats the Bb clarinet was usually chosen, while for keys with a signature of sharps the A clarinet was more suitable. At first the clarinet's purity and beauty of tone left much to be desired. As late as 1784 the *Musikalische Almanach* wrote: "Playing this instrument . . . is beset with difficulties which, if not overcome, can result in the most indescribable coos and squeaks. Run away, at such times, if you can!" However, the makers strove indefatigably to improve the instrument. Its range was constantly enlarged, until it reached almost four octaves, e–c⁴; while in the interest of purer intonation, the number of keys was gradually increased to 5, 6 and even 7 or 8. In the classical period the clarinet was notated as it sounded, the Bb clarinet a whole tone higher, and the A clarinet a minor third higher.

Clarinette d'Amour

The *clarinette d'amour* was a clarinet in low Ab, G or F, fitted with the barrel-shaped bell of the oboe d'amore; it was occasionally made in the last decades of the eighteenth century. The upper part of the clarinet was provided with a slightly curved brass tube, which made it possible to hold the rather lengthy instrument closer to the body. The instrument was first used by J. C. Bach in his opera *Temistocle*. It was especially appreciated in southern Holland, but since it was ultimately discovered that the barrel-shaped bell had hardly any effect on the tone, it had only a short career.

Basset Horn

Another kind of large clarinet was more successful: the *basset horn*, invented about 1770, possibly by Mayrhofer of Passau. The basset horn was an alto clarinet in F, with a narrower bore, whose compass extended a major third lower than that of an ordinary alto clarinet. The deepest note of the soprano clarinet in C is e; on an alto clarinet in F this would sound as A. The basset horn, however, went a third lower, to F, with an upper range to f³ (notated in the treble clef a fifth higher than the notes sound). On account of its great length the instrument was at first curved like a sickle (which was perhaps why it was called a "horn"), and later its body was bent at an obtuse angle. The lower end of the basset horn was bent twice, and enclosed in a wooden box, which sometimes had the shape of a book. This part of the tube served to produce the four deepest notes, which were controlled by the so-called "basset" keys. Mozart, a great lover of the clarinet, made repeated use of the rather cooler and duller voice of the basset horn. It is especially effective in certain passages—as in the *Requiem*, the *Magic Flute*, or the *Masonic Funeral Music*—when the composer wished to avoid the unduly sensuous effect of the clarinet. The career of the basset horn came to an end for the time being in the first half of the nineteenth century. Beethoven employed the instrument in *The Creatures of Prometheus*, in 1801, and Mendelssohn used it, together with clarinet and piano, in two concert pieces, Op. 113 and 114 (1833).

Bassoon

Whereas during the Baroque period the *bassoon* was used mainly to reinforce the bass strings, and separate parts were seldom written for it, in the classical period it gradually acquired an independent position. The instrument now assumed its natural function as the bass of the wind instruments. Its sound blended successfully with that of the oboes, horns and clarinets; and it achieved ever-increasing importance as a solo instrument. Its characteristic tones, now tender and pathetic, now hollow and

mysterious, now grotesquely nasal, recommended it as the inter-
preter of a great variety of moods and emotions.

The increased interest taken in the musical qualities of the
bassoon naturally stimulated its technical development, French
and German makers competing in their endeavors to perfect it.
While the best instruments of the Baroque period were fitted
with only four keys, by the time Beethoven had written the
majority of his symphonies, instruments were made with double
that number. At the same time the range of the bassoon was
extended upwards, so that the instrument covered more than
three octaves (Bb_1–c^2).

Double Bassoon (Contrabassoon)

The *double bassoon* or *contrabassoon* (Fr. *contrebasson*, Ger. *Kontra-
fagott*, It. *contrafagotto*), an octave lower than the bassoon, and
likewise sounding an octave lower than it is notated, shared to a
certain extent in the success of the parent instrument. Despite
its clumsiness and defective intonation—which was partly due
to the fact that no adequate tools were available for boring the
large billets of wood from which it was made—it was used by
the Viennese composers to obtain certain effects. In Haydn's
Creation, at the words *der Tiere Last* the composer produced the
impression of the animals' crushing weight by a single note of the
double-bassoon. Beethoven employed it in the Fifth and Ninth
Symphonies, and in the prison scene in *Fidelio* to evoke the dismal
atmosphere of the subterranean dungeon.

French Horn

A great transformation may be noted during the second half of
the eighteenth century in the part played by horn and trumpet.
The *French horn* turned into one of the most important members
of the orchestra. It was no longer used in the highest register;
the composers of the classical period were fond of employing the
warm and soft lower and middle registers. To some extent the
horn took over the role of the old continuo voices, filling the gap
between the melody and the bass. It was customary to assign the
higher notes to the first and (if there were four horns) third
players, the lower notes to the second and fourth players. The
latter also used, as a rule, a larger mouthpiece.

Circular tubes or crooks, which originated in the Baroque
period, were increasingly employed in the classical era; they

were fitted between the mouthpiece and the main tube of the horn, extending the length of the latter, and therefore lowering the pitch of the instrument. By means of a series of crooks of different lengths, two or three of which might sometimes be used together, it was possible to turn a C horn into a B♭, A, A♭, G or F horn, etc. Since in its lower register the horn could not produce much more than the notes of the fundamental triad, it became necessary to effect frequent changes of pitch. With the help of crooks this could be done with comparative ease without a change of instrument.

A further technical innovation introduced about 1750 supplemented the use of this device. At that time the horn-player J. Hampel, in Dresden, began to "stop" his horn. He plunged his right hand into the bell of the instrument, closing it more or less completely, which lowered the pitch of the horn by a semitone or a whole tone. This simple expedient made it possible to obtain more than twice as many notes from the same horn and enabled the player also to correct slight impurities of intonation; moreover, the new, rather dull and repressed timbre of the "stopped" horn helped to enrich the range of effects.

Very soon, however, it became apparent that the stopping of the horn was difficult or impossible if two or more crooks were employed, as these increased the distance between the bell and the player's body. Hampel then hit on the expedient of replacing the coiled crooks, interposed at the narrow end of the tube, by interchangeable, U-shaped tuning slides of different lengths, which were inserted in the middle of the hoop. These enabled the player to alter the pitch without increasing the distance of the bell from his body. The new inserted pieces were known as "inventions," and the instrument equipped with them was called the *Inventionshorn* (Ger.; Fr. *cor d'invention*). J. Werner, of Dresden, was the first to make such a horn in 1753. Crooks and inventions were the expedients by which the musicians of the classical and the early Romantic periods were enabled to tune their horns to the required key; but the more complicated inventionshorn was seldom employed save by solo performers.

During the classical period the French horn was notated in the treble or bass clef. The sounding pitch is ascertained by transposing down notes written in the treble clef and transposing up notes written in the bass clef. Thus, for instance, the notes of a horn in F would have to be transposed a perfect fifth down if they were written in the treble clef, and a perfect fourth up if they were written in the bass clef.

Serpent, Russian Bassoon, Bass Horn

While the cornetto had been eliminated from the classical orchestra, its larger variant, the *serpent*, was still indispensable as the bottom element among the wind instruments; moreover, in the last quarter of the eighteenth century the instrument, often fitted with three or four keys, played an important part in the vigorous development of military music. Attempts were also made to improve its serpentine form, which was troublesome to construct and difficult for the player to manage, by giving it the shape of a bassoon. This new form, the so-called *Russian bassoon*, was invented in about 1790, in the true home of the serpent, France, by an orchestral musician named Régibo. In construction it closely copied the bassoon of the period, except that it was more massive, and had a wider bore (Pl. LXIII/1). The bell was usually of metal, either trumpet-shaped or in the form of a grotesquely painted animal-head, an old fancy revived in the eighteenth century (cf. Pl. VI) and remaining in vogue for the larger military instruments for close on a century. About 1800 a similar instrument, except that it was made of metal, was constructed in London. The *bass horn*, as the newcomer was called, and the Russian bassoon made their way to all parts of the Continent, but they did not succeed in ousting the parent instrument, the serpent.

Trumpet

In the second half of the eighteenth century, the *trumpet* no longer held a position of pre-eminence. The art of "clarino" playing, requiring from the performer exceptional endurance and indefatigable practice, gradually declined. The trumpet parts were mostly confined to the middle notes of the so-called "principal" register, which had none of the magical quality peculiar to the highest notes. At the same time the social significance of the instrument declined. It sank to the status of an ordinary, and not even very highly esteemed orchestral instrument.

In these circumstances it is not surprising that during the classical period no important improvements were made to the instrument. Basically, the trumpet was content to take over what

PLATE XXXVII

Lid of a spinet made for the Nürnberg patrician Lukas Friedrich Behaim in 1619 (detail). Behaim is portrayed playing the bass viol. The center is occupied by the composer Johann Staden, who performs with his left hand on a positive organ, and with his right hand on the spinet from which this lid is taken. Next to him sits a player of an alto-tenor viol; in the background stand performers on violin and viola. Nürnberg, Germanisches Nationalmuseum.

PLATE XXXVIII

Musicians playing (from l. to r.): guitar, viola, recorder, theorbo lute, violoncello, spinet.
David Ryckaert III, 17th century. Vienna, Czernin Gallerie.

PLATE XXXIX

Players of theorbo lute and cittern. Jan M. Molenaer (1610–1668). London, National Gallery.

PLATE XL

A lady at the spinet, in the foreground a bass viola da gamba. Jan
Vermeer (1632–1675). London, National Gallery.

PLATE XLI

2.—Player of the tromba marina. From Filippo Bonanni, *Gabinetto Armonico*, 1722.

1.—Musicians playing on pochette and dulcimer. F. P. von der Schlichten, 17th century.

PLATE XLII

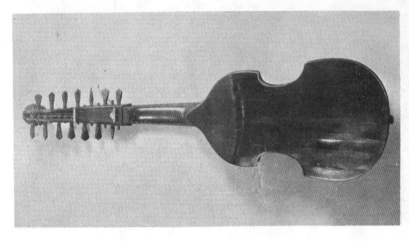

Viola d'amore with seven melody and seven sympathetic strings. 18th century. Private property.

PLATE XLIII

Musicians of the French court holding bass viola da gamba and transverse flutes. Attributed to Robert Tournières, 1705–1715. London, National Gallery.

PLATE XLIV

1.—Chitarra battente, 18th century. Formerly: Berlin, Staatliche Sammlung alter Musikinstrumente (lost during the war).

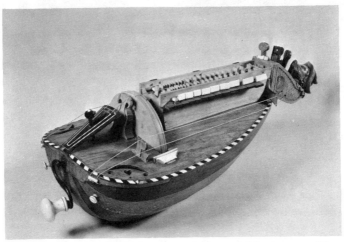

2.—Hurdy-gurdy (Vielle à roue). France, 18th century. New York, Metropolitan Museum of Art, Crosby Brown Collection of Musical Instruments, 1889.

PLATE XLV

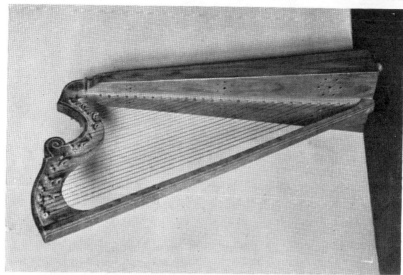

2.—Hook harp. Vienna, Gesellschaft der Musik-freunde, at present Kunsthistorisches Museum.

XLVII   *Arcileuto*

1.—Player of the chitarrone. From Filippo Bonanni, *Gabinetto Armonico*, 1722.

PLATE XLVI

1.—Fretted clavichord with "short" lowest octave and "broken" F♯ and G♯ keys (detail). Germany, early 18th century. Nürnberg, Rück collection in Germanisches Nationalmuseum.

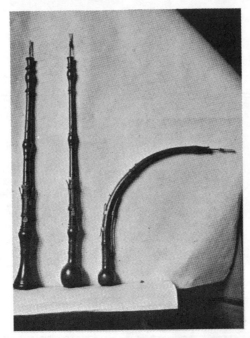

2.—Alto oboe, oboe da caccia, English horn. 18th century. Vienna, Gesellschaft der Musikfreunde, at present Kunsthistorisches Museum.

PLATE XLVII

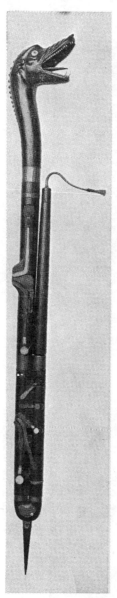

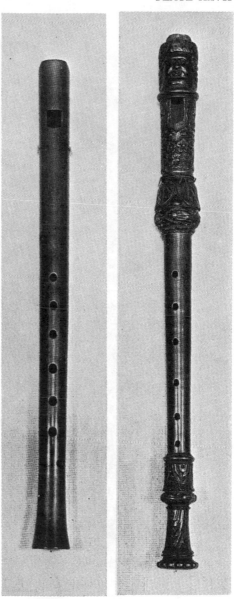

1.—Double bassoon by
Anciuti. Milan, 1732.
Salzburg, Museum
Carolino Augusteum.

2.—On the left recorder of the Renaissance,
on the right recorder of the Baroque period.
Vienna, Kunsthistorisches Museum.

PLATE XLVIII

Cembalo, may be folded for travel. Formerly in the possession of King Frederic II ("the Great") of Prussia. Made by Jean Marius, Paris, early 18th century. Berlin, Musikinstrumenten-Museum des Staatlichen Instituts für Musikforschung, Preussischer Kulturbesitz.

PLATE XLIX

Man with French horn. Unknown master, about 1730. London, David
Minlore.

PLATE L

Square piano by Johann Schantz, Vienna, after 1790, and baryton by Daniel Achatius Stadlmann, Vienna, 1732. According to tradition the two instruments belonged to J. Haydn, whose bust (without wig) is seen on the left. Vienna, Gesellschaft der Musikfreunde, at present Kunsthistorisches Museum.

PLATE LI

Harpsichord by Burkat Shudi and Johannes Broadwood. London, 1775. According to tradition the instrument belonged to J. Haydn. Vienna, Gesellschaft der Musikfreunde, at present Kunsthistorisches Museum.

PLATE LII

1.—Model of a German or Viennese piano action.

2.—Nail violin, about 1800. Vienna, Gesellschaft der Musikfreunde, at present Kunsthistorisches Museum.

had been done with the horn, which had gained as much in significance as the trumpet had lost. The latter became simpler and more compact in construction, and crooks—known since the seventeenth century—were now increasingly employed. The F trumpet, which gradually took precedence over the old D trumpet, could be transposed into E, Eb, D or C with the help of single crooks of varying length. If two crooks were employed the pitch could be lowered to B, Bb, A, or Ab. Trumpets are notated in the treble clef. Instruments pitched from F to D sounded a perfect fourth to a major second higher than written; instruments pitched from B to Ab a semitone to a major third lower.

Since trumpets fitted with crooks were more difficult to blow, owing to the greater number of convolutions, the *Inventionstrompete* was constructed, in about 1780, after the pattern of the Inventionshorn. At the beginning of the nineteenth century there were even semicircular or circular stopped trumpets in use, although the insertion of the hand into the bell infallibly destroyed the pealing tone of the instrument. Recourse was had therefore to the simple expedient which had been employed for centuries in the case of other wind instruments. Holes were made in the wall of the tube. In order to avoid the defects inherent in the serpent, the instrument was equipped with keys, which made it possible for holes to be bored which were acoustically correct in size and position. The *keyed trumpet* (Fr. *trompette à clefs*, Ger. *Klappentrompete*, It. *tromba a chiavi*) had as a rule five keys, which raised the pitch by successive semitones. They were arranged so that the performer could operate them with his left hand, holding the trumpet in his right.

The invention of the keyed trumpet has been ascribed by experts to the year 1801 and the Viennese Anton Weidinger. But the instrument is apparently older than that, for Haydn seems to have been acquainted with it as early as 1796. In that year the composer wrote his last and finest concerto *per il Clarino*, an instrument which can only have been a keyed trumpet. The melodic language of the work is mainly diatonic, and the composer indulges in chromatic passages even in the instrument's lower register. Great demands are made on the flexibility of the trumpet, and in the allegro passages runs of semi-quavers (sixteenth-notes) are not unusual.

Despite Haydn's efforts, the keyed trumpet had no real success.

The explanation may be sought in the fact that the holes and padded keys detracted greatly from the trumpet's brilliant tone. The instrument was occasionally used in military and operatic music (Rossini's *Guillaume Tell*, 1829). It did not succeed in obtaining admission to the symphony orchestra, however, and disappeared completely as soon as the valve trumpet started its victorious career (see p. 251).

Trombone

The *trombone*, which during the Baroque period was primarily employed in the Church and occasionally in operatic music, gradually came into more general use during the classical period. Composers of oratorios made increasing use of the now solemn, now menacing tones of the instrument. Moreover, from the end of the eighteenth century military bands employed it with ever-increasing frequency, on account of its powerful voice. Beethoven was one of the first composers to introduce it into the symphony orchestra (Symphony No. 5, 1805–1807).

In the classical period a trio of trombones was usually employed: the alto in E♭, the tenor in B♭, and the bass in E♭ or F. As a rule all three were used in conjunction, though they were by no means equally esteemed. The tenor was regarded as the principal instrument, being the most perfect in technical and acoustic respects. The alto, as compared with the tenor, sounded rather shrill, and was unsatisfactory in the low notes, while the bass demanded an excessive amount of wind, and made too great demands on the performer's strength.

So far, the technical construction of the trombone had undergone no essential modification. It is true that for use in military bands instruments were made with bells that were bent backwards, so that the troops marching behind the band could hear them better. In France and Belgium the bell was sometimes given the form of an animal's head (cf. p. 192) and an instrument so made was known as a *buccine*. By and large, however, the slide-trombone of the Renaissance—though equipped with a somewhat wider bell—was still in use during the classical period.

Organ

The *organ* at this time was less valued than in the Baroque era.

Despite all the efforts of the earlier period to make its voice more flexible and capable of expression, it was still regarded as too rigid and lifeless. The positive organs gradually disappeared during the second half of the eighteenth century, and only the great church organ remained in general use. It is characteristic of the age that the great Viennese composers wrote for the organ primarily during the earlier part of their lives, when they were still influenced by older models. Haydn, before 1778, composed organ concertos and two masses with important organ solos; Mozart wrote seventeen organ sonatas, the last of them in 1780; and Beethoven, at the age of eleven, composed "a two-part organ fugue in rapid movement," and two years later, two preludes "for the fortepiano or organ." But when the three composers had arrived at full maturity, none of them paid much attention to the organ, and it is significant that Beethoven never fulfilled his declared intention of writing an organ prelude to the Mass in C major.

In the history of the tremendous modern development of the organ, the period between 1750 and 1810 was thus comparatively static. One of the most prominent motives at work during this period was the desire, not to enrich and enlarge the instrument, but to simplify it. In 1791 the famous German organist, the Abbé Vogler, well known even in England through his concert tours, began a thorough transformation of the organ in accordance with his own ideals. He replaced the large costly pipes by smaller ones, which produced the deep fundamental notes required by sounding their partials (octave and twelfth). He discarded complex mixtures and certain registers which he did not regard as indispensable. The remaining pipes were arranged in a more practical manner and placed in chambers which could be gradually opened or closed with the help of a "Venetian swell," thus allowing the organist to produce crescendo and diminuendo effects. The Abbé Vogler's *Simplification System* was mainly concerned to make the organ cheaper, and easier to manufacture, repair and maintain, and to obtain a clearer and more limpid tone, in accordance with the taste of the classical period. But as such simplifications gave the organ a rather thin and commonplace tone, the Romantic period opposed these reforms, so that they had little lasting effect.

Kettledrum (Timpano)

In the second half of the eighteenth century the use of the *kettledrum* in the orchestra became more and more frequent. As of old, the drums were always employed in pairs, one being generally tuned in the tonic and the other in the dominant. Like the tuning, the role of the kettledrums was bound by tradition. They were mostly used in powerful tutti-passages to reinforce the sound of the wind instruments, especially the trumpets. The strange solo drum roll at the beginning of Haydn's Symphony No. 103, and the mysterious pianissimo effect of the kettledrums, as obtained by Beethoven at the close of the slow movement of his Fourth Symphony, were quite exceptional. Until about 1810 the instrument hardly underwent any technical modification. As the pitch of the kettledrum was never varied during the course of a movement, the arrangement of individual screws for tuning the instrument, inherited from an earlier period, was still adequate.

Occasionally the kettledrum was damped or muffled by laying a cloth over its skin or "head." Mozart was one of the first to prescribe this effect of *timpani coperti* in *Die Zauberflöte*.

Since the Turks had ceased to constitute a perpetual menace in Europe they were regarded, not perhaps with less interest, but certainly with less apprehension. The music of the once dreaded Janizaries now enjoyed remarkable popularity, and was adopted by the military bands of Europe and appeared also in the Turkish operas of the classical period.

Bass-Drum

One of the most important components of this "Janizary music" was the large Turkish *bass-drum* (Fr. *grosse caisse*, Ger. *grosse Trommel*, It. *gran cassa*), with a diameter of two to three feet, and a wooden shell of more than a foot in depth. The skins were stretched by means of cords. The instrument, which was played standing on its shell with the skins in the vertical position, was beaten with a single drumstick with a felted head or with a double-headed drumstick, to facilitate the execution of a roll. The sound of the bass-drum is dull and explosive, indefinite in pitch, and sometimes extremely loud. Mozart was one of the first to use the instrument, in 1782 in *Die Entführung aus dem Serail (Il Seraglio)*. Military bands availed themselves of its booming sound and Haydn employed it in 1794 in his Military Symphony.

Snare Drum (Side Drum), Tambourine

The ordinary *Snare drum*—also known as the *side drum* because it was often suspended at the side of a marching player—occurred in the classical period primarily as a military instrument. From 1800 onward the *tambourine* also found employment in the military bands of Europe.

Cymbals

Other important Janizary instruments were the *cymbals* and the triangle. The cymbals (Fr. *cymbales*, It. *piatti*, or *cinelli*, Ger. *Becken*) were among the first Turkish instruments to be introduced to Poland and from there to Germany. They consisted of pairs of large, circular, thin metal plates of indefinite pitch, which were held by leather straps attached to their centers, the rims being clashed together. These instruments, which diverged radically in size and character from the tiny medieval and Renaissance cymbals, were often sounded by the person who played the bass-drum. In that case one cymbal was fastened to the shell of the drum. The player held the second cymbal in one hand and the drumstick in the other, so that he could sound the two instruments together. The sharp, strident clash of the cymbals was often employed in operatic orchestras, in order to produce exotic effects. As early as 1680 N. A. Strungk used them in Dresden (*Esther*) and in 1703 R. Keiser in Hamburg (*Claudius*). In 1775 Grétry employed them in the Gypsy march of *La fausse Magie*, and four years later Gluck in the Scythian chorus of his *Iphigénie en Tauride*.

Triangle

In the last two of the scores just mentioned the *triangle*, now made in the basic triangular form and dispensing with the clanking rings, was also used. Mozart prescribed the instrument in *Die Entführung*. Steadily it made its way into the military band and the orchestra. (In Haydn's Military Symphony triangle and cymbals joined the bass-drum.)

Glockenspiel

A small *glockenspiel* of metal plates, with a keyboard but without dampers, was sometimes constructed in the eighteenth century.

The glockenspiel which Papageno plays in *Die Zauberflöte* is such an instrument.

Gong (Tam-Tam)

The *gong*, also known as the *tam-tam*, bears a certain relationship to the bell. It is a bowl-shaped instrument of bronze with an upturned rim, which is pierced to take the cord by which the gong is suspended. The center is set in vibration by a hammer or drumstick. The sound of the gong is dark in color, mysterious, uncanny, and of indefinite pitch. The home of the instrument is the Far East, and it was during the period of the French revolution that it found its way into European orchestras. In 1791 Gossec used it in his *Marche funèbre* on the death of Mirabeau; and in 1804 Lesueur introduced it into the score of his opera *Les Bardes*.

The unrestrained emotionalism of the period of *Empfindsamkeit*, culminating in the earlier part of the classical period, found expression in the construction of a whole series of curious instruments, which disappeared after a few decades. The inventors of these various instruments were mostly non-musicians.

Nail Violin

Some time before 1770 Johannes Wilde, in St. Petersburg, discovered the principle of the *nail violin* (Fr. *violon de fer*, Ger. *Nagelgeige*, It. *violino di ferro*). He assembled a number of round metal rods of different lengths and thicknesses, fixed them on to a round or oblong sound box (Pl. LII/2), tuned them to the chromatic scale and stroked them with a bow. The strange, mysterious, flute-like (though nerve-racking) tone of the instrument enabled it to achieve a certain popularity until the first few decades of the nineteenth century. It was, of course, never accepted by serious musicians.

Euphone, Clavicylinder

The results of the experiments of the physicist E. Chladni in Wittenberg were utilized when the *euphone* was constructed about 1790. Long, thin glass tubes, which were set in vibration by being stroked with moistened fingers, communicated the vibration to tuned metal rods, which produced a wavering flute-like tone. A more practical instrument was the *clavicylinder*, invented by

Chladni in 1799. In this the tuned rods were pressed against a rotating wet glass cylinder by means of a keyboard, and thereby set in vibration. Both these instruments were quite short-lived.

Musical Glasses (Verrillon)

In 1743 and 1744 an Irishman, Richard Pockridge, appeared in Dublin and in England as a performer on the *musical glasses*. He was followed by no less a musician than Gluck, who in 1746 played "a concerto on 26 drinking glasses tuned with spring water, accompanied with the whole band" at the Haymarket Theatre, London. The new instrument, also known as the *verrillon*, was soon extremely popular in England, and Goldsmith, in 1761, records in his *Vicar of Wakefield* that "fine ladies would talk of nothing but high life and high-lived company, pictures, taste, Shakespeare and the musical glasses."

Glass Harmonica

An improvement on this device was the *glass harmonica*, constructed in 1763 by Benjamin Franklin. His instrument consisted of a number of chromatically tuned, freely vibrating glass bells, which were arranged in series on a rotating axle. The individual bells were so close together that only the rim of each was visible, the rest being covered by the adjacent bell. The lower edges of the bells were dipped into a basin filled with water. The performer set the axle rotating by means of a treadle, while at the same time he set the wet bells in vibration by pressing on their rims with his fingers. The tones produced in this manner were soft, but peculiarly penetrating, with a lingering, flute-like quality. It was reported that at concerts listeners were moved to tears by the sound of the instrument, and the celebrated Viennese physician, Franz Mesmer, performed his magnetic cures to the accompaniment of the glass harmonica, since the sounds it produced made patients particularly susceptible to hypnotic sleep. The instrument, which had a range of up to four octaves ($c–c^4$), was soon accepted by the great masters. Mozart wrote an Adagio and Rondo (K. 617) for the blind harmonica virtuosa Marianne Kirchgessner, scored for harmonica, with flute, oboe, viola and 'cello; Beethoven, in his incidental music to Duncker's *Leonore Prohaska*, included a melodrama with harmonica.

Keyboard Harmonica

Since the friction of the sensitive finger-tips on the glasses led in the long run to nervous disorders, harmonicas were fitted, after 1784, with keyboards. By means of the keys, little pads were now pressed against the glass bells. The refined flexibility of tone which was obtained by playing with the finger-tips was naturally lost, and the *keyboard harmonica* never succeeded in rivalling the parent instrument, which held its own even in the early nineteenth century.

VII

FROM ROMANTICISM TO
AVANT-GARDE
(1810–1960)

1810–1900:
Romanticism

Nineteenth-century musicians worked under social conditions quite different from those of earlier times. Princely and aristocratic patronage, which had played such an important role in former centuries, was replaced by the support of middle-class music-lovers. Composers, whose output had been determined by the demands of their employers, now enjoyed a new freedom— with its obvious advantages and disadvantages—to create when and what they chose.

By and large freedom from fetters belonged to the artistic goals of the new era. Classical art of the late eighteenth century aimed at a perfect balance between form and content, between objective thinking and subjective feeling. The Romantic trend, which dominated nineteenth-century music, tried to reduce the control of the critical mind. Tender yearning, nostalgia and gloom replaced the serenity of the past. The creations of the romantic artist were emotional in character rather than guided by structural rules.

Throughout the Romantic period the human mind was peculiarly attracted by disproportionate and excessive features. The tiny piano piece and the brief lyrical song, forms which had been of no consequence during the classical period, now assumed the highest significance. On the other hand, the moderate length of the classical symphony and opera was doubled, tripled and quadrupled. Gustav Mahler (1860–1911) wrote symphonies whose length extended over a whole concert, Richard Wagner (1813–83) an opera that needed several evenings for its performance. While the eighteenth century pursued in its dynamic shadings an even middle course, avoiding extremes of loudness or softness, the nineteenth century produced the ear-splitting portrayal of the last judgement by Hector Berlioz (1803–69), which employs simultaneously a large chorus and orchestra, four additional brass bands and numerous kettledrums. On the other hand, Peter I. Tchaikovsky (1840–93) in his *Symphonie pathétique* prescribed *ppppp*, which seems almost to defy human perception.

The tight reins which tonality had kept on eighteenth-century musical thinking were gradually loosened. The increasing use of chromatic progressions, noticeable, for instance, in Wagner's *Tristan und Isolde*, or the gliding chains of unresolved dissonant chords favored by Claude Debussy (1862–1918), provided harmony with a hitherto unknown irridescent quality, while at the same time straining tonality to its utmost limits.

The clear separation and well-balanced contrast of movements in the classical sonata and symphony were frequently replaced by a method of tying the individual sections of a composition together, thus creating units of greater complexity. In the Symphony by César Franck (1822–90), for instance, the slow movement and scherzo are amalgamated, and in addition certain main themes are used throughout the composition. In *Also sprach Zarathustra* by Richard Strauss (1864–1949), a whole symphony consisting of introduction, slow section, scherzo and finale is squeezed into the form of a single movement, and in Wagner's *Der Ring des Nibelungen*, four mighty music-dramas are based on identical motive-material. Similarly, the dividing lines between the different forms of music, and beyond that the boundaries of the individual art-forms, were systematically obliterated. Beethoven's cantata-symphony, which introduced a chorus and vocal soloists into the hitherto uncontested domain of musical instruments, was imitated again and again (c.f. the *Faust-Symphonie* by Franz Liszt [1811–86], or Berlioz's *Romeo et Juliette*). In these and many other works of the Romantic period non-musical influences are very noticeable. "Program music," which drew inspiration from the composer's personal experiences, observations of nature, historical, literary and even pictorial sources, played a very big role in Romantic music. Its impact on the melodic language, format, and coloristic features of the compositions is unmistakable.

In this connection we might refer to so-called "impressionistic" music, cultivated at the turn of the century by Claude Debussy and to some extent also by Maurice Ravel (1875–1937). It was originally inspired by the paintings of the French impressionists, like Monet and Renoir, and partly by the work of contemporary poets, such as Verlaine and Baudelaire. Impressionistic music is a fragile, vague art, often based on programs intended to stimulate the listener's imagination while shunning intellectual concepts or traditional forms. Debussy's influence was strongly felt through the first decades of the twentieth century.

The combination of music with the other art-forms found its widest application, of necessity in the field of opera, which witnessed during the nineteenth century, apart from a host of highly talented and successful composers, the activities of the two giants, Richard Wagner and Giuseppe Verdi (1813–1901). Wagner, in particular, aimed at a fusion of the arts. For his "music-dramas," as he called his later operas, he wrote his own texts and often staged the works himself, in order to control even the visual aspects of their performance.

Retarding Elements

It would be wrong to assume that the Romantic movement developed in a single crescendo from its first beginnings in the eighteenth century to its last great manifestations early in the twentieth century. There were periods in which its impetus slackened, in which the turbulent forward motion was braked and even reversed. Men like Felix Mendelssohn (1809–47), César Franck and Johannes Brahms (1833–97) revived in their art elements of the past, thus temporarily leading the Romantic stream into a broader, less agitated channel. Brahms, in particular, who wrote no operas and disliked program music, introduced decidedly conservative features into Romanticism.

Coloristic Effects

During the Romantic period a strong sense of color was everywhere apparent. The painters of the Romantic school sacrificed careful drawing to a purely chromatic effect, and musicians too sought for means to enrich the range of color at their disposal. In the classical era instruments had primarily supported melodic, harmonic and contrapuntal ideas, whereas some nineteenth-century composers created orchestral effects for their own sake. This was the period of virtuosi of instrumentation. Composers like Berlioz, Wagner, and R. Strauss worked towards rich and massive coloristic ensembles; Debussy, on the other hand, preferred delicate, irridescent, and rather exotic sounds. They all aimed at a full exploration of the instruments' capabilities and, most of all, at enriching the musical palette through captivating and even startling new sound effects. Berlioz, in particular, was so strongly concerned with the problems of orchestration that in 1844 he published a treatise on instrumentation which soon became a standard work. Characteristically, it was revised and up-dated half a century later by R. Strauss.

The Instruments of the Romantic Era
While composers and performers made substantial new demands on the musical instruments, their makers revealed ingenuity in meeting or even anticipating any requests. Existing instruments were technically improved and a number of new ones added. By and large the bowed stringed instruments met the requirements of the time, but it was different with the wind instruments. Many highly gifted inventors now applied themselves with success to the final solution of a problem which in former times had seemed to offer insuperable difficulties: how to enable the wind instruments to produce in a satisfactory manner all the notes of the chromatic scale. The final result of their efforts was that most of the keys and modulations could be sounded on a single wind instrument. Similarly the harp, which was traditionally used for diatonic music, was transformed into an instrument which could hold its own in the harmonically complicated music of the time. Organs were drastically enlarged and the piano entered the most significant phase of its development.

The endeavor to conquer the lower registers was resumed with new zeal, and it was combined with the aim of increasing the volume of sound. Giant horn instruments owe their existence to the general tendency toward the ponderous and the super-human—a tendency to be observed also in the historical paintings of the period. Reed instruments were constructed with conical metal tubes of large bore, so that their tone gained in strength. The voice of the flute was made harder and sharper, as the instrument was provided with the cylindrical bore which since has become the rule.

The instrumental families of the later Renaissance were revived with a view to obtaining more harmonious effects. Wind instruments were made in various sizes and R. Strauss records, for instance, that in a performance of Mozart's great Symphony in G minor, given at the Brussels conservatoire, all the parts, from the highest to the lowest, were taken by different-sized members of the clarinet family.

After the first half of the nineteenth century had worked on improving the wind instruments, special attention was given to the percussion instruments. The last quarter of the century, in particular, found new means of expression in instruments which had either not been known before, or, if familiar, had not been employed in the orchestra. The xylophone, celesta, tubular bells, castanets, and rattle, for instance, were now incorporated in musical scores. Occasionally also pianoforte, organ and harmonium were used not as solo instruments, but as members of the ensemble to enrich the coloristic palette.

1900–1960:
Polyrhythm, Polytonality

At the beginning of the twentieth century the shimmering, luminous sound effects created by Debussy electrified the whole of the musical world. But a reaction to this delicate, ethereal idiom was already on its way. A new cult of vigor and even brutality led to a harsher, more assertive musical language. Complicated, rapidly-changing rhythms, as well as the simultaneous use of contrasting rhythms (*polyrhythms*) were repeatedly tried out; *polytonality*, employing two and even more different keys at the same time, was also one of the features of the new music. Sergey Prokofiev (1891–1953), Darius Milhaud (1892–1974) and, in particular, Igor Stravinsky (1882–1971), were among the enthusiastic protagonists of these powerful devices.

Influence of Jazz, Machines and Sports

On the other hand many composers saw in the idiom of American dance music a means of new artistic expression. The stimulating rhythm of *jazz* and, most of all, its striking coloristic effects influenced musicians on both sides of the Atlantic. Performance methods were employed which had hitherto been unusual—such as *vibrato* and *glissando* on wind instruments—and new instruments were introduced which were borrowed from popular or exotic sources (banjo, musical saw, vibraphone, marimba, etc.). The marked preference for wind instruments over bowed stringed ones and the subtly differentiated treatment of the percussion instruments likewise stimulated a young generation of composers. Among the countless compositions which show the influence of American dance music we mention only the piano concerto by Aaron Copland (b. 1900), Igor Stravinsky's *Ragtime* for eleven instruments, the ballet *La création du monde* by Darius Milhaud, the opera *Jonny spielt auf* by Ernst Krenek (b. 1900), *Porgy and Bess* by George Gershwin (1898–1937) and *Die Dreigroschenoper* by Kurt Weill (1900–1950).

Other sources of inspiration for twentieth-century composers were the sounds produced by *machines* or *sports* and *games*, which were portrayed realistically. Thus Arthur Honegger (1892–1955) wrote *Pacific 231*, eulogizing the motion of a locomotive, Alexander Mossolov (b. 1900) a ballet *The Factory*, and Bohuslav Martinů (1890–1959) an orchestral composition *Half-time*, glorifying a football game.

Atonality, Twelve-Tone (Twelve-Note) Technique

A different kind of experimentation was undertaken by Arnold Schoenberg (1874–1951) and his followers in Vienna. They wrote compositions in which all implications of tonality, as well as traditional harmonic progressions, were avoided. This system of *atonality* or *pantonality*, as they preferred to call it, went even further than the experiments with polytonality; it carried to its logical conclusion the systematic weakening of the tonal structure which had taken place during the Romantic period.

It was gradually discovered, however, that atonality needed a firm backbone to make up for the loss of tonal support. This was provided by the *twelve-tone (twelve-note) technique*, introduced in 1923 by Schoenberg and taken over before long by his adherents, Anton von Webern (1883–1945) and Alban Berg (1885–1935), as well as by other composers. For each work the author created a "series" of twelve notes which had to include all the components of the chromatic scale. This series, in which the order of the notes was left to the composer, could, as the piece progressed, be inverted, presented in retrograde order and transposed. The numerous possible permutations served, moreover, not only as the basis of the melodic, but also of the harmonic material. A certain structural solidity was thus achieved, which in turn also provided the basis for future musical developments.

Chamber Orchestra

In the first decades of the twentieth century the slogan "bigger and better," which seemed to have been valid for much of later Romantic music, began to lose a great deal of its magic attraction. In 1906 Mahler's Eighth Symphony was scored for 6 flutes, 5 oboes, 6 clarinets, 5 bassoons, 8 horns, 8 trumpets, 6 trombones, tuba, timpani, bells, mandolin, organ, harmonium, piano, celesta, a large string orchestra, a huge chorus, and 8 vocal soloists. In the same year, 1906, Arnold Schoenberg wrote his chamber symphony, op. 9, for 10 wind and 5 stringed instruments, requiring 15 performers in all.

A striving for clarity and lucidity replaced the former aim of rich color. The listener was supposed to be able to follow each voice of the composition, so instruments were assembled whose sounds resisted a blending of colors. In the sixth part of his *Pierrot lunaire*, written in 1912, Schoenberg accompanied the peculiar *Sprechstimme* (Speech-song) he had created with flute, bass clarinet and violoncello; and Stravinsky in the *Petit concert* of his *L'histoire du soldat* (1918) employed a quartet of clarinet, cornet à pistons, violin and double-bass only. In both cases a few instruments of sharply contrasting tone were used, as color was completely subordinated to polyphony.

Neoclassicism

In the second quarter of the century, a tendency to adopt features of earlier music could be observed. Such compositions, often designated as *neo-classical* in style, were likely to show a well-balanced structure and objectivity of expression. Absolute music, which kept itself free from any poetical program, was in vogue again. The Baroque suite of dances, passacaglia, fugue, toccata, concerto grosso, to be found in compositions from the sixteenth century to Couperin and Bach, stimulated the works of modern composers. The *Classical Symphony*, written in 1918 by Prokofiev, was in some respects prophetic of the trend. This reached its full development a few years later in works like the *Klaviermusik*, op. 37, by Paul Hindemith (1895–1963), the piano concerto by Igor Stravinsky, the *Prelude and Fugue* for orchestra by Walter Piston (b. 1894), and the *Introduzione, aria e toccata* for orchestra by Alfredo Casella (1883–1947).

These neo-classical tendencies were not conducive to an expansion of the orchestral resources. By and large composers were content to use the available means. The trend towards rebuilding instruments of the past, such as the recorder, harpsichord and members of the viol family, gained new impetus at this time. Certain organ-builders reverted not only to the aesthetic ideals of the Bach era, but even further back to those of the early seventeenth century. By following specifications offered by Michael Praetorius, instruments were built, first in Germany and later in the U.S.A., which recaptured the dignified simplicity and austere beauty of tone of the late-Renaissance organ.

Serial Music

The shock-waves emanating from the holocaust of the Second World War triggered off a new wave of dissatisfaction with the prevailing musical idiom. Avant-garde composers once more busily experimented to discover new modes of musical expression.

Anton Webern, whose fragmentation of sound, pithy forms and refusal to use clear-cut themes particularly appealed to the younger generation, might be regarded as the patron saint of the radical trends which developed around the middle of the century. The twelve-tone technique was subsequently enlarged into *serialism*, which proposed to organize rhythm, dynamics, and timbre according to similar, strictly mathematical principles. Thus total intellectual control of the elements of music was for some time one of the artistic tenets finding expression in works by such composers as Milton Babbitt (b. 1916), Pierre Boulez (b. 1925), and Karlheinz Stockhausen (b. 1928).

The application of serialism was promoted by the general mechanization of music, the increasing use of electronic instruments and of magnetic tape (see p. 210f). These technical advances introduced new dimensions into music, in particular an unlimited number of pitches, from the lowest to the highest audible to the human ear. While heretofore composers had at their disposal twelve notes to the octave and used, as a rule, less than one hundred different pitches, they could now free themselves completely from the fetters of the equal-temperament system. The early twentieth century had started to abolish tonality; the second half of the century began to destroy even the system of pitches on which western music had been based for centuries.

Chance Music

While composers aimed at total control of the means of expression, they also felt inclined to introduce the element of *chance* into their work. Thus *Piano Piece XI* by Karlheinz Stockhausen consists of nineteen fragments which the performer may play in any order he happens to choose, and with optional tempo, dynamics, etc. Similarly Pierre Boulez in his Third Piano Sonata offers the performer different alternatives, and John Cage (b. 1912) suggests in one of his pieces that the choice of clefs should be determined by the flipping of a coin: heads stands for treble, tails for bass, a far cry from the pedantic thoroughness of nineteenth- and early twentieth-century scores, which prescribed even minute details in the most exact manner possible.

New Forms of Notation

The decisive changes in the character of music obviously caused changes in its *notation*. For purely electronic music composers provided geometrical graphs, meant for the technician, who assumed here the role of the performer. While in other types of music many of the old symbols were still employed, they often no longer controlled the performance strictly, but served mainly as signals helping to regulate the flow of the music. Moreover, individual composers added new symbols depending on the character of the specific work. It says much for the ingenuity of the composers and the adaptability of modern performers that such reforms were cheerfully accepted as a rule and correctly interpreted by players and singers alike.

Coloristic Effects

The new spirit of experimentation manifested itself also in a striving towards unfamiliar *coloristic effects*. Composers started to use traditional instruments in a decidedly unorthodox manner. They plucked the strings of a piano with the fingers or produced eerie glissando effects by passing the hands over the strings. Likewise they hit the piano strings with mallets, without resorting to the keys and hammers of the instrument. In John Cage's "prepared piano," nuts, bolts, pieces of felt and rubber were inserted between the strings; the resulting softly muffled sounds seemed to approach the tone-quality of Indonesian gongs and drums. The strings of a harp were hit with drum sticks, producing strange clanging sounds. The body of a stringed instrument, such as the viola or 'cello, was rubbed or tapped with the finger. Frightening noises came forth when the bow was applied between bridge and tailpiece, instead of above the bridge. A nasal tone-quality was obtained when the player used the wooden stick instead of the hair of his bow. Percussion instruments of various kinds were favorites of the time. In ensemble music melodic progressions and rhythms were often indicated in very general terms only, a method requiring some kind of improvisation on the part of the performers and apt to produce unusual sound effects. Krzystof Penderecki (b. 1933) and George Crumb (b. 1929), for instance, made use of such ideas with eminent success in various compositions.

Magnetic Tape

Recent technical advances also offered composers an opportunity to manipulate the tone-qualities of instruments played in the traditional manner. In particular, the invention of the *magnetic tape* opened up a host of new possibilities. If a sound recorded on tape was played faster or slower, not only did the speed change but with it the pitch and, most of all, the timbre. A high note played on the piano could thus be made to sound like a full-bodied gong. Tapes were also played backwards, achieving a very curious effect, as the tone seemed to grow out of nowhere, then gain in strength and end with an explosive attack. Tapes might be cut to pieces and the fragments spliced together in a different order. Several tapes could be superimposed and the result recorded afresh. Thus, for instance, Thea Musgrave (b. 1928) in *From one to another* produced a rich texture of the most variegated sonorities, all gained from music played by a single viola. This sophisticated complex of sounds was used, moreover, to accompany the live performance of a viola player.

Musique Concrète, Electronic Music

Traditional instruments or human voices were not the only basis for sound manipulations with magnetic tape. *Musique concrète*, practised primarily in France by composers like Olivier Messiaen (b. 1908) and Pierre Boulez, started out with non-musical sounds, such as bird-songs, the noises of machines, the bustle and stir of cities. Purely synthetic sounds created by electronic devices and combined through the operation of magnetic tapes, proved even more attractive to the minds of avant-garde composers, since here pitch, duration of note and timbre could be controlled to an extent previously unknown. Electronic instruments had been made since the end of the First World War, but they were technically too primitive to find more than a limited use. This changed around the middle of the century, when efficient electronic generators and synthesizers were constructed. In various parts of the world experiments were made in an attempt to create by electronic means timbres and complex combinations of sound that had not existed previously.

A rather startling type of synthetic music has been produced with the help of digital computers. Carefully punched cards are fed into a digital computer, which is programed to produce corresponding signals on a magnetic tape. They in turn serve as the basis for performance on a recording machine. Bell Laboratories in the U.S. have done pioneer work in this field.

Synthesizers and computers are apt to eliminate the person of the performer. Music can be created in a laboratory, projected on to a magnetic tape, and finally reproduced with the help of a loudspeaker. No intermediary need be involved in this process.

Clearly, electronic music has not yet outgrown its experimental stage, and there is little doubt that it will lead to surprising developments. Twentieth-century music is bound to be stimulated increasingly by the expansion of technical means.

Let us now examine specific instruments of the era:

Violin Family
If we take a general survey of the *bowed instruments* from the Romantic period to the present day, we find that the resulting picture does not differ in its main features from that of the preceding period. The violin, viola, 'cello and double-bass are still, though not the only bowed instruments, the only ones of any importance. On the whole the nineteenth and twentieth centuries

found little need to alter their classic form. Constant progress was made, but it was in the technique of the performer rather than in the technique of construction. One of the greatest virtuosi of the violin, Niccolò Paganini (1782–1840), whose career fell in the Romantic period, and the double-bass player Domenico Dragonetti (1763–1846), who made nothing of playing works written for the 'cello on his large, ponderous instrument, evoked storms of applause from thousands of listeners. But of even greater importance than the supreme achievements of individual artists is the fact that during the nineteenth century the general standard of orchestral performers was enormously improved. The tasks which Liszt, Wagner and Richard Strauss required of the whole body of the strings were far more arduous than those demanded of the solo instrument in the violin concertos of Haydn and Mozart. The two classic masters hardly ever took the solo violin higher than a^3; but Berlioz, in his *Traité d'instrumentation* (1844), asserted that the violin of the orchestra could go a third higher— that is, to c^4—and Strauss declared, in his supplement to this work (1909), that even this assertion was out of date, since the members of a symphonic or operatic orchestra could play up to g^4. With the help of such devices as tremolos, trills, arpeggios, pizzicatos, executed by either hand, and their combination, new effects are always being obtained, and it seems as though after a history of more than 300 years, the possibilities of the stringed instruments are by no means exhausted (cf. also p. 210).

Violin

To the *violin* (tuned in g, d^1, a^1, e^2) is assigned the undisputed leadership of the strings. The number of violinists in a full-sized orchestra is usually as great as, or even greater than, that of all the rest of the strings together. In tutti and solo passages alike the most important tasks are allotted to them, and they also provide the basis of chamber music no less than of orchestral music. Following the example of Bach, Max Reger (1873–1916) and Paul Hindemith have written sonatas for the unaccompanied violin.

Viola

The *viola* (tuned in c, g, d^1, a^1) is not only appreciated as the essential central voice of the string group; it has also attracted the attention of composers through the more subdued, drier, less sensuous quality of its tone, which distinguishes it from both violin and 'cello. Berlioz employed it as a solo instrument in his symphony *Harold en Italie*, to describe the rather problematic personality of the hero. R. Strauss in *Don Quixote*, on the other hand, availed himself of a solo viola to portray the down-to-earth character of Sancho Panza. The viola was the favorite instrument of Brahms, and among more recent composers Hindemith, a viola player himself, had a special predilection for it. Concertos for viola have been written by Béla Bartók (1881–1945), Darius Milhaud, and Boris Blacher (b. 1903).

Violoncello

Like the viola, the *violoncello* (tuned in C, G, d, a) plays a double role. It serves as an essential foundation-element in orchestral and chamber music; at the same time the sonorous quality of its lower and middle range and the penetrating, yet sweet timbre of its higher notes have been used for special purposes. It is characteristic of the important position allotted to the violoncello in the Romantic period that G. Rossini (1792–1868), in the overture to *Guillaume Tell*, introduced a quintet of five solo 'cellos accompanied by the rest of the 'cellos. A large number of sonatas for 'cello and piano, as well as concertos for solo 'cello, were written during the nineteenth and twentieth centuries. Thus mention may be made of sonatas by Beethoven, Brahms, R. Strauss, Debussy, Ravel, Honegger, Z. Kodály (1882–1967), F. Martin (1890–1959), and D. Shostakovich (1906–75); and concertos or concerto-like pieces by R. Schumann (1810–56), P. I. Tchaikovsky (1840–93), A. Dvořák (1841–1904), P. Hindemith and A. Khachaturian (b. 1903).

Double-Bass

The long-standing conflict between the three-stringed *double-bass* tuned in fifths (G_1, D, A) and the four-stringed instrument tuned in fourths (E_1, A_1, D, G) was decided, in the course of the nineteenth century, in favor of four strings. Recently instruments have occasionally been seen which have in addition a fifth, bottom string in C_1. More often the four-stringed double-bass is equipped with an extension enabling the player to tune the E_1 string down to C_1. Music for the double-bass is always written an octave higher than it actually sounds. The thick, heavy strings of the instrument are generally tuned with the help of steel cog-wheels.

The high opinion which was held of the capabilities of the double-bass, even at the beginning of the nineteenth century, is evident from the great unaccompanied bass recitative in the finale of Beethoven's Ninth Symphony; while Wagner, in Act III of *Tristan und Isolde*, and above all, Verdi, in Act IV of *Otello*, have given proof of the impressive quality of a solo double-bass. A celebrated example of the naturalistic effect of the instrument is that obtained by R. Strauss in the opera *Salome*. In order to represent the death-rattle of the murdered Jochanaan, one of the strings of the double-bass is bowed below the bridge, instead of above it, as is usual. The instrument's capacity for producing exotic sounds has been increasingly explored. Its pizzicato is effectively used in modern dance music. It is also significant that the great double-bass virtuoso, Sergei Koussevitzky (1874–1951), eventually developed into one of the most celebrated conductors in the United States.

Effective though the supremacy of violin, viola, 'cello and double-bass has been in practice, it was by no means uncontested. Many experiments were made in the construction of stringed instruments, but none of the "improvements" were really success-ful. The old-established instruments were not excelled, and their pre-eminence has been undisturbed.

Some of the "improved" forms may be mentioned here, though to deal with them all would require a special chapter.

Variants of the Violin
François Chanot, of Mirecourt, France, believed that the sharp corners of the violin inhibited the diffusion of the tone, and from 1817 onwards he accordingly built instruments which had some-what the shape of a guitar. Contemporaries of Chanot's declared that in the quality of their tone these violins could rival the creations of Guarneri and Stradivari, and the famous violinist Giovanni Battista Viotti (1755–1824) is said to have played on them occasionally. However, the Chanot violins had no more enduring success than the trapezoid box-fiddle of the French physicist Felix Savart (1819), or the elliptical instrument of the Dresden composer Dr. Alfred Stelzner (circa 1890). Practical tests subsequently established their acoustic inferiority. An

interesting experiment was made in London. At the close of the nineteenth century, violins were constructed in which the sound-box was replaced by a diaphragm and a trumpet like that of the old gramophones. These instruments had a powerful tone, but a grotesque appearance. In recent decades violins have once more been made without sound-boxes. They are provided with electronic equipment and a loudspeaker, and with the help of a pedal any desired loudness of tone can be obtained, from the softest *ppp* to the most powerful *fff*.

Variants of the Viola

Attempts were made to combine the characteristics of the viola and the violin, the viola being given, as a fifth string, the highest string of the violin (e²). An instrument of this kind was the *viola alta*, which Hermann Ritter of Würzburg produced in 1876.

Tenor Violins

As a connecting-link between viola and 'cello various *tenor violins* were constructed, tuned an octave lower than the violin (G, d, a, e¹). Charles Henry in Paris built such instruments around the middle of the nineteenth century, and so did Valentino de Zorzi in Florence in 1908 (*controviolino*). The elliptical *violotta*, introduced by Alfred Stelzner in 1891, had a fine full tone and was even admitted occasionally to the opera orchestra. These three instruments were held like the violin, whereas the *Tenor-Geige*, made by Hermann Ritter and by A. von Glehn in Reval (1912), was held between the legs like a 'cello.

Variants of the Violoncello

A 'cello in the cornerless form devised by Chanot was the *Arpeggione* or *Bogenguitarre* (Pl. LIV/1), invented by G. Staufer in Vienna (1823). This had the frets and the six strings of the guitar and was tuned like it, in E, A, d, g, b, e¹. Franz Schubert (1797–1828) wrote an admirable sonata for this instrument. A larger variant of the violoncello was the elliptical *cellone* of A. Stelzner (circa 1890), which was a fourth lower than the 'cello and therefore two octaves lower than the violin (G₁, D, A, e). This was intended especially to replace the all-too-unwieldy double-bass in chamber music. Stelzner himself and A. Krug wrote compositions for this instrument.

Variants of the Double-Bass

An enlarged variant of the double-bass was the *octobass*, invented in 1849 by J. B. Vuillaume in Paris. It was thirteen feet in height (Pl. LIV/2) and had three strings in C_1, G_1, C; they were tuned from the tail-piece and were shortened by means of a key mechanism operated with the help of seven pedals. Berlioz, who was an enthusiast for all innovations, praised the octobass in his *Traité d'instrumentation*. I have had the opportunity of hearing this instrument, and I was surprised by the weak tone of its rather loosely stretched strings. This defect, no less than its unwieldy dimensions, must have hindered any wide use of the instrument. As far as I know, only three octobasses have been made in all (preserved in Russia, Paris and Vienna respectively). Even this mammoth instrument was overtopped in America by the *grand bass* of John Geyer (1889), which was fifteen feet in height.

Historical Instruments

While all these instruments were devised as innovations and improvements—even when unsuccessful—the historical tendencies of the period led to a conscious reversion to old forms. *Viole da gamba* in various sizes, as well as *viole d'amore* (tuned to d, f♯, a, d^1, $f♯^1$, a^1, d^2), were not infrequently constructed, and there are many schools of music in which a student can learn to play them. The viola d'amore in particular has never become entirely obsolete. Among the Romantic composers G. Meyerbeer (1791–1864) employed it in *Les Huguenots* and W. Kienzl (1857–1941) in *Der Kuhreigen*. Hindemith has composed a sonata and a concerto for the viola d'amore.

Guitar

In the course of the nineteenth century the classical *guitar* was gradually transformed into a heavier, stronger and more efficient instrument. Instead of wooden tuning-pegs, metal screws were employed. The lower part of the guitar's body was widened, and to enable it to withstand the pull of the heavier strings, the whole instrument was more solidly built. The rose of earlier guitars disappeared from the sound-hole, which was left open. In our time the finger-board has been equipped with brass frets, and its length extended all the way to the sound-hole.

Throughout the Romantic era the guitar's popularity was

very great. Weber wrote songs with guitar accompaniment. Berlioz was a guitar player; so was his friend Paganini, who wrote some masterly chamber music for the instrument. To this day the guitar holds its own, not only as the people's instrument, but also as a means for virtuosi to display breath-taking technical skill. Especially in its homeland, Spain, a high level of playing was achieved. Andrés Segovia (b. 1893) attained a mastery reminiscent of the art of the old lute players. In the younger generation, the Englishman Julian Bream (b. 1933) is one of the leaders in this field. From among the various modern composers who have written for the guitar one might single out Manuel de Falla (1876–1946), who wrote his profoundly stirring *Homenaje*, dedicated to the memory of Debussy, for unaccompanied guitar.

The guitar also finds employment in jazz music. Here it is at times accompanied or replaced by its variants.

Ukulele, Hawaian Guitar, Electric Guitar

The *ukulele* is a small guitar of Portuguese origin equipped with four steel strings, which are shortened by means of a metal bar and played with a ring-shaped plectrum. The *Hawaian guitar*, on the other hand, is a large guitar equipped with a high bridge. It too uses metal strings and a movable metal bar placed across the finger-board. Both instruments foster sentimentality through ample use of vibrato and portamento effects. The *electric guitar*, invented in America in 1936, replaces the sound-board by electronic devices. With their help the tone of the instrument can be altered and reinforced until it is audible above the strongest orchestra.

Banjo

The guitar-like *banjo* was originally used in West Africa and later taken over by the North-American Negroes. Its body consists of a shallow metal drum, open at the back, and a long neck. This instrument, which is made in various sizes, used to be provided with from five to nine gut or nylon strings, the highest (known as the "thumb string") lying immediately beside the lowest. A common tuning was, for instance, g^1, c, g, b, d^1. Jazz musicians prefer the tenor banjo, with four metal strings in viola tuning. When wire-strung, the instrument is played with a plectrum and produces hard metallic sounds admirably suited to the creation of rhythmic effects.

Mandolin

The *mandolin* (with four pairs of metal strings tuned to g, d^1, a^1, e^2 and plucked with a plectrum) is diligently cultivated to this day in Italy and also in Austria. Whole orchestras are formed of mandolins and their larger relatives, which perform light music with an often astonishing degree of technical skill. The mandolin sometimes appears even in symphonic and operatic music, e.g. to produce the atmosphere of a serenade. The Austrian composers Mahler, Schoenberg, and Webern made use of it; Verdi employed it in *Otello* and Stravinsky in the ballet *Agon*.

Balalaika, Dombra, Gusli

Russian folk-music relies largely on the use of three primitive instruments with plucked strings. Two of these, the *balalaika* and *dombra*, are like the guitar or lute; the third, the *gusli*, is a kind of psaltery or zither. Late in the last century V. V. Andrejeff modernized these instruments and made them the basis of an All-Russian orchestra, with which he toured Europe.

The balalaika has a triangular body, with a central "rose" in the table, and a fretted neck carrying three strings. At first the modern instrument was made in five sizes, which are, with their tunings: *prima* (e^1, e^1, a^1), *secunda* (a, a, d^1), *alto* (e, e, a), *basso* (E, A, d), and *contrabasso* (E_1, A_1, D), the last being stood on the ground to use. Soon a sixth instrument, the *piccolo* (b^1, e^2, a^2), was added. The balalaika is usually strung with gut strings and plucked with the fingers, or swept by the open hand; professional players, however, like to use wire strings and pluck them with a piece of leather. This adequately reproduces the effect of gut strings while saving the wear and tear inseparable from their use.

The dombra resembles a long-necked mandolin. It has three wire strings, which are played with a hard plectrum. The performer produces a tremolo similar to that employed on the mandolin, but with the difference that it is made on single and not on paired strings. The six sizes of the dombra correspond to those of the balalaika, the *prima* being tuned e^1, a^1, d^2, and the others to the same intervals at different pitches.

The gusli is made in triangular or trapezoid form. It appears in various sizes and is equipped with from 12 to 36 strings, which are plucked with the bare fingers by a player who holds the instrument on his lap.

Harp

The *harp* was one of the instruments which were radically transformed and improved during the Romantic period. As early as 1782 Georges Cousineau in Paris was experimenting with a view to transforming the single-pedal harp into a double-action pedal harp. Before long the problem was tackled by the celebrated maker of pianos, Sébastien Érard, who in 1801 applied for a patent in connection with a new type of harp. But this type still did not satisfy him and he made even further attempts to better the instrument's construction. Around the year 1820 he finally reached his goal. Érard's new double-action pedal harp had a range of Cb_1-gb^4, that is of $6\frac{1}{2}$ octaves, and eventually the range of the instrument was still further enlarged, to close on eight octaves (Cb_2-bb^4). Like the older harp, Érard's instrument was furnished with seven pedals, each pedal acting on one note of the diatonic scale throughout the instrument's range. The pedal could be depressed to an intermediate position or pushed right down. When half-way down it raised the pitch of the strings connected with it, in all the octaves, by a semitone; when fully depressed it raised them by a whole tone. The mechanism of the double-action pedal is shown schematically in Fig. 5. Figure 5a shows an unshortened string, the pedal being in the up position. Figure 5b shows the effect of depressing the pedal halfway. The upper disc has rotated, and the pins attached to it have shortened the string by such an amount that it is now tuned a semitone higher. Figure 5c shows the result of depressing the pedal fully. The lower disc and fork have also rotated, and the string is so far shortened that it sounds a whole tone higher. As already mentioned, the depression of a pedal produces its effect not merely on a single string, but on all the strings tuned to the same note. Since the pedals can be fixed in either position, it is possible, in a harp tuned to the key of Cb major, by depressing the pedals through half their range or through their full range, to obtain all the major and minor keys, as well as numerous tonal combinations.

The Romantic period discovered that the harp was a very

versatile instrument. Not only melodies with an accompaniment, chords, arpeggios and glissandos, but also harmonics of a peculiar charm can be played upon it. Nicolas Bochsa (1789–1856), harper to Napoleon I and Louis XVIII, enjoyed international celebrity as a virtuoso and composer for the harp. His fame was even surpassed by that of his pupil, Elias Parish-Alvars (1808–49), who explored all the technical possibilities of the Érard instrument. The harp, whose tender and ethereal sound contrasts most

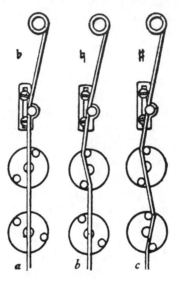

Fig. 5. Mechanism of a double-action pedal harp

effectively with the tone of wind and bowed stringed instruments, is also often employed in chamber music, besides symphonic and operatic orchestras. The list of composers who made special use of the harp is over-long. We might single out only Berlioz, Wagner, Debussy, Ravel, Stravinsky and Bartók.

The double-action pedal harp, although it was by far the most important, was not the only harp of the nineteenth century. G. C. Pfranger's *chromatic harp* of 1804 needed no pedal, since it had a string for every note of the chromatic scale; the strings for the notes of the C major scale were white, while the rest were dark blue. More efficient than this instrument, in which all the strings lay in the same plane, was the chromatic harp invented by

Jean-Henri Pape in 1845, in which those strings which corresponded to the white keys of the piano lay in one plane, while the rest of the strings formed a separate row. The two sets crossed each other at the level of half their length. This instrument was still further improved in America, and more particularly by Gustave Lyon, the director of the firm of Pleyel in Paris (1903). It found many exponents in France, Belgium and Switzerland. The fact, however, that in *forte* passages the strings collided with one another where they crossed, and the rather poor tone of the instrument, prevented its wide diffusion.

Aeolian Harp, Piano Éolien

Aeolian harps were still in use during the second half of the nineteenth century, and inventors continued to improve their construction. Following the tremendous advances made by various keyboard instruments, the Aeolian harp, although certainly less adapted for such a device, was also provided with a keyboard. As early as 1789 J. J. Schnell in Paris had built an instrument with a compass of five octaves and three strings for each note. The depression of keys directed a current of air against the strings, producing a very light and delicate tone. An improved version of this instrument was the *piano éolien*, built in Paris by Isouard and Herz about the middle of the nineteenth century. Since the notes took some time to build up, the ingenious instrument failed to achieve wide distribution.

Zither

During the nineteenth century the *zither* of the Alpine regions increasingly attracted the attention of tourists and consequently gained in importance. The instrument was technically improved, exchanging its plain rectangular structure for a more sonorous curved form. Two different types now made their appearance. The Salzburg form, which was rounded on the bass side, and the Mittenwald form, rounded on both sides. At times the instruments were also artistically finished or, for use in dilettante circles, provided with gadgets facilitating their use. For players of bowed instruments Petzmayer in Munich invented in 1823 the *Streich-Zither* (bowed zither). This heart-shaped instrument was usually provided with a rounded and fretted finger-board and four wire strings, tuned as in the violin, though the order is the reverse of that found in the violin.

Recently, in America, *electric zithers* have been employed which are equipped with a microphone and loudspeaker. This adaptation makes it possible to produce tones of any desired strength. But, as with other instruments, the simple basic form of the zither displayed more vitality than the various "improved" types.

Cimbalom

The *cimbalom* of the Hungarian gypsy orchestra is a descendant of the ancient dulcimer. In the form improved by J. Schunda of Budapest, the instrument is trapeze-shaped, struck by leather or wooden mallets, and supported on four legs. It has a compass of four octaves ($E–e^3$) and is equipped with three to five metal strings for each note. Dampers are often fitted which can be lifted by means of a pedal, as in the piano. Cimbalom players, most of whom perform without music, attain an astonishing degree of virtuosity. Bartók and Kodály (1882–1967), introduced the instrument into their compositions to emphasize the element of Hungarian folk-music, and Liszt used imitations of cimbalom music for the same reason in his piano compositions.

Piano

The upward career of the *piano* during the nineteenth century was quite unprecedented. Steadily advancing, it became one of the most important instruments of the period. While in Haydn's work compositions for the piano take a comparatively modest place, Mozart, twenty-four years his junior, wrote pieces for the instrument which are among his very finest achievements. In the work of Beethoven, born fourteen years after Mozart, compositions for the piano play an even more significant part, while the creative output of Chopin (1810–49), Liszt, Schumann, Brahms and Debussy was largely based on compositions for the piano.

This increasing interest in the piano was obviously bound to be accompanied by an enlargement of its technical possibilities. Many excellent pianoforte manufacturers, in England, France, the U.S.A. and Germany, helped to transform the delicate, fragile instrument of the eighteenth century into the powerful grand piano of the present day.

English makers must be credited with the perfecting of the English action, with its beautiful tone, whose superiority over the German action was admitted by Beethoven. They were also largely responsible for the wider compass and more robust construction of the piano. The Parisian manufacturer, Sébastien Érard, who had also improved the harp by his ingenious inventions, gave the piano thicker and therefore more sonorous strings, with hammer-heads of corresponding dimensions. Above all, his improvements to the action of the piano were of decisive importance. In 1822 he patented the *double escapement*, which makes it possible for the same note to be repeated as often and as rapidly as the performer pleases. As long as the finger continues to depress the key, the hammer, having struck its blow, does not fall back into quite the initial position, but only halfway, so that it is ready for another quick blow. Hummel (1778–1836) and the young Liszt were not slow to realize the importance of the new invention; yet almost twenty years were to pass before it gained general acceptance. Then, indeed, it was adopted by almost all piano manufacturers, though naturally with various modifications of detail.

In America, where such makers as Meyer, Chickering, and above all Steinway were at work, decisive improvements were made in another important respect. The adoption of heavy, thickly-felted hammer-heads, and the consequent employment of thicker and more tightly stretched strings, together with the constant extension of the compass, which sometimes exceeded eight octaves, resulted in an enormous increase in the tension which the frame of the instrument had to withstand. Even in the nineteenth century it amounted to no less than sixteen tons, while in our day tensions of up to thirty tons are to be found. After various experiments, in which European makers also played an important part, a heavy *cast-iron frame* was produced in 1825 by Babcock of Boston, Massachusetts, of the kind in use to this day. Babcock, and later the firm of Steinway & Sons of New York, also adopted the practice of *over-stringing* or cross-stringing, in which the bass strings run diagonally above the rest. Thanks to this more compact arrangement of the strings, the over-strung piano is shorter than the older type. At the same time—if the dampers are raised—the close proximity of the strings increases the wealth of overtones, and therefore the richness of sound. The tone of the overstrung piano has not, however, the limpidity of the older instruments. It is less well adapted for polyphonic playing, and chords in the lower octaves, such as recur in classical compositions, may assume the character of a buzz or growl. Such chords were therefore avoided by composers of the Romantic period.

England, France and America were not alone in making structural improvements to the development of the piano; there were also Germany and Austria, where experts such as Bechstein, Blüthner and Bösendorfer were at work. However, central Europe no longer played such an important part as in the days of Silbermann, Stein and Streicher.

The various forms of piano case adopted in the classical period were retained in the Romantic era. The prevailing form of the instrument, now as then, was the *grand piano* or *Flügel*. It underwent a gradual increase in size, weight and structural solidity. The keyboard projected from the case, and was covered with a lid of its own, which could be opened independently of the lid closing the case of the piano. Three heavy legs with Baroque protuberances replaced the many thin legs of bygone days. The pedals were given a strong, wooden, lyre-shaped support. Their number was now reduced, since the Romantic period began to regard the many subtly differentiated registers of the classical period as a sort of toy. The right pedal served to lift all the dampers, and the left to shift the keyboard so that the hammerheads no longer struck all three strings assigned to the note. Modern pianos are also often equipped with a third pedal, placed in the middle. This serves to sustain individual notes or chords which are struck when the pedal is pressed down. The respective dampers are raised and only return to the strings when the pedal is released.

The piano of the late Romantic period, and still more the modern concert grand, can easily make itself heard against a full orchestra, and fill a big concert hall with its powerful sounds. In the twentieth century, however, it is also used occasionally as a regular, non-privileged member of the orchestra.

Neo-Bechstein
For music in the home, the smaller baby grand piano is preferred, as better adapted to the comparatively small rooms of twentieth-

century dwellings. Similar conditions are fulfilled by the *Neo-Bechstein*, built in the nineteen-thirties by the physicist Nernst in Berlin. In lieu of the usual three strings for each note, only one is employed, or two at most, while the iron frame and the soundboard have disappeared. In their place the Neo-Bechstein is fitted with 18 microphones and a loudspeaker, which effect the necessary amplification of tone. The instrument possesses two pedals. The right-hand pedal performs the traditional function of lifting the dampers and allowing the strings to vibrate freely, but the left enables the performer to regulate the volume of sound from the most powerful fortissimo to the softest pianissimo. Both a crescendo and a decrescendo can be obtained without moving the fingers, while chords can be sustained for a long time with the greatest facility. Whereas in a normal piano the resistance to be overcome in depressing the keys is from $2\frac{1}{2}$ to 3 ounces, and sometimes even more, in the Neo-Bechstein it is only a fraction of this amount. It is doubtful, however, whether the undeniable qualities of the instrument can make up for the mechanization of the tone.

Square Piano

The *square piano* underwent the same development as the grand piano in its more important phases. The strings were thickened, the compass was extended, and in America it even preceded the grand piano in adopting the iron frame and over-stringing. Large and powerful instruments were built, which were hardly smaller than a grand piano; but they were inferior to the latter in beauty of tone, and this sealed the fate of the square piano. It disappeared first in Europe, and the 1880s saw the last of it in the U.S.A.

Upright Piano

France and England had the greatest share in the development of the *upright piano*. In England T. Loud (1802), W. Southwell (1807) and above all T. Wornum the younger (1811) worked at the improvement of the instrument. Wornum's "Piccolo Piano" of 1829 already contained the essential features of the modern upright. In France H. Pape in particular made important improvements in the structure of the instrument. America, where the need to save space was less urgent than in Europe, did not start making upright pianos until the second half of the nineteenth century, though it had done much to further the development of the instrument by the introduction of over-stringing. In recent decades inexpensive upright pianos of small dimensions have found wide circulation under the name of "spinet."

Experimental Pianos

It is impossible, within the limits of this survey, to note, in addition to the Neo-Bechstein, all the many attempts to modify the structure and the technical possibilities of the piano. We will mention only two of the numerous experiments. The "reformed keyboard," invented by P. v. Jankó in 1882, consisted of six rows of short keys arranged in tiers, which made it possible to strike any note in three different places. The advantage of this keyboard was that all major and all minor scales could be played with the same fingering, while the execution of large intervals and great leaps, as well as interesting *glissandi*, was made easier. Like Jankó, E. Moór was a native of Hungary. His "duplex coupler" was suggested by the structure of the harpsichord. Moór placed two keyboards, of which the upper sounded an octave higher than the lower, so close together that it was possible to play on both simultaneously with one hand; or, if desired, the upper could be coupled to the lower. Among the advantages of this device was again the ease with which octaves and large intervals and leaps could be played. However, the tenacious conservatism of pianists prevented any wide diffusion of either invention.

Mechanical pianos have been in use since the beginning of the nineteenth century. Modern player-pianos, often known as "pianolas," employ punched paper rolls; they have an electric-pneumatic mechanism and are able to reproduce the performance of a pianist with great fidelity. However, following the development of the gramophone, interest in mechanical pianos has greatly declined.

Keyboard instruments in which the strings are not struck with a hammer, but are set in vibration by means of a bow, have been built since the year 1600; indeed, Leonardo da Vinci examined the problem more than a century earlier. Well over fifty types have been constructed—the latest in the twentieth century—but none has been able to take its place among serious musical instruments, for the effect of a mechanically-operated bow is always rigid, lifeless and unsatisfying.

Clavichord, Harpsichord

Clavichords and especially *harpsichords* have often been built by Dolmetsch, Pleyel, Neupert and others. Players have to use modern copies, as the original old instruments are, as a rule, too brittle to be tuned to modern pitch and can no longer stand prolonged use. Modern harpsichords are sometimes equipped with a third manual, and in order to leave the hands free, the change of stops is usually effected by means of pedals; also, the strings may be plucked by tags of plastic. It is to be questioned, however, whether the technical "improvements" to Renaissance and Baroque instruments do not alter the character of the music of the past which they interpret. The possibility of changing register stops quickly and without interrupting the performance can induce players to adopt an unsettled, irridescent style, foreign to the character of early compositions. On the other hand, harpsichords are now also employed for the performance of contemporary music. Following the neo-classical trend, composers such as M. de Falla, W. v. Waltershausen (1882–1954), F. Poulenc (1899–1963), and K. Thomas (b. 1904) have written original compositions for the harpsichord. In 1961 Elliott Carter (b. 1908) wrote a double concerto for harpsichord, piano and orchestra, a combination tried out by C. P. E. Bach in 1788.

Wind Instruments

While only a certain number of the stringed instruments underwent any important modifications during the Romantic period, all the *wind instruments* passed through a decisive development. Their construction was completely revolutionized, for the makers had the courage to shake off the bonds of tradition. Every smallest detail was carefully investigated; nothing was accepted without criticism. The result was a richness and purity of tone quite unknown in the preceding period.

Flute

The life of Theobald Boehm, the reconstructor of the *flute*, who was born in Munich in 1794 and died in that city in 1881, may be cited as confirmation of the proverb *nemo propheta in patria*. He brought to the manufacture of the flute a new impulse of decisive importance, and the results of his efforts were received with enthusiasm in France, England and America, but his native

Germany always regarded his innovations with a certain degree of aversion. Boehm, who was himself a distinguished flutist, had felt even as a youth that his instrument suffered under a very great disadvantage, in that even with the eight-keyed flute, which was then the best, certain passages and keys—as, for instance, the scale of E major—could be played only with difficulty, while their intonation was far from perfect. Inspired by the achievements of the English flutist C. Nicholson in the 1820s, Boehm constructed a flute with holes bored for all the chromatic tones; these holes had the acoustically correct diameters and were placed in the acoustically correct positions. The possibility of covering the holes with the fingers, which had hitherto played an essential part in their arrangement, was at first disregarded. Next,

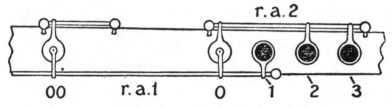

Fig. 6. Action of a Boehm flute

Boehm furnished his instrument with a number of open keys, to be closed by the player's fingers. Here a difficulty was immediately apparent: there were more holes in the flute than fingers on the human hand. In order to overcome this deficiency, Boehm employed an ingenious device invented earlier in England by the Rev. Noland. He surrounded certain holes with ring-keys, which were connected by rotating axles to key-covers that closed those holes for which no finger was available. An example of this procedure is offered in Fig. 6. The performer's right hand is supposed to cover hole 3 (D) with the third finger, hole 2 (E) with the second finger, and hole 1 (F) with the first finger. However, these fingers control not just their own holes; when either of them is shut, the hole 0 (F♮) is also closed, by means of the rotating axles r.a. 1 or r.a. 2. The first finger even has a third task. As soon as notes above G are played it would be idle; however, with the help of r.a. 1, it can be used to close the hole 00, higher up the tube, thus offering the performer another way of playing B♭.

These and similar ingenious devices on the Boehm flute were naturally bound to revolutionize fingering and therefore the performer's whole technique, which explains why, in spite of its enormous advantages, Boehm's method of construction met with violent opposition in many flute-playing circles.

The first model, which Boehm produced in 1832, still had the traditional and predominantly conical form of bore, tapering towards the instrument's open end. However, Boehm continued his improvements. Working on the basis of exhaustive experiments undertaken in conjunction with his friend, the physicist K. F. E. Schafhäutl, Boehm produced a new model in 1846–47 which was now cylindrical in bore, apart from the head-piece containing the embouchure, which was parabolic. The new flute was remarkable for its great purity and evenness of tone throughout its compass. The thin, delicate, ethereal tone of the older flutes was replaced by a much fuller, more robust and powerful tone, which is perhaps the reason why the cylindrical flute has never been completely naturalized in Germany. Nevertheless, recent instrument-makers have been obliged to equip even the traditional conical flute with many of Boehm's devices.

In its present form the flute has a chromatic range of b–e^4 (though in exceptional cases even f$\sharp^4$ might be prescribed). It is made of wood or metal; the wooden flutes are considered to have greater beauty of tone, while the metal instruments are reputed to "speak" more easily. The lowest notes have a full and warm quality, but are very soft; the middle range sounds bright and brilliant, and the highest notes rather hard and shrill. The flute is one of the most nimble instruments in the orchestra, being capable of the greatest variety of nuances.

Giorgi Flute

Since Boehm's time there have been no really important changes in the structure of the flute. But mention might be made of the instrument built by Giorgi in Florence, in 1888. The material of the *Giorgi flute* was ebonite, and it dispensed with keys altogether, having a separate hole for every semitone of the octave. But since only ten fingers were available for the eleven holes of the instrument, the left index finger had to cover one hole with the tip of the finger and one with the second joint. Giorgi's flute is not held transversely before the face, but in the same position as the oboe and clarinet, the embouchure being pierced in a separate bulbous head-piece. The difficult fingering and the wide intervals between the holes, which can be reached only by performers with unusually large hands, have prevented any general adoption of this instrument.

Piccolo

Since the Romantic period the *piccolo* (compass d^2–c^5, best performance g^2–g^4, scored an octave lower) has attained a position of almost greater importance than it held in the classical period. For the expression of wild passion or the description of storm and tempest, its hard, sharp utterance, which is unpleasantly shrill only in the highest register, is extremely valuable; and it can also be used with good effect in delicate *piano* passages. It is an indispensable component of the Romantic and the modern orchestra. Wagner employed two piccolos in the smithy scene of *Siegfried*, and three in the storm scene of *Der fliegende Holländer*.

In this description of the various kinds of flute only the more important types have been included. Flutes, which were among the favorite instruments of the eighteenth and nineteenth centuries, were made in twenty different sizes, in about 1830, as is shown by the price-list of a Belgian instrument-maker; and even since 1900 they have been obtainable in various tunings, some of them only for use in military bands.

Alto Flute

The powerful, mellow, expressive *alto flute*, a fourth lower than the ordinary flute (compass g–e^3, scored a fourth higher), has gained an ever-increasing number of devotees since its structural improvement by Boehm. Among other composers, N. Rimsky-Korsakov (1844–1908) used it in *Mlada*, G. Holst (1874–1934) in *The Planets*, M. Ravel in *Daphnis et Chloé* and I. Stravinsky in *Le Sacre du Printemps*.

Bass Flute

Bass flutes are pitched an octave below the ordinary soprano flute and should therefore really be called tenor flutes. They have made appearances in the nineteenth and twentieth centuries, but in practice they are not employed very often. Special mention should be made of the *Albisiphone*, constructed by Abelardo

Albisi of Milan in 1910, whose metal tube, on account of its great length, is bent twice, near the embouchure; the body of the instrument—as in the oboe and the Giorgi flute—points downwards and away from the performer. Other forms of bass flute with the tube bent back are used increasingly.

Electric Flute

The *electric flute* is an ordinary flute to which a contact microphone has been attached. With the help of a special gadget (a "Multi-Vider"), an amplifier, and a loudspeaker, the player is able to transpose the instrument's pitch one or two octaves down, and to modify volume and tone-quality. Electric flutes are mostly used in film studios and in modern dance music.

Recorder

In the Romantic period the *recorder* was not much used. But since 1912 or thereabouts the late Arnold Dolmetsch and his family have paved the way for the instrument's revival, which has reached considerable dimensions, particularly in England, the U.S.A. and Germany. Recorders in various sizes—mostly without keys—are now made for the interpretation of old music, for use in schools and for the performance of folk-music. During recent decades various exercises and original compositions for the recorder have been published.

Ocarina

The *ocarina* is a globular flute which belongs among the cheap instruments of amateur music. It has a hollow body of terracotta or porcelain, made in the shape of an egg, and is played by means of a mouthpiece similar to that of the recorder. Its sound is hollow, sweet and rather dull. These characteristics might be responsible for the unusual name of the instrument (the Italian word *ocarina* meaning "little goose"; the French sometimes call it *coucou*). The ocarina is supplied with 9–10 finger-holes, and occasionally also with keys and tuning-slides; it has a compass of more than an octave. The instrument was first devised in 1860 by Donati at Budrio in Italy, and achieved such popularity that it was made in various sizes, from soprano to bass.

Oboe

The development of the *oboe* during the nineteenth century was such as to make it all but the equal of the flute. Even before 1800 Grundmann and Grenser of Dresden attempted to improve the intonation of the instrument through the addition of keys. During the first quarter of the nineteenth century the number of keys was gradually increased, until at last there were up to ten. About 1825 the leading maker was the Viennese S. Koch, who was guided by the advice of the celebrated oboe-player J. Sellner. The instrument was constantly improved, and by 1840 the number of keys had increased to fourteen. But now the example of Boehm's flute began to influence the oboe. French makers—above all F. Triébert—took the initiative, and we may trace through several decades a period of reformation in the construction of the oboe. The climax and conclusion of these efforts were represented by an instrument (Pls. LVI, LVII) which was made about 1880, and which to this day has hardly been excelled: the Parisian "Conservatoire model" (compass b♭–a³), an instrument equipped with a key-mechanism as complicated as it is ingenious, which makes playing easier by providing two, three, and sometimes even four ways of obtaining the same note. Oboes are no longer made of boxwood, as of old, but more frequently of ebony or rosewood. Recently, as an exception, metal or ebonite has been used. The double reed is fashioned of cane by the player himself, as its thickness and elasticity decisively influence the instrument's tone. The sound is, generally speaking, nasal and poignant, but since the middle of the nineteenth century a difference between the French oboe, also used in England, America, Belgium and Italy, and the German–Austrian instrument has become increasingly marked. The French oboe has a thinner and more delicate tone; the German is harsher and more powerful. The reasons why the French oboe found an enthusiastic advocate in R. Strauss are not without interest. In his supplement to Berlioz's work on instrumentation he praises it for its finer workmanship, its more equable voice in the various registers, and its greater flexibility and power of expression, while he criticizes the thick, trumpet-like tone of the German oboe, and the incompatibility of its sound with that of the flutes and clarinets. Since this criticism came from their own camp, there has been no lack of German makers to copy the French model. But on the whole central Europe has remained true to its own ideal of the oboe.

Oboe d'Amore

The *oboe d'amore*, which is equipped with a bulbous bell and is pitched a third lower than the ordinary oboe, was unknown in the early Romantic period. In the 1870s, however, V. C. Mahillon, in Brussels, resuscitated the instrument for historical performances, and since then it has again been produced— equipped with the mechanism of the modern oboe—by a number of different makers (Pl. LVII). R. Strauss employed the instrument in his *Sinfonia domestica*, for the melody associated with the innocent child, and M. Ravel in *Bolero*. The compass of the oboe d'amore as scored is b–e³, but it sounds a third lower, so that the actual range is g#–c#³.

English Horn

While the oboe d'amore is a rare member of the orchestra, the *English horn* is very often to be found in larger ensembles. Until the middle of the nineteenth century the body of the instrument had the sickle-shaped curve or the obtuse angle adopted in the eighteenth century. Later, however, the English horn was given the straight body and the key mechanism of the oboe. Apart from its greater length, the bent metal crook carrying the double reed, and the pear-shaped bell (Pl. LVII), the English horn looks like the parent instrument; as a rule it is also blown by oboe players. The English horn is therefore scored as a transposing instrument, a fifth higher than it sounds. Its written compass is b–f³, its actual range e–bb². The instrument's tender and noble utterance has been successfully employed for solo passages of a melancholy and expressive character. It is in special demand for the description of languorous pastoral moods. Berlioz so used it in his *Symphonie fantastique*, Schumann in *Manfred*, and Wagner in *Tannhäuser* and above all *Tristan und Isolde*.

Baritone Oboe, Heckelphone

A fourth lower still than the English horn, and therefore an octave below the oboe, is the *baritone oboe*, which is more than three feet long, built with a bassoon-like butt, an upturned lower end and pear-shaped bell. It is also made in straight form, and blown through a curved metal crook. The instrument's voice is akin to that of the English horn. A German version of the baritone oboe is the *Heckelphone*, constructed in 1904 by Wilhelm Heckel, of

Biebrich-am-Rhein. This instrument, with its wide, conical bore, is made of maple-wood and has a barrel-shaped bell with lateral openings. Despite its considerable length of more than four feet it has the same key-mechanism as the oboe. Its compass is A–g^2, and it is usually scored an octave higher than it sounds. The rich, noble voice of the Heckelphone has been employed by R. Strauss in *Salome*, *Elektra* and *Alpensinfonie*. A small variant of this instrument is the *Piccolo-Heckelphone* in F, with the compass e^1–a^3 (scored a fourth lower).

In our survey of the oboes of the Romantic period and the present day we have been able—as with the flutes—to mention only some of the more important forms. Various other sizes, most of which have been made for use in military bands, have been omitted because of their comparative rarity.

Clarinet

The *clarinet* was one of the favorite instruments of the Romantic era. The warm, lyric quality of its middle range and the sonorous sounds of its low notes won it universal admiration among composers of the nineteenth and twentieth centuries. Solos were entrusted to it in practically every orchestral composition. It was used in significant chamber-music works by Schumann, Brahms and Bartók; clarinet concertos were written by Rimsky-Korsakov, Milhaud, Hindemith and Copland (b. 1900). In the swing music of the 1930s clarinet virtuosi like Benny Goodman and Artie Shaw excelled.

The constructional development of the clarinet resembled that of other contemporary wind instruments. The beginning of the nineteenth century saw it provided with a number of extra keys, which were added in an attempt to remedy the unreliability of the chromatic semitones produced by cross-fingering. In 1812 the clarinettist Ivan Müller appeared in Paris with a thirteen-keyed instrument, which showed a great acoustic improvement and had a separate key for every semitone. But Müller was evidently in advance of his time. A commission which was appointed to examine it gave an unfavorable opinion of Müller's instrument, and it was not until the years 1825–35 that the thirteen-keyed clarinet really established itself. In 1840 a new type appeared in the form of the so-called *Boehm clarinet*, which was produced by H. Klosé, professor at the Paris Conservatoire, and the instrument-maker A. Buffet. In this Boehm's improvements were fully adapted to the clarinet, and the result was an instrument distinguished by great uniformity of tone, on which trills and legato passages could be played more satisfactorily than on any clarinet hitherto constructed. Of course, the inventors came up against the same opposition as Boehm himself. Since the new instrument often entailed changes in the traditional fingering, it was a long while before French clarinettists would accept it. In Germany, also, where R. Mollenhauer had constructed a Boehm clarinet in 1867, and where the German *Normalklarinette* (based largely on Buffet's and Mollenhauer's devices) made its appearance in 1890, opposition to the Boehm clarinet has never been completely overcome. The cheapness and simplicity of the old Müller clarinets, with their thirteen or fourteen keys, have always been appreciated, especially by military bands.

Today clarinets are usually made of a hard, dark wood like grenadilla (Pl. LX) or of ebonite, or metal. The written compass of the instrument is e–c⁴, but its upper quarter is extremely sharp and strident, whereas the lowest notes are distinguished by a particularly noble tone. The instrument is made in about twenty different sizes, of which a few are described below.

Of the *soprano clarinets*, in C, B♭, and A, the highest is in C. It is particularly suitable for strong and brilliant or convivial effects. Beethoven used it in the finale of the Fifth Symphony, and Mendelssohn at the end of the Reformation Symphony. On the other hand, R. Strauss employed it in the tavern music in *Rosenkavalier*. Apart from such special effects, the C clarinet has its place today in military and dance bands. The standard instruments are the B♭ and A clarinets. Until late in the nineteenth century, the choice between them was still made according to the easier way of fingering, A clarinets being prescribed for sharp keys and B♭ clarinets for flat keys. Even in our day some players use both clarinets, according to the score. The improvements in the key-mechanisms have made it possible, however, to play in all keys on the same instrument, so that the performer no longer has to carry two instruments about with him. This being so, for use in the orchestra the clarinettist will prefer the more powerful and robust B♭ clarinet (Pl. LX), which is equally capable of heroic strains and of tender or dreamy passages. The gentle, intimate A clarinet is perhaps better suited for chamber music.

It was for this instrument that Brahms wrote his Clarinet Quintet and his Clarinet Trio.

Among the high *sopranino clarinets*, in F, E♭ and D, a fourth above the principal clarinets in C, B♭, and A, the extremely shrill F clarinet has always been virtually restricted to military music and German dance music. The E♭ clarinet (Pl. LX), on the other hand, since its classic employment in the caricature of the *idée fixe* in Berlioz's *Symphonie fantastique*, has found its place in operatic and symphonic orchestras. Modern composers are fond of employing its clear, penetrating tones to give sharpness to the woodwind section. The effect of the brilliant D clarinet was cunningly employed by Liszt in *Mazeppa*, and by Wagner in the fire music of *Die Walküre*. R. Strauss used its biting quality in *Till Eulenspiegel* to portray the execution of the hero. The F clarinet is notated a perfect fourth below its actual sound, the E♭ clarinet a minor third below, and the D clarinet a whole tone below.

Alto clarinets, in F or E♭, are rarely used. They are constructed like soprano clarinets, although they exceed them considerably in length and are provided with a metallic bell. The instruments are notated a perfect fifth or a major sixth above the actual sound.

Basset Horn

The *basset horn* is an alto clarinet in the key of F. It is, however, narrower in bore and has a thinner wall. Its tone is duller and cooler, and its range extends a major third lower. After various experiments had been made during the nineteenth century, the instrument adopted the straight form and the mechanism of the modern clarinet, but it is equipped with a crook and a metal bell. The range of the basset horn is F–f³. It is usually notated in the treble clef a fifth higher than it sounds, but also occasionally in the bass clef a fourth lower than it sounds. The instrument is employed mainly in performances of Mozart's music, though R. Strauss used it in *Elektra* and *Die Frau ohne Schatten*.

Bass Clarinet

Bass clarinets, an octave below the soprano clarinets, have been made since 1772, and have varied in shape. However, the instrument first achieved importance in the 1830s. In 1836 G. Meyerbeer introduced the bass clarinet into *Les Huguenots*, but it was not until 1839 that Adolphe Sax made a model which attracted attention by its efficiency and its beauty of tone. Since then the bass clarinet has been made with the metallic bell turned upwards (Pl. LX), and with the same key-mechanism as the soprano clarinet. In the nineteenth century instruments in C, B♭ and A were in use. Today we are content with the bass clarinet in B♭. It is scored either in the treble clef (compass e–g³), the actual sound being a major ninth lower; or in the bass clef, the actual sound being a major second lower. Owing to its soft, expressive tone, the instrument seems even better fitted to form the bass of the woodwind section than the bassoon. It is also greatly esteemed as a solo instrument. Schumann, Wagner, R. Strauss and Milhaud have made use of its noble voice in passages of a particularly expressive character.

Contrabass Clarinet

Contrabass clarinets, an octave lower than the bass clarinets, were made for use in military bands as far back as the first half of the nineteenth century, but it was only in 1890 that Besson, in Paris, succeeded in constructing an efficient contrabass clarinet in B♭, which consisted of three wooden tubes of different lengths connected by metal U-bends. This powerful instrument, whose sonorous tone is like that of an organ, has a range of A_1–f^1. For the convenience of clarinet players it is usually notated in the treble clef, sounding two octaves and a major second lower. The costliness, weight and sensitivity of the instrument have hitherto prevented its extensive use. According to Adam Carse, "It seems to be the destiny of contrabass clarinets to end their days as museum exhibits."

Saxophone

Around 1840 Adolphe Sax fils, in Brussels, constructed metal clarinets with a broad reed and a conical bore, the *saxophones*, which, when overblown, sound not the twelfth, but the octave. All the holes are closed with keys, and the mechanism is akin to that of the oboe. The instrument is easier to play than the clarinet, since fewer keys are required, and its voice is more brilliant and powerful, with a characteristic vibrato. Sax gradually built up a family of fourteen members; seven of them, intended for use in military bands, were tuned in E♭ or B♭, and seven, meant for operatic and symphonic orchestras, in F or C. They were all scored in the treble clef, their compass being from b♭–f³. The highest instrument, the sopranino in E♭ or F, sounds a minor third or a perfect fourth higher, the lowest, the contrabass in E♭ or F (Pl. LXI/1), a twentieth or a nineteenth lower. Later, yet another was added, a subcontrabass in B♭, a fourth below the contrabass in E♭. The two highest members of the family (sopranino and soprano) are straight, the others are curved at their upper end and have an upturned bell. The military bands of the Latin countries adopted the new instrument with enthusiasm. Before long it found use also in operatic and symphonic works, by composers such as Bizet (1838–75), Debussy, Ravel, Honegger, Stravinsky and Bartók. Germany alone was at first extremely averse to the instrument, and for a long while the saxophone quartet which R. Strauss introduced *ad lib.* into his *Sinfonia domestica* could not be performed. The situation changed around 1920, when jazz music cast the saxophone for a leading part. Berg and Hindemith made use of the versatile instrument and today, in all parts of Europe as in America, the saxophone is one of the most familiar and most extensively employed wind instruments. The soprano in C, the alto in E♭ and the tenor in C (known as "melody saxophone") enjoy particular favor.

Tárogató, Heckelklarina

A relative of the B♭ soprano saxophone is the *tárogató*, an instrument frequently used in Hungary; it is a straight, wooden saxophone with a somewhat sombre tone-color. The tárogató was first made in Budapest in 1900, by W. Schunda, by modifying a popular Hungarian wooden shawm. The instrument has also been constructed in various other sizes.

The firm of Heckel in Biebrich made a variety of the saxophone, the *Heckelklarina*, in B♭ with an oboe mechanism (compass a–c♯³). It has a clear and robust tone and was specifically intended by the inventors for the playing of the joyous shepherd's tune in *Tristan und Isolde*.

Bassoon

The *bassoon* is one of the most versatile instruments of the orchestra. It serves to reinforce the bass section of the strings and provides the natural foundation for the wind instruments. Used as a solo instrument its tone is penetrating, almost menacing in *forte* passages, gently expressive and intimately tender in *piano* ones. The bassoon has a conical bore and is usually made of maple in four sections: the wing joint, which carries the metal crook with the double reed; the butt, in which the tube makes a U-turn; the long bass joint; and finally the bell joint (Pl. LVIII). The instrument has a range of $3\frac{1}{2}$ octaves, A_1–e^2, and is scored as it sounds, in the bass or tenor clef.

As regards the constructional development of the instrument, a divergence between French and German methods may be noted somewhat similar to that in the case of the oboe. The efforts of the French makers were directed mainly toward improving the mechanism and the technical possibilities of the instrument; at the same time they were anxious to preserve its individual tone-quality, which is characterized by distinct contrasts of color between the different registers. The Germans, however, were not content with producing purer intonation; they also endeavoured to give the instrument a softer and more equable voice, which is less characteristic than that of the old bassoon, though it blends better with the tone of other wind instruments. Up to the present time each country has remained faithful to its own ideal of the bassoon. Belgium and Italy chose the French type, while in England and America both types are found, though preference is usually given to the German model.

In France, the Parisian manufacturers F. G. Adler, G. Triébert and above all J. N. Savary fils, were the first to work at the improvement of the bassoon. In their hands the eight-keyed bassoon developed, by the middle of the nineteenth century, into a seventeen-keyed instrument, which in technical respects was greatly superior to the old type. Small improvements were repeatedly made during the third quarter of the century, and up to five additional keys were fitted. The bassoon constructed at this time, in accordance with the system perfected by the performer Jancourt and the maker Buffet, was equipped with twenty-two keys and six open finger-holes. It represents the highest achievement of the French manufacturers.

German instrument-makers were working along other lines. The bassoon-player, conductor and composer, K. Almenräder of Nassau, guided by the researches of the musical theorist, G. Weber, rearranged the finger-holes of the bassoon in accordance with acoustical requirements, thereby doing for the bassoon what Boehm was soon to do for the flute. The fifteen-keyed bassoon made by Schott in Mainz in 1820, in accordance with Almenräder's data, was distinguished by greater purity of intonation and a more uniform utterance throughout its compass. After Almenräder, the two Heckels, father and son, continued to work on the improvement of the bassoon. Around 1880—that is, at about the same time as the French makers—they called a halt to their efforts. Apart from minor improvements, the German bassoon of to-day, which is equipped with five open finger-holes and up to twenty-two keys, is still in essentials the practically-planned, even-sounding, tonally-true instrument of the Almenräder-Heckel type.

Double Bassoon (Contrabassoon)

In the days of Haydn and Beethoven the *double bassoon* (*contrabassoon*), an octave lower than the bassoon, was greatly valued in Germany and Austria for the production of special effects. But the need to have the holes small and close together, so that they could be covered by the finger-tips, made true intonation quite impossible. As a result, in the German-speaking countries the contrabassoon steadily lost ground during the second quarter of the nineteenth century; in other parts of Europe, even during the classical period, its employment had been restricted to military music. It is characteristic of the opinion held of the instrument that in 1830 Parke derisively compared its long tube to the funnel of a steamer. During the following decades various attempts were made, in the interests of the military band, to solve the problem of the contrabassoon (Pl. LIX/2), but not until 1877 was a serviceable instrument constructed, by the firm of Heckel. Its wooden tube was bent back on itself three times, the sections being connected by the butt and metal U-pieces. The instrument was equipped with a modern key-mechanism and had a compass of Bb_2–f, notated an octave higher. The English and French models are rather shorter and larger in bore than the Heckel type so widely employed in Germany. They have a more powerful tone than Heckel's, and a wider compass (C_1–c^1). They owe their various features to two Englishmen, Stone and Morton, a Frenchman, Thibouville, and a Belgian, Mahillon. Schoenberg (*Gurrelieder*), Mahler (Symphony No. 9) and Stravinsky (*Sacre du Printemps*) are among the more recent composers who have made use of the contrabassoon.

Tenoroon, Alto Bassoon, Soprano Bassoon, Subcontra Bassoon

The bassoon has occasionally been made in other sizes than the two described. The *tenor bassoon*, or *tenoroon*, is pitched a fourth or fifth higher than the usual bass instrument, while the *alto bassoon* is pitched a sixth and the *octave* or *soprano bassoon* an octave higher. Perhaps the most significant of the rarely-employed types is the *subcontrabassoon* (Ger. *Subkontrafagott*), produced in 1873 by the Czech instrument-maker Cerveny, which was an octave below Heckel's contrabassoon, so that it went down to $B\flat_3$.

Sarrusophone

An interesting attempt to replace the various kinds of oboes and bassoons by a single new type—mainly for use in military bands—was made in France. In 1856 a patent was taken out for the *sarrusophone*, which was invented by the military bandmaster Sarrus and constructed by the Parisian instrument-maker Gautrot. The sarrusophone is a brass instrument with a pronounced conical form, which is equipped with eighteen keys and blown with a double reed. No less than nine different sizes were made, from the small sopranino in high $E\flat$ to the contrabass in low $B\flat$, all of which can be played with the same fingering. The lowest written note for all types is $b\flat$, the highest varies from c^3 to g^3; but the sopranino sounds a third higher, and the contrabass three octaves and a whole tone lower. The other sizes transpose correspondingly. The two highest types are straight, the others doubled back. The sarrusophone, which has a powerful but rather coarse and common tone, has not gained any real footing outside the military band. Only the contrabass is sometimes employed in place of the contrabassoon. Thus C. Saint-Saëns (1835–1921) and J. Massenet (1842–1912) have occasionally used it.

(French) Horn

In the nineteenth century the construction of the circular (*French*) *horn*—like that of the trumpet—underwent an almost more decisive change than that of the flutes, oboes, clarinets and bassoons. Neither the crooks nor the "inventions" of the classical period proved equal to the increased demands made upon them by music of the Romantic period. Skilful performers could, of course, change the key of their instruments in the middle of a composition. But it would obviously have been impossible to make such a change in the course of a passage, and the expedient which was often employed, of using conjointly horns in different keys, so that, for example, the notes which were difficult to obtain on the first horn, were played on the second, was not really satisfactory.

In 1818 J. B. Dupont in Paris, and in 1824 Sax (the elder) in Brussels, attempted to fix all the crooks for the various tunings to the instrument, and to make them available at will in the windway by means of a slide. The *cor omnitonique*, which was so constructed, and on the improvement of which both French and German instrument-makers labored for decades, did not find acceptance, as the addition of several crooks made the instrument unduly heavy and unwieldy. Moreover, at the same time as the cor omnitonique was being produced, another ingenious invention was made, which solved the problem of the chromatic horn in a simpler and more practical manner.

In the second decade of the nineteenth century F. Blühmel, of Silesia, and H. Stölzel, in Berlin, constructed the valve mechanism, which they patented jointly in 1818—the same year that saw the appearance of the cor omnitonique. The principle on which it is based is essentially a development of the old "inventions." The valves are devices which make it possible by a single touch to insert in the main tube of the horn short pieces of extra tubing which increase the total length of the instrument and so lower its pitch. At first only two valves controlling different lengths were employed, but a third was soon added. Without the valves the horn player can produce most partials from the second to the sixteenth harmonic (cf. p. 278). The valves, which may be used individually or in combination, enable him to bridge the gaps between the harmonics and to play a chromatic scale throughout the instrument's range. A horn equipped with valves requires a much shorter length of extra tubing than the cor omnitonique and is therefore lighter and easier to manipulate.

The mechanism by which the extra tubing is included or cut

out in the valve horn takes many forms, but they can all be referred to two basic types, rotary valves and pistons. *Rotary valves,* which were invented about 1830 in Vienna, are particularly favored in Germany, but also in the U.S.A. (Pl. LXII). The effect of this device is shown schematically in Fig. 7. Here the wind is diverted when a cylinder is rotated. In the primary position (Fig. 7c) the wind passes only through the main tube; but if the cylinder is rotated (Fig. 7d) by pressing the lever, the wind has to pass through the additional length of tubing. *Pistons,* which were originally employed by Blühmel and Stölzel, and are still—in an improved form—preferred in France (cf. also.

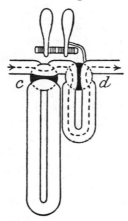

FIG. 7. Rotary valve of a wind instrument. In c the valve is in the resting position, in d it is activated

Pl. LXIII/3) and England, use a kind of plunger system to control the air supply.

It is impossible to mention in these pages even a fraction of the many great instrument-makers who have done good work on the improvement of the valves, and especially of the pistons. We might only single out L. Uhlmann, of Vienna; W. Wieprecht and J. G. Moritz, of Berlin; E. F. Périnet, G. A. Besson and Adolphe Sax, of Paris; K. Embach, of Amsterdam; and the Englishmen J. P. Oates and H. Distin. Thanks to the efforts of these and many others, it has been possible gradually to overcome the serious faults of the oldest models, which affected both beauty of tone and accuracy of pitch.

Owing to the imperfections which were at first inherent in the valve horn, its general acceptance was very slow. Until after the 1830s the old valveless natural horn held the undisputed lead, and the new invention was accepted without prejudice only in military bands, where tonal beauty and accuracy of pitch were not of the first importance. The situation changed in the following decades. About 1850 the natural horn and the valve horn were considered equally legitimate. Wagner, in particular, used both types together in his earlier compositions. It was after the middle of the century that the modern instruments began to throw the original horn into the shade. Nevertheless, in 1865, Brahms still employed the natural horn for his Horn Trio, as he thought the valve horn too coarse for chamber music.

The unqualified victory of the valve horn towards the close of the century also put an end to the old multiplicity of horn tunings. Since that time the favorite instrument has been the F horn (compass G_1–f^2), on which performers can play almost any part, even if it was originally written for an instrument in quite another key. The F horn is usually notated in the treble clef, a fifth higher than it sounds; the lowest notes appear in the bass clef, a fourth lower than they sound. The instrument is blown by means of the traditional long, funnel-shaped mouthpiece.

The national difference to be noted in respect of the woodwind instruments may also be observed in connection with the horn after the latter half of the nineteenth century. French instruments have retained the slender shape of the older horns. They are distinguished by a peculiar nobility of timbre, for the sake of which the performer is willing to put up with the greater difficulty of playing them. The horn preferred in Germany and Italy is somewhat larger in bore, which makes it rather easier to play; however, the tone is a little less refined. The English-speaking countries originally favored the French type of horn, but now they prefer the German-Italian model with rotary valves.

Since the beginning of the twentieth century the first and third horn players have sometimes been equipped with a valve horn in B♭ alto, a fourth above the main tuning in F, in order to produce the higher notes better. For the same reason increasing use is being made of the *double horn*, in which a fourth valve is employed to change an F horn into an instrument in B♭ alto. The length of the valve tubing is altered automatically, as that used on the B♭ horn would be too short for the F horn; but the player operates the same basic three keys in both tunings of the instrument.

The practice of stopping the horn, which is inevitable in the case of the natural horn, is also applied to the valve horn. This instrument, however, is no longer stopped in order to alter its pitch, but because the stopped tones, with their dull, depressed timbre, have a completely different color from the natural tones. The stopping is effected either with the right hand, or with the help of a damper or mute, a wooden or metal cone inserted in the bell. In any case the valves are so placed that they can be operated with the left hand, so that the right is free for stopping.

Keyed Bugle

Horns with finger-holes occasionally made their appearance as early as the latter half of the eighteenth century, but they played no important part until, after 1810, when the Irish bandmaster Joseph Halliday supplied the English bugle with keys. The *keyed bugle* looked externally like a keyed trumpet; however, the bore was not cylindrical, but conical. The keyed bugle was at first fitted with five keys; later, more commonly with six, or even seven, and in exceptional cases with up to twelve. Its compass was b–c³; it was made in C, B♭ and A, and sometimes, as a sopranino, in E♭ and F. It used to be employed principally for the soprano parts in military music, and in the second and third decades of the nineteenth century it was often entrusted with solo parts. In 1831 Meyerbeer included it in the orchestra of his opera *Robert le Diable*. But because of its harsh and rather common tone, and its unreliable pitch, the instrument suffered increasing neglect after the middle of the nineteenth century. Its successors were the *Flügelhorn* and the *cornet-à-pistons* (cf. p. 247f), both of which were made with valves.

Serpent, Ophicleide

The *serpent*, which even in the classical period seemed a little out of date, survived surprisingly enough through half the nineteenth century. It was employed principally in churches, but also in military bands; and it was even prescribed in works by Rossini (*Le Siège de Corinthe*), Mendelssohn (*St. Paul*) and Wagner (*Rienzi*). In order to overcome to some degree at least the defects of unreliable pitch and poor quality of tone, due to the too-small finger-holes, the serpent was given an ever-increasing number of keys. On the Continent, particularly in France, it expanded into a remarkable variety of forms.

By about the middle of the nineteenth century the serpent had disappeared from general use, and the annihilating attack which Berlioz made on the instrument shows how little the progressive composers of his day thought of it. Berlioz, who had himself employed the instrument in a youthful mass, wrote in his *Traité d'instrumentation* (1848): "The essentially barbaric timbre of this instrument would have been far more appropriate to the ceremonies of the bloody cult of the Druids than to those of the Catholic religion. There is only one exception to be made—the case in which the serpent is employed in masses for the dead, to reinforce the terrible plainsong of the Dies Irae. Then, no doubt, its cold and abominable howling is in place."

A rival of the serpent was the more successful *ophicleide*, a sort of bass keyed bugle (Pl. LXIII/2). The unusual name is derived from the Greek words *ophis*, serpent, and *kleides*, keys; *ophicleide* meaning "keyed serpent." This instrument, which was first constructed in 1817 by Jean Hilaire Asté, better known under the name of Halary, was made entirely of metal with a conical tube folded back upon itself. The instrument was at first fitted with eight to nine, and later with eleven keys, which replaced the open holes of the English bass horn. The ophicleide was usually built in C or B♭, with the compass B_1–c^2 or A_1–b♭^{1} respectively. Halary also constructed double-bass ophicleides, an octave below the standard instrument, and alto ophicleides, in F or E♭, a fourth higher. The latter Halary called "quinticlaves," because they were a fifth lower than the keyed bugle. The (bass) ophicleide was distinguished by its easy utterance and its suitability for legato playing. In view of its slightly raw, rough tone, and the fact that its accuracy of pitch was not entirely satisfactory, it seemed more suitable for use in military bands than elsewhere. However, it played a not insignificant part in the Romantic orchestra. Meyerbeer employed it in *Les Huguenots*, Wagner in *Rienzi* and Berlioz in *La Damnation de Faust*. Most delightful is the burlesque way in which Mendelssohn used the ophicleide in his *Midsummer Night's Dream* Overture.

Despite these limited successes, the career of the ophicleide did not greatly outlast that of the superseded serpent. By 1850 it had been largely displaced by the far more efficient bass tuba (cf. p. 248f), which was equipped with valves, but it lingered in the hands of a few performers down to the last quarter of the century.

The horns equipped with finger-holes or keys were doomed by nineteenth-century technical innovations; the future belonged to the numerous horns of various shapes and sizes which, like the circular (French) horn, adopted the valve mechanism.

Cornet-à-Pistons

In France in the late 1820s, the cornet (also known as the *cornet de poste*), a small instrument with a narrow, conical bore, was fitted with two and then three valves. The new *cornet-à-pistons* had the form of a short, rather broad trumpet, and was blown by means of a cup-shaped mouthpiece (Pl. LXIII/3). It was made in various sizes, of which the cornets in B♭ (compass e–b♭²) and A (compass e♭–a²) are the most frequent. The soprano in E♭, a fourth higher than the B♭ cornet, is employed as the highest voice of the English brass band.

France, England and Belgium gave the new instrument a very ready welcome, for it is extremely mobile, and has a far better tone than the keyed bugle. The cornet was employed mainly in military and brass bands, and as a solo instrument in light compositions and dance music. However, it not infrequently made an appearance also in the Romantic orchestra. It was a favorite instrument of the composers of French opera, such as Meyerbeer and Bizet. Elgar (1857–1934) introduced it into his *Cockaigne* overture, and Hindemith employed it in his Violin Concerto.

Formerly, in point of tone the cornet was midway between the trumpet and the horn. It was less brilliant than the trumpet, but its sound was fuller, and it blended excellently with the tones of other instruments. Berlioz, and many more recent composers after him, complained that the cornet was a trivial instrument, and that its tone was shrill and vulgar, yet it may well be that they were unconsciously attributing to the instrument itself the qualities of the light music for which it was most often employed. Because it is easy to play the cornet has been eagerly accepted as a substitute for the trumpet, and as a result it has more and more frequently been given the cylindrical bore of the trumpet; today indeed, the two instruments are sometimes indistinguishable.

Flügelhorn

The *Flügelhorn*, which came into existence in Austria at about the same time as the cornet-à-pistons in France, represents the direct offspring of the keyed bugle, being made with valves instead of keys. This valved bugle appeared in the same sizes and with the same compasses as the cornet. At first, however, it was larger in bore, had a deeper mouthpiece, and a somewhat wider bell, so that its tone was fuller, softer, and less brilliant than that of the cornet. Gradually these differences disappeared, and the Flügelhorn adopted a narrower bore, the only distinguishing feature then being the wider bell. The instrument is employed mainly in military bands. It has been in especial favor in Germany and Austria; but in many other countries, too, it is a much-appreciated constituent of the brass band.

Alto Horn, Tenor Horn (Baritone)

Lower-pitched valved bugles were also made before long under various names. The *alto horn*, in F or E♭, has a compass of B–f², or one tone lower; the *tenor* horn (in England known as the *baritone*), in C or B♭, has a compass of F♯–c², or one tone lower. These instruments have the conical bore and the deep mouthpiece of the original Flügelhorn, and also its full, soft tone. Their form is not subject to any rule; they are made in trumpet-like shape, or in the form of the ophicleide, or in the circular form of the French horn. Instruments of this type, which since 1830 have been made in most countries, are intended principally for military bands.

Euphonium, Bass Tuba, Sousaphone

The *euphonium* (Fr. *basse à pistons*, Ger. *Barytonhorn*, It. *eufonio*) was first constructed in the 1840s by Sommer of Weimar. It appeared as a successor to the ophicleide, and was made in C and B♭ with a range of three octaves (C–c², or one tone lower). On this bass instrument, constructed with a wide bore, the fundamental note could be sounded, so it was equipped with four, eventually even with five valves (cf. p. 297).

The principal instrument of the group is the *bass tuba* (Fr.

contrebasse à pistons, Ger. *Basstuba,* It. *tuba bassa*), which was constructed as early as 1835 by Wieprecht and Moritz in Berlin. In military bands it is also known as the *bombardon.* The instrument is made in F or E♭, with a range of C–f¹ or one tone lower, and it is generally provided with five valves. Sometimes, for the use of troops on the march, the bass tuba is given a circular form, so that it can be carried round the shoulder (the usual name for this form is *helicon,* from the Greek *helikos,* winding). But the most frequent shape is the bassoon-like "tuba-form," shown in Pl. LVI. Since the middle of the nineteenth century *contrabass tubas,* in B♭ or C, have been made, with a range of F_1–c¹ or one tone lower. They too are mostly constructed in tuba or helicon form. The sonorous, warm sound of the bass tuba found frequent use, not only in military bands but also in the opera and symphony orchestra. Even the contrabass tuba is no stranger in the concert hall or theater.

Apparently more for its optical effect than for acoustical reasons, the American bandmaster J. P. Sousa had the *sousaphone* built, an instrument in helicon form, equipped with a movable bell of around 30 inches in diameter. It was made as a bass in E♭ and a contrabass in B♭, and is still to be found in military bands as well as occasionally in jazz orchestras.

Wagner Tuba

In the score of *Der Ring des Nibelungen* Wagner included, in addition to the contrabass tuba proper in C, two tubas made to his own design, a tenor in B♭ and a bass in F. These instruments of Wagner's, which were first constructed in about 1870, are much narrower in bore than the ordinary tubas. They are blown with a funnel-shaped French-horn mouthpiece, and since they are usually entrusted to French-horn players, the bass tuba having the range of the F horn and the tenor tuba that of the B♭ horn, their valves are usually operated with the left hand. The voice of the *Wagner tubas* or *Waldhorntuben,* as they are called in Germany, is full of unction and majesty. Since Wagner's day they have been employed in particular by A. Bruckner (1824–96) and R. Strauss for the expression of lofty nobility.

In France the Wagner tubas were replaced by the related *cornophones,* instruments with a conical bore and a conical mouthpiece, made by the firm of Fontaine-Besson and patented in 1890.

Saxhorn
In 1845 the celebrated Parisian instrument-maker, Adolphe
Sax, the inventor of the saxophone, took out a patent for the
family of *saxhorns* which he had created. This comprised some ten
members of different sizes, from the tiny "saxhorn sopranino"
to the mighty "saxhorn bourdon," with a tube length of 36 feet.
They are all made in upright form and scored in the treble clef
between f♯–c³, while the actual sound varies according to the
size and tuning of the instrument. The saxhorns were by no means
an original invention, for they had borrowed their principal
features from the various valved bugles, so Sax's right to name his
instrument after himself was hotly disputed. Adam Carse reports
that when the Italian maker Pelitti was asked "if he made Sax's
instruments in Milan," he replied: "It is Sax who is making my
instruments in Paris." Sax's real merit was that, in place of all the
innumerable varieties of horn and tuba instruments, he created
one uniform family, the members of which were all carefully
constructed and of excellent tone.

The development of the trumpet resembles in some respects
that of the members of the horn family, but there is by no means
such a variety of forms to be observed.

English Slide Trumpet
In the *English slide trumpet* we see an assimilation of the trumpet
to the structure of the trombone. While in the case of the slide
trumpet of the Baroque period the whole instrument moved to
and from the player, in the nineteenth-century instrument the
U-shaped section lying next to the mouthpiece was made to draw
out. A spring returned the draw-tube to the resting-point after
use. The slide made it possible to correct faults of intonation and
to lower the pitch of the whole instrument by a semitone, and
sometimes even by a whole tone. The instrument was usually
made in the key of F, and provided with crooks for lower keys.
According to tradition the English slide trumpet was invented
by John Hyde in 1804. In its native country it held its own during
much of the nineteenth century, and was until recently employed
for Handel performances. However, it never gained general
acceptance outside of England.

Valve Trumpet

Of incomparably greater importance than the slide trumpet is the *valve trumpet* (Pls. LVI and LXIV), which makes use of the Blühmel and Stölzel system. It was introduced into German military bands during the second quarter of the nineteenth century, and adopted by orchestras in the third quarter. From Germany the valve trumpet spread with the greatest rapidity to all parts of Europe and America. At first the classical alto trumpet in F was equipped with the customary three valves. However, the exacting technical demands which were soon to be made on the trumpet led to a gradual replacement of the F trumpet by the shorter, higher-pitched and more flexible soprano trumpets in C or B♭, which were equipped as a rule with pistons. A special slide on the B♭ trumpet enabled the player to transform it into an instrument in A. This B♭ trumpet is the one most frequently employed to-day. Its range is approximately f–d³, but jazz trumpeters like Louis Armstrong have been able to produce notes up to g³ and higher. On this comparatively short instrument, which is not nearly as long as the Baroque trumpet, the harmonics from the second to the sixth can be sounded comfortably, the seventh to the twelfth with increasing difficulty. The tone-quality is full and pealing in the lower register, taking on an increasingly sharp and penetrating quality as the pitch rises.

Muted Trumpet

As long ago as 1707 Alessandro Scarlatti employed *muted trumpets* in his opera *Mitridate*. But the first composer to make really significant use of the damper-effect was R. Wagner, who in his scores repeatedly directed the muting of the trumpets; this was done by means of a hollow, pear-shaped piece of wood placed in the bell of the instrument. The trumpet so treated has a strongly nasal, discontented sound, which is eminently suitable for the characterization of Mime and Beckmesser. Of recent years the muted trumpet has been employed a great deal, and dance bands in particular are fond of using it for humorous effects. If the mute is employed in *piano* passages the tone of the trumpet can assume a dream-like, unreal quality, as A. Berg has shown in his Violin Concerto.

Bach-Trumpet, Sopranino Trumpet

A so-called *Bach-trumpet* in A, made in straight form and often equipped with only two valves, was produced late in the nineteenth century, specifically for the execution of Baroque clarino parts. Occasionally also high Bach trumpets in sopranino D were constructed. They greatly facilitate the execution of high-pitched parts, but their tone-quality is unsatisfactory. *Sopranino trumpets* in D and E♭ in conventional form have also been used in compositions of the late nineteenth and twentieth centuries. Particularly successful were the D trumpets equipped with a mechanical contrivance to change the tuning rapidly to E♭.

Bass Trumpet

Richard Wagner introduced the *bass trumpet*, which was employed in the military bands of the Austrian cavalry, into the operatic orchestra. This instrument was usually made in C or B♭, an octave below the ordinary soprano trumpet, and reached even further down than the Baroque trumpet; in point of timbre it resembled the trombone. The original tone-quality is better preserved in the somewhat smaller bass trumpet in E♭, which is equipped with a fourth valve lowering it to D. Since Wagner, R. Strauss, Schoenberg, and Stravinsky have made use of this instrument, with its noble and solemn utterance.

Trombone

In the Romantic period the *trombone* (Pl. LVI) was an important and highly esteemed member of the symphony orchestra. The chief instrument of the family, the tenor trombone in B♭, achieved through the seven positions of its slide (cf. p. 295f) a range of E–d² (written in the tenor or bass clef, and sounding as written), to which must be added three slightly rough, muffled notes, B♭₁, A₁ and A♭₁, being in fact the fundamental notes of the first three slide positions. H. Berlioz employed these pedal notes for special effects in his *Requiem*, and E. Elgar in his *Cockaigne* overture. As a rule, however, they are avoided.

The tenor, in the course of the nineteenth century, supplanted the alto, which stands a fourth higher and is apt to be unsatisfactory in its upper notes. The earlier trio of alto, tenor, and bass trombones was replaced by two tenor and one bass trombone, with the higher notes entrusted to a trumpet rather than a trombone. Even the bass, which was up to a perfect fifth lower than the tenor, was cast into the shade by the tenor. After 1900 it was gradually replaced by the tenor-bass trombone, which by means of an extra valve changed from a Bb tenor into a F bass trombone.

In 1816 Gottfried Weber suggested the construction of trombones with a double slide, in which the effect of the draw would be increased, since four instead of two tubes would be involved. In 1830 Halary in Paris made a *contrabass trombone* on this principle, and similar instruments have also been constructed in other countries (Pl. LXI/2). This instrument achieved a special importance, for in the 1870s Wagner introduced it into the score of *Der Ring des Nibelungen* and had it made for the purpose by C. Moritz in Berlin. His contrabass trombone in Bb was an octave below the tenor trombone, and had a compass of E_1–d^1 (scored as sounding). R. Strauss used it in *Elektra* and Schoenberg in *Gurrelieder*, but the tremendous demands which this instrument makes upon the lung-power of the performer are, of course, an obstacle to its wide distribution.

The trombone is a very versatile instrument, whose full and solemn tone blends as well with the sounds of wind and stringed instruments as with those of human voices. From a delicate *pianissimo* to a menacing *fortissimo* it offers a rich variety of tonal nuances. Beethoven was so impressed by the potentialities of the instrument that he wrote his *Equale* of 1812 for an unaccompanied quartet of trombones. Recently the trombone has been employed in jazz bands with *vibrato* and *portamento* effects; it is even played with a mute, which is apt to give its tone an ominous quality.

Valve Trombone

Although the trombone is inherently chromatic, so that the addition of valves is hardly necessary, several makers have provided it with such a mechanism. The new *valve trombones*, in which the valves are sometimes made to lengthen the tube and sometimes to shorten it, have found employment mainly in military bands, though they are used occasionally in symphonic and operatic orchestras. In shape they often differ completely from the slide trombone, so that the bond which connects them with the parent instrument is a very loose one. The valve trombone may be technically more efficient than the slide trombone, but it is decidedly inferior in beauty and purity of tone, so that it cannot really replace the older instrument.

Organ

Hardly any other instrument has undergone such decisive changes during the nineteenth and twentieth centuries as the *organ*. For a long time the Romantic tendency to increase coloristic variety and to enlarge dynamic possibilities was reflected in the instrument's development. Organs were no longer confined to churches. They were built for concert halls, theaters, cinemas, and even for department stores. In power of tone and variety of sound these instruments dwarfed the modest organs in use during the classical era.

This was the outcome of important structural alterations. A discussion of all the details would fill a whole book, but a few significant improvements can be mentioned here.

Up to the beginning of the nineteenth century the *bellows* were operated by man-power. It became more and more evident, however, that the immense quantity of wind required by the organ of the Romantic era could not be produced in such a way. F. Haas of the monastery of Muri, Switzerland, was the first to have the bellows operated by machinery, early in the nineteenth century. His invention was soon taken up in other countries. Steam, hydraulics, gas and in later years electricity have been used as power-sources for the necessary wind pressure.

To provide the evenness of pressure needed for the satisfactory working of the instrument, small bellows or "feeders" were installed, which worked alternately. There were also devices which automatically cut off the feeders as soon as the necessary pressure was reached in the reservoirs.

The instrument's *action* likewise underwent significant changes. In order to connect a key to several pipes the organist had to overcome a considerable wind pressure. It required quite an effort to depress several of the valves or "pallets" simultaneously, so as to allow the wind to enter the pipes. At first little bellows, or "puff-valves," were installed which, with the aid of wind pressure, relieved the player of some of the effort. An improvement on this idea was the "pneumatic lever," used for the first time in 1841 by the famous French organ-maker, A. Cavaillé-Coll, for the organ of St. Denis, France. Here a pneumatic lever, depressing a key, opened the valve of a small auxiliary bellows, which in turn opened the valve proper of the pipe. In 1868 the "electro-pneumatic action" was invented by Charles S. Barker of Bath,

England, in which the levers were operated partly by electricity. Before long this system was considerably improved by the firm of Schmoele & Mols in Philadelphia. In the twentieth century, all-electric organ actions have been most successful. In the case of some organs in concert-halls the console can be placed on any part of the platform. The modern electric action makes it possible for the console to be connected with the rest of the organ merely by electric cables. As a special trick the consoles of theater organs are sometimes built so that they make their appearance—with the player—from a trap, into which they return at the end.

While the older organs were usually equipped with two or three *manuals*, instruments of the nineteenth, and especially of the early twentieth century might be equipped with five, six, or even seven manuals, connected with a varying assortment of pipes. The second manual from the bottom, known as the "great organ," usually operates a number of good-sized basic stops with a serious and majestic tone-quality. There might then be a "choir organ," "solo organ," "echo organ," "swell organ" and "tuba organ." The pipes of the choir organ—originally designed to accompany the choir—have a rather pungent quality. In the past they were often situated behind the player (the German name then being *Rück-Positiv*). The stops of the solo organ are used mainly for playing solo melodies. The registers of the echo organ are soft-toned and often fixed at some distance from the bulk of the other pipes. A "Venetian swell" opens and shuts the wooden box which encloses the pipes of the swell organ. The registers of the solo organ, echo organ, and choir organ are also often placed in swell-boxes with shutters. The tuba organ is connected with particularly brilliant stops played with a high wind pressure. Even the pedals were occasionally given two tiers, but these were subsequently abandoned as uncomfortable for the player and technically superfluous. The large number of manuals was also gradually reduced, as "combination stops" made it possible for the performer to prepare a certain mixture of registers in advance, so that a single touch on the respective stop during the performance was enough to bring the whole group of registers into action.

The *concave pedal-board* was introduced by J. F. Schulze of Paulinzelle in the middle of the nineteenth century. In order to bring the keys for the highest and the lowest notes within easier reach of the player's feet these are slightly raised, thus giving the whole pedal-board a concave form. Many modern organs are so equipped.

An important feature of the Romantic organ is the *crescendo-pedal*, invented in the second half of the nineteenth century. It consists of a cylinder, which, when rotated by the foot, brings in further stops of increasing power. By rotating the cylinder backwards these stops are again disconnected. Most effective crescendi and decrescendi can thus be achieved.

In their striving for new coloristic effects organ-builders of the nineteenth century also introduced registers unknown in earlier centuries. There were, for instance, pipes equipped with "free reeds," used in lieu of the traditional "beating reeds" (cf. p. 257, as well as p. 293). A Cavaillé-Coll introduced the *flûte harmonique*, a stop of overblowing flue-pipes, which, for the first time, sounded the second partial instead of the fundamental note. They require a high wind pressure, and the result is an uncommonly full and powerful tone. Certain devices for imitating percussion instruments are also included in the modern organ. The theater organ, in particular, makes ample provision for triangle, xylophone, timpani, drums, and many others. The *tremulant*, giving a fluttering quality to any note, had already been invented in the Baroque period, but its excessive use has been reserved to theater organs of our own century.

The development of the organ reached a peak during the first third of the twentieth century. Builders in Europe and the U.S. competed with each other in creating instruments of ever-larger proportions. Thus the organ set up in 1917 in Wannemaker's department store, in Philadelphia, was equipped with 18,000 pipes and more than 200 stops. It was dwarfed, however, by the organ erected in 1932 in the Convention Hall in Atlantic City, New Jersey, which boasted more than 30,000 pipes and over 1,200 stops, operated with the help of seven manuals.

A reaction against such exaggerations seemed unavoidable, both from an aesthetic and an economic point of view. It was sparked off by the efforts of two twentieth-century scholars. The great Albert Schweitzer extolled the beauty of the organs built by Bach's contemporaries, the brothers Silbermann, while the Freiburg musicologist Wilibald Gurlitt suggested a return to the ideals of Michael Praetorius, to whom we owe a thorough

PLATE LIII

2.—Upright "giraffe" piano. Early 19th century. Vienna, Gesellschaft der Musikfreunde, at present Kunsthistorisches Museum.

1.—Grand piano by Johann Andreas Stein. Augsburg, 1788. Nürnberg, Neupert collection in Germanisches Nationalmuseum.

PLATE LIV

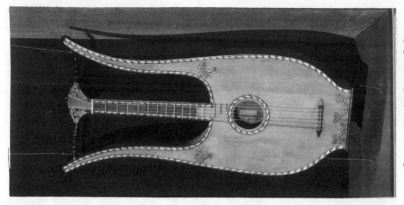

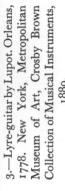

3.—Lyre-guitar by Lupot. Orleans, 1778. New York, Metropolitan Museum of Art, Crosby Brown Collection of Musical Instruments, 1889.

2.—Octobass by J. B. Vuillaume. Paris, 1849. Vienna, Gesellschaft der Musikfreunde.

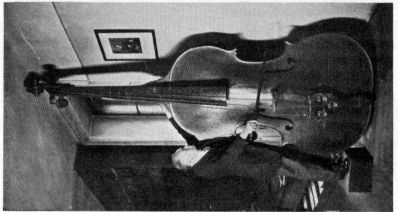

1.—Arpeggione. From *Caecilia*, 1824.

PLATE LV

Alice Chalifoux of the Cleveland Orchestra playing the double-action pedal harp. Photo G. Landmann. Courtesy Cleveland Orchestra.

PLATE LVI

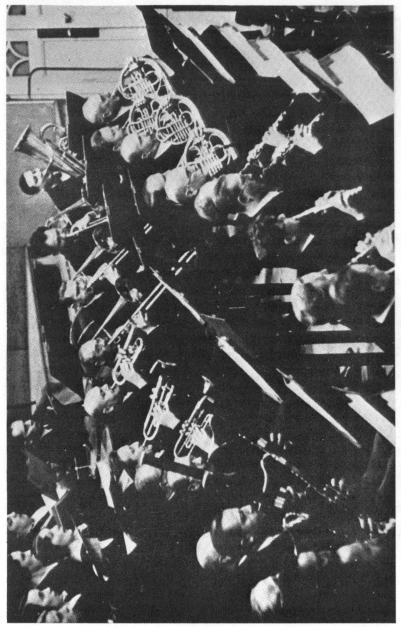

Members of the Vienna Philharmonic Orchestra performing an oratorio. In the third row a player of the kettledrums; in the second row players of bassoons, trumpets, trombones, bass tuba; in the front row players of flutes, oboes, and horns. Photo A. Fischer, Wiener Neustadt.

PLATE LVII

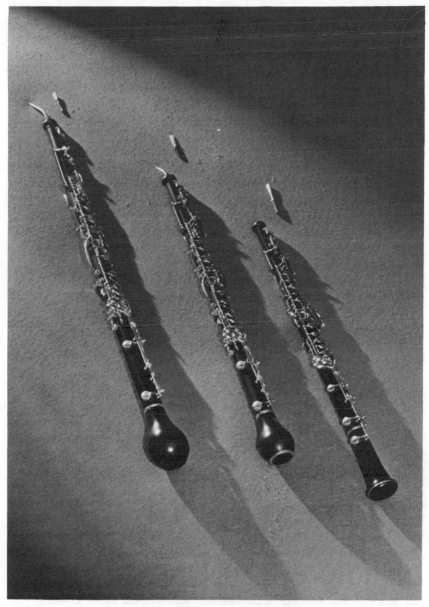

Oboe, oboe d'amore and English horn of the 20th century. Courtesy
Cleveland Orchestra.

PLATE LVIII

Bassoon players of the B.B.C. Orchestra. By kind permission of the British Broadcasting Corporation.

PLATE LIX

1.—Serpent, 18th century. Salzburg, Museum Carolino Augusteum.

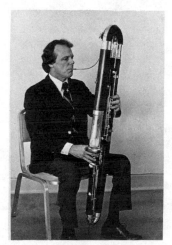

2.—Stanley Maret of the Cleveland Orchestra playing the double-bassoon. Photo Hastings-Willinger & Associates. Courtesy Cleveland Orchestra.

PLATE LX

Bass clarinet, B♭ and E♭ clarinets. Courtesy Cleveland Orchestra.

PLATE LXI

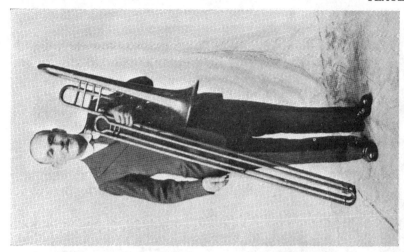

2.—Player of a contrabass trombone by Boosey, London. By kind permission of Mr. A. Falkner, London.

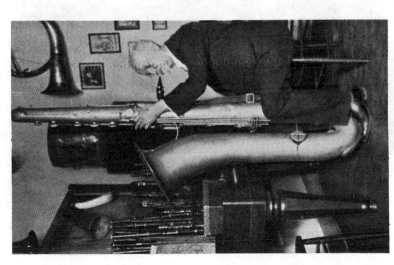

1.—Player of the contrabass saxophone.

PLATE LXII

Myron Bloom of the Cleveland Orchestra playing the French horn.
Courtesy Cleveland Orchestra.

PLATE LXIII

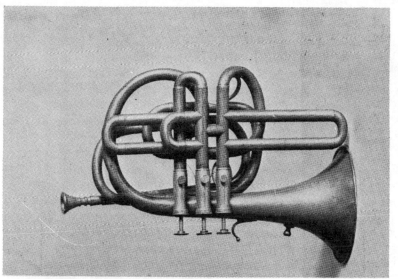

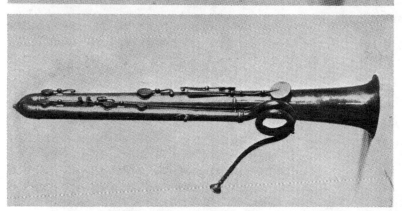

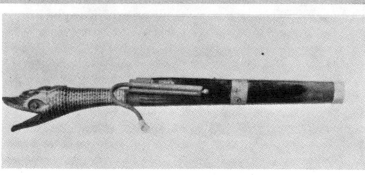

1.—Russian bassoon. Paris, Conservatoire National de Musique. Reproduced by permission of Boosey & Hawkes Ltd., London.

2.—Ophicleide. Vienna, Gesellschaft der Musikfreunde, at present Kunsthistorisches Museum.

3.—Cornet à pistons. Vienna, Gesellschaft der Musikfreunde, at present Kunsthistorisches Museum.

PLATE LXIV

Trumpet players of the B.B.C. Orchestra. By kind permission of the British Broadcasting Corporation.

PLATE LXV

Richard Weiner of the Cleveland Orchestra surrounded by cymbals of various sizes, snare drums, bass drum, and timbales. On the left are whip and maracas, on his right temple blocks. Photo Hastings-Willinger & Associates. Courtesy Cleveland Orchestra.

PLATE LXVI

Professor Emma Lou Diemer of the University of California, Santa Barbara, explaining a Moog synthesizer to a student. Stacked on top of the synthesizer are two amplifiers (lighter color), a tape recorder and a timer.

PLATE LXVII

Woodcut from Franchinus Gafurius, *Theoria Musicae* (Milan, 1492).
It shows in four different ways the mathematical relationships producing
the intervals of fifth, octave, ninth, twelfth and double octave.

description of the early seventeenth-century organ. Both scholars demanded a lighter, clearer, more transparent tone for the instrument, suitable for the realization of Baroque polyphony. Organ-builders have been receptive to the new mood. By and large they have stopped constructing gigantic instruments and started to create smaller organs with fewer registers, fewer pipes, and lower wind pressure, relinquishing the enormous volume of sound and much of the gadgetry acquired during the Romantic era.

Harmonium

The *harmonium*, the accordion and the mouth organ belong to a special group of "free-reed" instruments, which were introduced into Europe around 1800. The free reeds (cf. p. 293) are so called because a flexible metal tongue, under the impact of a stream of air, vibrates freely within a frame and thus produces a musical sound. The shape and material of the tongue determines the pitch and quality of the tone. Like the beating reeds of the regal and the organ, the free reeds do not require a tube.

Experiments with free reeds, which had already been used by the Chinese in their mouth organ or *cheng*, were made in the early nineteenth century in various parts of Europe. In Paris, the versatile Sébastien Érard, in conjunction with Grenié, experimented in the use of free reeds in a keyboard instrument of the organ type. In 1816 two Germans, Eschenbach and Schlimbach, constructed the *Äoline*, a keyboard instrument with a compass of six octaves, whose bellows were operated by the player's knee. Improvements on this instrument were the *Physharmonika*, produced in 1818 by Haeckl of Vienna, and the *aeolodicon*, constructed from 1820 onwards by various makers. In England John Green of London produced the *seraphine* in 1833. Although its sound was rather harsh, the public was attracted by the novelty of the instrument, and it was sold at the considerable price of forty guineas. These experiments culminated in 1840 in the construction of the *harmonium* by Auguste Debain, of Paris. His instruments were built much more carefully than most of the older free-reed organs, and were provided with several registers of different tone-colors. Later inventors found reason to alter only a few details in the construction of the instrument. In 1843 the harmonium was built with the "expression" stop—a slide enabling the player to cut out the wind reservoir, so that the air travelled direct from the feeder to the sound-board. The player could then control the wind-pressure, and thus the strength of the tone, with his feet. Even crescendi and decrescendi could be produced in this way. About the same time another Frenchman, L. P. A. Martin, invented the "percussion"; as soon as the key was pressed, a small hammer hit the tongue, making it "speak" more promptly. The *prolongement*, also invented by Martin, made it possible to hold certain notes after the finger had left the key. The "melody attachment" of W. Dawes, London (1864), enabled the player to give prominence to the highest voice by making it sound more strongly than the rest of the notes, while the "pedal substitute," introduced by Dawes and Ramsden, did the opposite, by emphasizing the lowest part of the composition.

While European instruments work mainly with pressure-bellows, those built in the U.S.A., and somewhat misleadingly called *American organs*, are operated by suction. The air is drawn in through the reeds, producing a softer and more organ-like sound. The invention of the American organ was due mainly to Mason and Hamlin, Boston, who, making use of earlier European experiments, produced their first reliable instrument in 1860.

American organs are sometimes constructed with two manuals and one pedal. They have various stops, which usually bear names adopted from the organ. The newer instruments are provided with a swell and the inevitable device for producing a tremolo effect.

As far cheaper substitutes for the organ, which are also, incidentally, much easier to play, the harmonium and the American organ are still popular on both sides of the Atlantic. R. Strauss used the harmonium in *Ariadne auf Naxos* to reinforce the rather small wind section of his chamber orchestra.

Mechanized harmoniums and American organs of various sizes, controlled by strips of perforated cardboard or metal discs, were frequently used in the nineteenth and early twentieth centuries. They were usually operated by hand with the help of a crank.

Accordion

The *accordion* is a small portable organ of the free-reed type. On this instrument one key can produce two different notes, as the reeds are arranged in such a way that one reed sounds as the bellows are expanded and another when they are compressed. The left hand works the bellows and a large number of studs, which are used mainly for the bass parts and the accompaniment. The melody is usually played with the right hand, for which the larger instruments provide a keyboard with a compass of four or more octaves.

The instrument was first built in 1822 by Friedrich Buschmann of Berlin, under the name *Handäoline*. It was improved in 1829 by Demian of Vienna (who gave it the name *Akkordion*). In the same year Sir Charles Wheatstone in London constructed the hexagonal *concertina*, in which expanding and compressing the bellows produced the same note. The concertina was then provided with a complete chromatic scale.

An improved form of the concertina is the *Bandoneon*, invented in Germany shortly before the middle of the nineteenth century, an instrument on which up to 200 notes can be produced.

The various members of the accordion family are frequently in use for popular and dance music. Their wide diffusion is illustrated by the fact that they hold a place both in American jazz music and in the traditional *Schrammel* quartets of Austrian folk music (known there as *Ziehharmonika*). Chamber music works and concert pieces have been written specially for these instruments, and virtuosi on the accordion are numerous.

Mouth Organ

The smallest member of the free-reed family is the *mouth organ*, commonly known as the *harmonica*. It consists of a box containing sometimes scores of reeds. The player moves it along his lips according to the notes he wishes to produce. Different pitches result from blowing and from sucking. The instrument was probably invented in 1821 by Buschmann, the constructor of the accordion. His *Mundäoline* or *Aura* had a length of only 2½ inches. To-day mouth organs are constructed either in quite primitive form, as a sort of toy, or as a rather elaborate and expensive instrument. In both forms the mouth organ belongs among the instruments of folk-music, and even the best performers, who sometimes achieve a quite surprising virtuosity, are mostly amateurs.

Kettledrum (Timpano)

The vast improvements which the first half of the nineteenth century made in the wind instruments were extended to the most important of the percussion instruments, the *kettledrum*, usually known under its Italian name as *timpano* (Fr. *timbale*, Ger. *Pauke*). As in the past, the drum was most often employed in pairs, but composers occasionally prescribed three timpani (Meyerbeer, *Robert le Diable*) or four (Wagner, *Der Ring des Nibelungen*, Mahler, Seventh Symphony). Berlioz, in his *Requiem*, even asks for sixteen kettledrums, to be played by ten timpanists. The adjustment of six or more screws, which had to be made in the classical period whenever the instrument was retuned, proved to be much too laborious when it became necessary to alter pitch not merely between movements, but sometimes during the course of a single, unbroken piece. This difficulty was overcome by the device of a crank fitted to the side of the drums, which made it possible to tighten all the screws simultaneously. It was first applied in 1812 by G. Cramer of Munich, then, in 1837, by the English maker C. Ward, and in 1840 by the Italian C. A. Boracchi. Even to-day this method is preferred by many. Another device was adopted by J. C. N. Stumpff in 1821. On his kettle-drums the whole frame of the instrument was revolved in order to tighten or slacken the skin, and thereby alter the pitch. From Paris, about 1830, came kettledrums in which the pitch was altered by means of pedals. But here two different principles were applied. In the older pedal kettledrums the area of vibrating skin was reduced by pressing rings or cylinders against it, while in the later type the tension of the skin was altered. Kettledrums with pedals are so efficient that all the semitones within a compass of at least an octave can be quickly and accurately obtained.

Beethoven was one of the first to depart from the tuning of the kettledrums in perfect fourths or fifths (tonic and dominant), which was usual in the classical period; for example, in the Seventh Symphony his kettledrums are tuned in sixths, and in the Eighth and Ninth Symphonies in octaves. To-day four different sizes of kettledrum are commonly used, the compass of the highest being d–a, that of the lowest an octave deeper, D–A. The two intermediate instruments have compasses of F–c and B♭–f. Occasionally a *timpano piccolo* is needed, with a higher range. Stravinsky in *Sacre du Printemps* prescribes b♭, and N.

Rimsky-Korsakov in *Mlada*, d♭[1]. Since about 1800 the timpani have been notated as they sound.

The technical demands on the instrument have increased sharply in the present century. It is expected in particular that changes of pitch can be performed quickly, a requirement best met by pedal drums. Thus V. d'Indy (1851–1931) in *Jour d'Été à la montagne* prescribed a sequence of chromatically ascending and descending notes unbroken by any rests, and B. Bartók in *Music for Strings, Percussion and Celesta* demanded a *glissando* consisting of a drum-roll beginning on G♯ and ascending without a break to c♯. The newly-acquired flexibility of the instrument even enabled A. Tcherepnin (b. 1899) to write a *Sonatina* for timpani and piano.

Snare Drum (Side Drum)

The *snare drum* or *side drum* (Fr. *tambour*, It. *tamburo*, Ger. *Trommel*) was greatly improved in the nineteenth century, so that it was able to make its way from the military band into the orchestra. In 1837 C. Ward patented "a mode of dispensing with the use of cords to all drums." Instead of the troublesome tightening of the skin or head by means of a cord, he introduced the method of applying tension by screws, as in the kettledrum. This drum, which before long was in general use, is small and shallow, with a brass shell and tuning-screws (Pl. LXV). Stretched across the lower skin are one or more catgut or coiled-wire strings, known as "snares," which rattle when the drum is played. This pattern of drum has not, however, ousted the deep-shelled side drum, tightened by cords, which can still be found in most military bands and some orchestras.

As a rule the roll is sounded, or single short strokes are given on the drum's *batter head*. They produce rattling, banging sounds of indeterminate pitch, which have been employed, since the days of the Romantics, as an important means of expression in opera, oratorio and symphonic music. If the snares laid across the drum's *snare head* are loosened, the pitch drops considerably and the sound assumes a dull character. Bartók uses this effect in his *Concerto for orchestra*. If the snares are wrapped in cloth, a hollow, subdued sound is produced, which is peculiarly appropriate for funeral marches.

Tenor Drum, Tambour de Provence

The *tenor drum* (Fr. *caisse roulante*, It. *cassa rullante*, Ger. *Rührtrommel*) is about twice as large as the snare drum and uses no snares. Tenor drums with deep wooden shells and cord tension were employed, for example, by Wagner in *Rienzi, Die Walküre* and *Parsifal*. Their tone is much duller and heavier than that of the side drum, but like the latter, is of indeterminate pitch.

A French variety somewhat resembling a long tenor drum, which possesses a snare and is beaten with a single large drumstick, is known as the *tambour de Provence*. It was used especially to accompany the *galoubet* (the Provençal tabor-pipe). G. Bizet (1838–75) employed the instrument in his second *L'Arlésienne* suite.

Bass Drum, Gong Drum

Like the small side drum, the big *bass drum* (Fr. *grosse caisse*, It. *gran cassa*, Ger. *Grosse Trommel*), without snares, has come down to us both in the older form, with wooden body and cord tension, and in a modern form, with brass body and screw tension (Pl. LXV). Here the wooden drum certainly ranks first, for its tone is fuller. In some of R. Strauss's compositions, and in Mahler's Second Symphony, one head of the bass drum, or even the wood of the rope-hoop, is beaten with a switch of birch. The sound of the bass drum is hollow and resounding in *fortissimo*, but gloomy and mysterious in *pianissimo*. Since the early nineteenth century the instrument has been employed for the expression of exceptional power and energy, and also for mournful and mysterious effects.

A variant of the bass drum is the English *gong drum*, with a shallow metal body and only one head. In modern dance music the big drums that are used have sticks operated by a pedal (Pl. LXV).

Tambourine

The *tambourine* (Fr. *tambour de Basque*, Ger. *Schellentrommel*, It. *tamburino*) came into its own during the Romantic era after a long period of neglect. It is a small drum with a diameter of about ten inches and a single head. Jingles made of brass are inserted loosely into its shell. The instrument is usually made of wood, rarely of metal. It is played with the bare hand, by hitting or rubbing the skin, or by shaking the whole tambourine so that only the jingles sound.

This instrument has been employed not only in military bands, but also in symphonic and operatic orchestras, in wild dances, scenes of carnival, and especially to conjure up the Spanish atmosphere. Thus Berlioz used it in the *Carnaval Romain* overture, Bizet in *Carmen*, Rimsky-Korsakov in *Capriccio Espagnol*, Debussy in *Iberia* and Ravel in *Rhapsodie Espagnole*.

Timbales (Tom-Toms)

Timbales or *tom-toms* are small exotic drums equipped with a single head and employed in pairs. They are mounted on a separate stand and played with drumsticks (Pl. LXV).

Cymbals

Like the drums, the *cymbals* won the freedom of the orchestra in the nineteenth and twentieth centuries. The two plates, which are made now in various sizes, are either clashed together softly in the medieval manner, so that a gentle vibration results, or they are swept past each other violently in the Turkish fashion, producing a, sharp hissing sound. Frequently, too, a single plate; hanging freely, or supported underneath by a special spring (Pl. LXV), is played by means of a kettledrum-stick. Wagner uses this mysterious ringing sound to portray the glitter of the Rhine gold.

In jazz music a single cymbal is frequently swished with a wire brush.

Antique Cymbals

Tiny tuned cymbals (Fr. *cymbales antiques*, Ger. *antike Zimbeln*, It. *crotali*), on the pattern of the Greek and Roman cymbals preserved in various museums, were resuscitated by Berlioz. He required them in *Roméo et Juliette* and *Les Troyens*. Following his example, Debussy used them in *L'Aprèsmidi d'un Faune*, Ravel in *Daphnis et Chloé*, Milhaud in *L'homme et son désir*, and Boulez in *Le visage nuptial*. Outside of France these instruments, which are difficult to obtain, are frequently replaced by the glockenspiel.

Castanets

Castanets have remained the national dance instruments of Spain—

widely used, for instance, by Flamenco dancers—and as such are known throughout the world. No composer will write a Spanish dance piece without employing the highly sophisticated rhythmic effects they produce. One of the best known examples of their use is in the second act of Bizet's *Carmen*. The castanet parts in modern scores are generally played, not with real castanets fastened to the fingers, which are very difficult to use, but with a more convenient, though aesthetically not quite satisfactory substitute. This consists of a stick, to one or both ends of which the shells of the castanets are loosely attached, with an intermediate plate between them. The desired rhythm is produced by shaking the stick.

Maracas
Maracas (Pl. LXV) are exotic gourds filled with dry seeds. They produce rustling sounds when they are shaken.

Triangle
In the course of the nineteenth century the *triangle* became an important and much-used member of the percussion family. It now has the form of an equilateral triangle, and is set in vibration by means of a small metal rod or, rarely, by means of a wooden stick. The tinkling sound is clear and penetrating, and although it is of indeterminate pitch, it seems to fit well into any harmony.

Musical Saw
Jazz bands make use of ordinary hand-saws, which the player bends more or less in order to alter the pitch. The *musical saw* is usually played with the help of a violoncello bow or a hammer with a rubber head. The instrument's tone is tremulous and bell-like in the low notes, and it is employed mostly for the performance of slow melodies, allowing for slurring from note to note.

Xylophone, Marimba
The *xylophone* consists of small tuned bars of wood, which are usually arranged, for the convenience of the player, in two rows, like the keys of a piano, and are played with spoon-shaped or round-headed wooden hammers. The usual compass of the instrument is f–c⁴, but xylophones are also made with a smaller compass. Thanks to its peculiar, dry, hollow timbre, the

instrument has found its way into the symphonic and operatic orchestra. C. Saint-Saëns (1835–1921) employed it in his *Danse
macabre* to portray the clatter of skeletons; Mahler introduced it
into his Sixth Symphony, R. Strauss into *Salome*, and Debussy
into *Iberia*. The xylophone is used also in jazz bands, when very
great demands are made upon the technical skill of the performer.
The *marimba* was originally a kind of xylophone, common among
the native Africans, in which the sound was reinforced by gourds
placed under the bars to act as resonators. Taken to America by
slaves, it was developed and became extremely popular, especially
in central America. The marimba of north America and Europe
is a large xylophone with a compass of four octaves (C–c^3). The
bars are of rosewood and under each one is suspended an
accurately-tuned metal resonator. The marimba's tone is rounder
and warmer than that of the xylophone, and it has been used as
a solo instrument. The marimba may be played by two or more
performers, and this is commonly done in Central and South
America.

Temple Blocks

Temple blocks (Pl. LXV) are of Chinese origin. They are made of
wood, round in shape, and with a slot in the middle. Usually they
appear in sets of five supported by a special stand. The temple
blocks are tuned to the notes of the pentatonic (five-tone) scale
and played with drumsticks or with hammers equipped with a
felt head. Their tone is dry and hollow.

Glockenspiel

The *glockenspiel* of the nineteenth and twentieth centuries consists,
as a rule, of small tuned metal bars, which are arranged in a row,
or in two rows, like the keys of a piano, and are struck with
hammers, whose round heads may be made of wood, rubber or
metal. To-day the compass is usually g^2–c^5, notated two octaves
lower. Wagner used the glockenspiel in the fire music of *Die
Walküre* and in the Apprentices' Dance in *Die Meistersinger*, and
G. Puccini (1858–1924) in *La Bohème*. The glockenspiel with a
keyboard, as used by Mozart in *Die Zauberflöte*, is rare to-day.

Celesta

The place of the glockenspiel equipped with a keyboard has been taken in modern times by the *celesta*, the bars of which are mounted on tuned wooden resonators. The tone of the celesta is soft, gentle and almost harp-like. The instrument has a compass of c^1–c^5, and is usually scored an octave lower than it sounds. The celesta was invented in 1886, by Victor Mustel in Paris. Since then it has often been prescribed in works by Tchaikovsky, Puccini, Mahler, and others. Best known is probably the beautiful blending of the celesta-tone with the sound of woodwind, harp and muted solo violins in the second act of R. Strauss's *Der Rosenkavalier*.

Vibraphone

The *vibraphone*, invented in the 1920s, is one of the most valuable contributions made by dance bands. Its tuned metal bars are arranged in two rows, as on a keyboard, and are played with soft-headed sticks. The range of the instrument is f–f^3. Tuned resonators in tubular form are placed under each bar. Above the openings of the resonators there are rotating discs driven by an electric motor. These prolong the sound and produce the peculiar tremolo or vibrato which is characteristic of the instrument's full and soft tone. A. Berg made use of the vibraphone in *Lulu*, Boulez in *Le marteau sans maître*, and T. Musgrave in *The voice of Ariadne*. D. Milhaud composed a concerto for vibraphone, marimba and orchestra.

Bells

In the modern orchestra the *bells* (Fr. *cloches*, Ger. *Glocken*, It. *campane*) usually take the form of hollow steel tubes, hung in a frame and struck with a hammer, as real church-tower bells would be both too heavy and too costly for use in a theater or concert hall. The tubular bells can be tuned to a definite pitch—commonly from c^1–f^2—and they have a full and mellow tone, owing to the air enclosed within the tube. Among composers who have used them are Mahler, in his Second Symphony, Moussorgsky-Ravel, in *Pictures at an Exhibition*, and O. Messiaen (b. 1908), in *Oiseaux Exotiques*.

Gong (Tam-Tam)

The modern *gong* (*tam-tam*) appears in various sizes, from instruments with a diameter of about 20 inches to ones which are twice as large. It is struck with a soft-headed stick. The persistent clangor of the gong, now mysterious, now ominously solemn, then again throwing off scintillating sparks, found ready acceptance in dramatic and symphonic compositions. Meyerbeer employed it in *Robert le Diable*, Strauss in *Tod und Verklärung*, Puccini in *Madama Butterfly*, and Ravel in *La Valse*. More recently, Boulez and Stockhausen have made use of this versatile instrument.

Rattle

The wooden *rattle* (Ger. *Ratsche*, Fr. *crécelle*, It. *raganella*), in which a flexible tongue is caused to vibrate by the rotation of a toothed wheel, was once used in Catholic churches in Easter Week, as a substitute for bells. Its clattering tone is sometimes employed in the symphonic orchestra, as in Strauss's *Till Eulenspiegel* and *Don Quixote*.

Whip

The *whip* (Ger. *Peitschenknall*, Fr. *fouet*, It. *frusta*) consists of two pieces of wood hinged together at one end (Pl. LXV). If they are hit against each other, they produce a noise similar to the crack of a whip. Milhaud uses this effect in his Second Symphonic Suite.

Wind Machine

The *wind machine* (Ger. *Windmaschine*, Fr. *éoliphone*, It. *eolifono*), which is used in the theater to represent the voice of the storm, consists of a rotating barrel covered with silk, which is stroked by a piece of pasteboard. If it is turned faster, both the pitch and the volume rise. This curious sound was employed by Strauss in the *Alpensinfonie* and by Ravel in *Daphnis et Chloé*.

Electro-Mechanical Instruments

While most twentieth-century instruments are firmly rooted in the music of the past, one group is pioneering into unchartered territory. These instruments profit from the technical advances made in recent times in the field of electrical engineering. In *electro-mechanical instruments*, such as the Neo-Bechstein piano (cf. p. 224f) and the electric guitar (cf. p. 217), the tone is produced in the traditional manner but the sound-box is eliminated. The vibrations are picked up by electronic devices, and then, by means of amplifiers and loudspeakers, given a stronger tone. A similar treatment can also be applied to the violin, viola, 'cello, and double-bass; likewise, tuned springs of coiled steel, played with the help of a keyboard, provide the perfect basis for the electronic reproduction of the sound of bells in a carillon. Even flutes (cf. p. 23) and saxophones have at times been equipped with microphones to start the electronic process.

It is among the peculiarities of the electro-mechanical method that usually not only the volume but also the quality of the resulting tones can be changed. It is possible to strengthen certain harmonics and to eliminate others. Plucked strings can be made to assume the character of bowed strings, and even of percussion instruments. In certain respects the electronically treated tone is far more flexible than that of the original instrument.

Electronic Instruments

A growing number of instruments produce music synthetically, by *electronic* means, without recourse to mechanical devices. In most of these instruments the basis of the sound is provided by "oscillators," electric circuits which produce alternating currents of controlled frequency. The pitch of the tone in the loudspeaker depends on the frequency of the oscillation, and changes if the frequency is modified. Instruments equipped with only one or two oscillators are usually confined to monophonic music; for the performance of polyphonic music several oscillators are needed.

We can deal here with only a few of the most successful electronic instruments.

Aetherophone (Theremin)

A characteristic representative of the early instruments is the *aetherophone* (*Theremin*), invented around 1920 by the Russian physicist Leon Theremin. In this two generators produce oscillations of different frequencies. The pulsation created by combining them, the so-called "beat," is filtered and made audible with the help of a loudspeaker. The aetherophone gives a quaint and rather magical impression, as the performer regulates the pitch simply by movements of his arm. The nearer his hand approaches an upright rod-antenna connected with one of the generators, the higher is the resulting note; the farther his hand recedes, the deeper. By his movements the player alters the frequency in the variable generator, and with it the beat and hence the pitch of the tone. The aetherophone is a purely melodic instrument, with a compass of about three octaves. Its sound resembles that of a musical saw. The instrument's volume can be controlled, but not its timbre. A *Symphonic Mystery* for aetherophone and orchestra was written in 1923 by the Russian composer A. F. Pashchenko (b. 1883).

Ondes Musicales (Ondes Martenot)
The same idea of using the difference between the frequencies of two generators is employed in the *ondes musicales*. This highly successful instrument was built in 1928 by the Paris music-educator Maurice Martenot. The player wears on his finger a ring which is fastened to a cord. A kind of manual indicates the exact position of the hand to produce a given note. A special key makes it possible to cut off the electric current and thus avoid wailing glissandos between notes. The ondes musicales is a homophonic instrument, but attractive variations of timbre are possible. Some fifty compositions have been written for it, largely by French composers such as Honegger, Milhaud, and Messiaen.

Trautonium
In the *Trautonium*, which was developed in 1930 by Friedrich Trautwein in Berlin, a single neon tube serves as oscillator. Changes in pitch are achieved with the aid of a wire stretched above a metal rail. The performer has to press the wire against the rail at the proper place, thus closing the electric circuit. Volume is controlled with a foot pedal, and with the help of harmonic filters various tone-colors can be built up. Although the Trautonium was originally a monophonic instrument it was later built as a Mixtur-Trautonium, with doubled generators and "manuals," thus enabling the player to produce two notes simultaneously. R. Strauss, Hindemith, W. Egk (b. 1901), and other German composers have employed the Trautonium in their works.

Hammond Organ
The *Hammond organ* is one of the most widely used electronic instruments, as it is comparatively small and movable, yet

equipped with two manuals and a pedal-board and fully polyphonic. It was constructed in 1934 by L. Hammond in Chicago
and has since been improved repeatedly. In this instrument, 91
iron discs with faceted rims are rotated in an electro-magnetic
field to produce alternating currents of various frequencies,
corresponding to those of the equally-tempered scale. It is provided with combination registers, and some models are equipped
with stops which can be drawn out to seven different positions,
whereby harmonics of varying intensity are produced. Votaries
of the Hammond organ claim that by mixing and combining
all its possibilities no less than 25 million different sound-colors
can be obtained.

Connsonata Organ

The *Connsonata organ* is not meant to explore novel timbres; it
aims rather at imitating and replacing small pipe organs. This
instrument, produced by Conn Ltd., in Elkhart, Indiana, is a
polyphonic organ equipped with 167 generators consisting, in
newer models, of transistor oscillators, four-fifths of which belong
to the two manuals, the rest to the pedal-board.

Novachord, Baldwin Organ

The *novachord* is equipped with a single manual only, which has
a range of six octaves. Twelve tube-oscillators of fixed frequency
are provided for the semitones of the highest octave. Five dividers
reduce the frequency of each of these master oscillators to produce the pitches of the lower octaves. The first divider reduces
it to half the original frequency, the second to a quarter, and
each successive divider again halves the frequency of the one
before. In addition, a variety of timbres can be produced on the
novachord, and the "attack," duration and "decay" of the tone
widely modified. The sounds of stringed and wind instruments, as
well as of the piano, can thus be imitated by means of the controls, which are conveniently located above the keyboard, or
operated by pedals.

The idea of frequency-division found application in a number
of other electronic instruments too. Mention might be made, in
particular, of the *Baldwin organ*, which is built in various sizes,
from large instruments with three manuals, pedal-board and
fifty-six speaking stops to small instruments for the home.

Generator, Synthesizer

A new and most important phase in electronic music started around the middle of the twentieth century. In fact, many musicians believe that electronic music proper did not begin until that time, earlier manifestations being regarded as mere preparatory stages. As a rule the new type of electronic music no longer needs the personality of the performer. The composer, who at the same time must be a technician, creates his music synthetically on the new electronic instruments and puts it straight on to a magnetic tape. Thereupon it can be further manipulated or amplified, and performed through one or more loudspeakers. Electronic music is usually created in studios which are attached to radio stations or form part of a university's music department.

One of the earliest studios was established in Cologne. It emphasized at first the use of so-called "sine" wave-forms, electronic phenomena which lead to the production of pure notes without any overtones. By mixing such notes of different frequency and intensity provocative new timbres could be created. The inventors of the mighty *RCA synthesizer*, operated in New York by staff-members of Columbia and Princeton universities, attempted to solve the problem in a different manner. The synthesizer is equipped with twelve tuning-fork oscillators tuned to the notes of the equally-tempered scale. For those composers who prefer to use their own tonal system there are in addition twenty-four variable oscillators, which enable the musician to divide the octave differently. The oscillators produce so-called "saw-tooth" wave-forms, which, unlike sine waves, include harmonics. Even "white noise" can be created, i.e. hissing noise which contains all the frequencies at the same time. Through a process of filtering these basic sounds can be reduced to any desired frequencies and timbres. Next, the sound might be amplified (Pl. LXVI), and its duration, mode of "attack" and "decay" might be modified; it can be transposed, and altered through the use of an echo chamber. Even after a recording on tape (Pl. LXVI) has been made, the process of sound-transformation can go on, as it is possible to play the tape backwards, to cut it up and reassemble the pieces in a different way, or to combine the output of several tapes. The possibilities for an inventive mind are practically unlimited.

The RCA synthesizer is operated by means of fifteen-inch wide paper into which holes are punched. This is done through a perforator equipped with forty keys. One group of these keys determines the note that is to be sounded, another the octave in which it is to appear, a third controls the "envelope" (attack, sustaining level and decay of the tone), a fourth the timbre and a fifth the loudness of the tone. Some synthesizers are equipped with two perforators, so that two tone-generating processes can take place simultaneously.

The RCA synthesizer and similar models are extremely efficient, but very large, very heavy, and very costly. In the 'sixties the construction of small and comparatively inexpensive synthesizers was started. These consist of a number of little boxes, or "modules," enclosed in a cabinet, the connections between the modules being either prewired or made by the player on the front panel with the help of "patch cords." These modules vary in the different systems of small synthesizers, but the basic components are similar to those in the large models.

Among them are, again, a number of sound generators which create varying wave-forms, filters which eliminate certain frequencies, and mixers which combine the signals; the sound can be "shaped" in various ways and its loudness controlled by means of amplifiers. Some models, like the *Moog* (Pl. LXVI) and the *Arp*, are equipped with a keyboard, while in the *Buchla* a set of plates, touched by the performer's fingers, serves a similar purpose.

The *modular* synthesizer is based on the principle of voltage control. Every stage of its operation is guided by a separate set of "control voltage" generators. These modules form the real core of the machine, as they direct all aspects of its work.

Computer

It is hardly surprising that the *computer*, which plays such an important part in modern life, has also entered the field of music. Scholars use it for musical analysis and for the compilation of thematic indices. In a way it can even assume the role of a creative artist. When it is programed to obey strict stylistic rules, the random sequences of notes produced by the computer take on a certain musical sense. One result of such experiments was the famous "Illiac" Suite, created in 1956 at the University of Illinois. The computer produced a numerical "score," which was transcribed into musical notation and played by a string quartet of human musicians. Somewhat similar kinds of chance music—like minuets composed with the help of dice—have been known for centuries.

The situation is quite different, however, when the computer is used as a sound generator and thus as a musical instrument proper. In this case the composer has complete control over every detail of his work. Nothing is left to chance; furthermore, he is not obliged to use any other instrument apart from the computer. The composer transfers every facet of his ideas, pitch, timbre, loudness and shape of the sound, on to punch-cards, which are fed into the machine. From these, the computer produces a "digital" tape, which is then transformed, by means of a converter, into a magnetic "analog" tape, supplying the continuity of signals necessary for the production of acoustical wave-forms. This magnetic tape can finally be played over a loudspeaker. In theory the computer is an ideal instrument with great possibilities, but the formidable difficulties involved in the proper preparation of the punch-cards have so far been overcome only by a very small number of hardy technician-composers.

APPENDIX
RUDIMENTS OF THE ACOUSTICS
OF MUSICAL INSTRUMENTS

In the following pages no attempt is made to deal with the complex topic of musical acoustics in an exhaustive manner. A limited amount of basic acoustical and technical information is provided, simply because it might contribute to a better understanding of the historical sections. Certain repetitions of statements made in the main part of the book have not been avoided, if continuity of presentation seemed to warrant them.

Sound
Sound is produced by the vibration of an elastic body. If a tongue of steel is clamped to the top of a table with the greater part of it

Fig. 8. Diagram of a vibration

projecting above the edge (the section from A to B in Fig. 8), and if the end B is then pressed sideways (phase 1) and suddenly released, it will at once begin to vibrate like a very rapid pendulum. Because of its elasticity it will immediately return to the point of rest (phase 2), but instead of remaining there it will swiftly travel to the opposite extreme (phase 3); and from here once more, because of its elasticity, the tongue will return to phase 1. This process would repeat itself to infinity, if the manifold hindrances to free movement—internal friction and, above all, the resistance of the air—did not gradually absorb the initial effective impulse.

The course from phase 1 to phase 3 and back again to 1 is known as a *vibration* or *cycle*. The distance from 2 to 3 or from 2 to 1 is the *amplitude* of the vibration. The term *frequency* denotes the sum of vibrations or cycles effected in one second.

If we leave a very large part of the tongue projecting into the air the vibration will be slow, and we shall hear no sound. If, on the contrary, we shorten the free part of the tongue (i.e. A–B) it will vibrate more rapidly and a sound will be audible. And if the tongue is gradually drawn farther on to the table, so that the vibrating part is correspondingly curtailed, the vibrations will become more and more rapid, while at the same time the pitch of the sound will be raised. In addition, the strength of the sound can be influenced according to how forcefully the tongue is plucked. A greater amplitude of vibration results in a louder sound. We can therefore state the following basic rules: 1) the frequency increases as the length of the vibrating body decreases; 2) as the frequency increases, the pitch of the sound is raised; and 3) as the amplitude of the vibration grows, so does the loudness of the sound.

A graphic picture of vibrations can be obtained by attaching a pen to the upper end of the tongue and drawing a strip of paper rapidly across it as it vibrates. If the frequency is increased, the waves will move closer together; if the amplitude is increased, the wave-crests will get higher, the wave-troughs lower.

Not every sound can be perceived by man. The human ear will not respond to fewer than 16 vibrations per second, while at the other extreme it cannot discern more than 20,000 vibrations per second. Music makes use of only a part of this immense range. Usually it is content with the middle frequencies, between 30 and

4,000 vibrations. This embraces a range of some seven octaves, i.e. $C_1 - c^5$.

Longitudinal and Transverse Vibrations

The sound-impulses that are set up by the sound-generator (in our case the metallic tongue) are imparted to the surrounding air, and thereby transmitted farther. The process is as follows:

When the tongue (Fig. 8) reaches phase 3 at the end of its first vibration, the air-molecules at this spot are pushed and hustled against the neighboring molecules. The result is a compression of the air. But the tongue at once swings back to phase 1, and since it drags the adjacent air-molecules back with it, the pressure is reduced, and there is a rarefaction of the air. This phenomenon of compression and rarefaction, which is the characteristic of vibrations in air, repeats itself as long as the tongue is in motion. The vibrations of the air, however, are not confined to the immediate neighborhood of the initial impulse; they are taken up by the adjacent air-molecules, which transmit them still farther. Nor does the sound travel in one direction only; it is propagated in all three dimensions, in the form of spherical fronts.

It should be clearly understood that the individual air-molecules are not themselves transmitted; they merely swing to and fro on the spot, as it were; what is transmitted is simply the local *movement*. Thus an object floating in water is not really carried forward by the motion of the waves, but is merely raised and lowered in a vertical plane.

A similar image may be obtained if we take one end of a rope and swing it vigorously up and down like a pendulum. Here, too, a wave-movement is set up, which travels along the length of the rope in a horizontal plane, while the rope itself, at any point, is moving vertically, up and down. The pendulum-like vibrations of the separate points are thus set up in a direction at right angles to the direction in which the waves are proceeding. Vibrations of this kind are called *transverse vibrations*. On the other hand, in the case of waves transmitted by alternate compressions and rare-factions of the air, the separate molecules vibrate in the same direction as that in which the waves are travelling. Vibrations of this kind are called *longitudinal vibrations*.

Transverse and longitudinal vibrations both play their part in the functioning of musical instruments. Here we are dealing, not with a progression of waves, as in the sea or the air, but with static waves. Longitudinal vibrations are restricted to wind instruments (scientifically termed "aerophones"), while transverse vibrations occur in the stringed instruments ("chordophones"), in drums ("membranophones") and other percussion instruments ("idiophones").

Tone and Noise

Both the sound produced by a vibrating string and the sound produced by blowing into a wind instrument cause in the human ear a smooth, harmonious sensation. A sound of this kind we call a *tone*. But the crunching of a cart-wheel or the clash of cymbals produces a rough, inharmonious sound-sensation in the ear. A sound of this kind we call a *noise*. Both tones and noises are composed of various components, called *partials*.

If we listen to the ringing of a bell, we hear, pretty clearly, that the sound which to our ears determines the pitch of the bell, and is called the "strike note," is accompanied at the same time by the sound of a whole series of higher notes, known as *overtones* or *upper partials*. In other sounds the overtones are fused into a single composite sound, which can be analysed only with the aid of acoustical apparatus; but their existence can be established objectively, and they play an important part in determining the color of the sound. The difference between tones and noises, physically speaking, is that in a tone the frequencies of the over-tones stand in a simple and unalterable relation to one another, while in a noise the frequencies of the overtones stand in a complicated relation to one another, which, moreover, can be subject to unlimited variation. The sum of the frequencies forming a sound is known as its "spectrum." When the frequencies of the partials constituting a sound are in the ratio of $1 : 2 : 3 : 4 : 5 : 6 : 7$, etc., the partials are called *harmonics*, and we speak of a "natural series of harmonics." If in the natural series of harmonics the first harmonic, or *fundamental tone*, has the frequency n, the second harmonic will have the frequency $2n$, the third the frequency $3n$, and so on. If we assume that the fundamental tone has a frequency of 110 cycles, the second harmonic will have a frequency of 220 cycles, the third harmonic, 330 cycles, and so on. Musically speaking, a tone of 110 vibrations per second has the pitch A, a tone of 220 vibrations the pitch a, a tone of 330 vibrations the pitch e^1, and a tone of 440 vibrations the pitch a^1. The complete series in musical notation, as far as the 16th harmonic, consists of the following notes:

The 7th, 11th, 13th and 14th harmonics, written here in brackets, are out of tune in any musical scale.

This series of overtones (cf. Pl. LXVII) may be built up on any other fundamental note; so if we take C as our first harmonic, the series will be:

Tone-Color

As already stated, in a tone the frequencies of the harmonics stand in a simple relation to each other. On the other hand, no single tone includes the whole series of harmonics, and those that are represented are not equal in strength. The fundamental tone, which also determines the pitch, is by far the strongest; the distribution of the other partials is subject to considerable variation. These differences in the structure of tones are the most important cause of the differences in *tone-color*. A few examples may serve to illustrate this.

In the tone of a tuning-fork (a U-shaped piece of steel furnished with a stem, such as is often used to tune instruments), or of a flute blown very gently, only the first harmonic—the fundamental note—is present. The effect is soft and pleasant to the ear, but at the same time insipid and lacking in character. A tone of such simplicity is exceptional in music. Combinations of harmonics are much more frequent.

In the tone of a gently-blown horn or a softly-struck piano note the first five or six harmonics are present. The tone is now fuller and more powerful, but still comparatively expressionless.

A hard-blown horn or a powerfully-struck piano note includes a whole series of soft harmonics in addition to the first six strongly-sounding partials. The effect is more solid and vigorous. In the violin, the oboe, and the human voice, a whole series of harmonics is present besides the first six. All these harmonics serve to produce a strong and individual effect.

If, as in the trumpet, the higher harmonics (above the sixth or seventh) are more pronounced than the lower, the tone will be particularly sharp, penetrating and brilliant. If, as in the clarinet, the even-numbered harmonics are missing and only the odd-numbered (1, 3, 5, 7) are represented, the result may be a somewhat hollow-sounding tone.

As already stated, the pitch of the fundamental note is invariably the pitch of the whole tone. In noises with partials in complicated and unstable relations there is no question of a definite pitch. But if in such sounds there are, besides the overtones in unstable relations, also harmonics which stand in a simple relation, and remain constant for some time (as e.g. in the kettledrum), then even a noise may have a pitch that can be established.

Intervals

In our discussion of overtones we saw that the frequencies of two tones separated by the interval of an octave stand in the ratio of of 1 : 2, just as the frequencies of two tones separated by the tones separated by the interval of an octave stand in the ratio octave is expressed by the ratio 1 : 4, the double octave and a major third by the ratio 1 : 5, and so on. From the series of overtones in the example on page 278 we are able to draw further conclusions as to the relations between the frequencies of two tones. Between the second and third harmonics of this example— i.e. between c and g—there lies the interval of a perfect fifth. The ratio of these two frequencies is 2 : 3. As we have already seen, the series of harmonic overtones can be built up on any fundamental note, and this helps us to realize the significant point, that when any two tones are separated by the interval of a perfect fifth their frequencies stand in the ratio of 2 : 3. Similarly, the frequency-ratio of a further series of important intervals can be established. Between the third overtone (g) and the fourth (c^1) lies the interval of a perfect fourth. Thus the frequency-ratio of a fourth is 3 : 4. Between the fourth and fifth overtones (c^1 and e^1) there lies a major third, the ratio accordingly being 4 : 5. Similarly we can determine the ratio of the major sixth as 3 : 5, of the minor third as 5 : 6, of the major second as 8 : 9, of the major seventh as 8 : 15, and of the minor sixth as 5 : 8. Thus, for the individual notes of the major scale, we have established the following ratios:

$$1, \tfrac{9}{8}, \tfrac{5}{4}, \tfrac{4}{3}, \tfrac{3}{2}, \tfrac{5}{3}, \tfrac{15}{8}, 2.$$

In a harmonic minor scale, we have the following ratios:

$$1, \tfrac{9}{8}, \tfrac{6}{5}, \tfrac{4}{3}, \tfrac{3}{2}, \tfrac{8}{5}, \tfrac{15}{8}, 2.$$

Just Intonation

In the major scale, outlined above, all the intervals are also derived from the natural fifth ($\tfrac{3}{2}$) and/or the natural major third ($\tfrac{5}{4}$). If in the C major scale we designate C as 1, the note D would result from two superimposed fifths ($\tfrac{3}{2} \times \tfrac{3}{2} = \tfrac{9}{4}$) transposed an octave down so as to return to the basic octave; E stands to C in the relation $\tfrac{5}{4}$; F results from the subtraction of a fifth ($1 : \tfrac{3}{2} = \tfrac{2}{3}$) transposed an octave up, so as to be restored to the basic octave; G stands to C in the relation $\tfrac{3}{2}$; A results from the subtraction of a fifth from a third ($\tfrac{5}{4} : \tfrac{3}{2} = \tfrac{5}{6}$), transposed an octave up so as to be restored to the basic octave; B results from superimposing a third over a fifth ($\tfrac{5}{4} \times \tfrac{3}{2} = \tfrac{15}{8}$); C stands to C_1 (an octave below) in the relation of $\tfrac{2}{1}$.

Using the ratios established here, we find that in so-called *just intonation* the three main chords of C major—the subdominant (F–A–C), the tonic (C–E–G) and the dominant (G–B–D)—sound perfect and harmonious. On the other hand, the chord of the supertonic (D–F–A) is not satisfactory, as the fifth D–A is slightly flat. This is due to the fact that the scale of C major—like every major scale in just intonation—contains two different sizes of whole tones: major ones (C–D, F–G, A–B) with the relative vibrations of $\frac{9}{8}$ (i.e. $1 : \frac{9}{8} ; \frac{4}{3} : \frac{3}{2} ; \frac{5}{3} : \frac{15}{8}$); and minor ones (D–E, G–A), with the relative vibrations of $\frac{10}{9}$ (i.e. $\frac{9}{8} : \frac{5}{4} ; \frac{3}{2} : \frac{5}{3}$). The fifths F–C, C–G, and G–D contain two major and one minor whole tone; the fifth D–A, however, contains one major and two minor whole tones. This disparity obstructs key changes within a composition. Thus, for instance, in C major the interval D–E (supertonic to mediant) would be a minor whole tone; in D major, on the other hand, the same interval would have to be a major whole tone (tonic to supertonic). If we use the major whole tone in the key of C it would sound as badly as if we used the minor one in the key of D. Similarly, in the C major scale, the note A has the frequency-ratio $\frac{5}{3}$ ($\frac{80}{48}$), but in the D major scale, it has the frequency-ratio $\frac{9}{8} \times \frac{3}{2} = \frac{27}{16}$ (or $\frac{81}{48}$). Any attempt to obtain the interval of an octave by building up three major thirds or four minor thirds would be equally unsuccessful. The more chromatic notes we use, and the further we move from C major, the worse are the results.

Mean-Tone Temperament, Equal Temperament

These serious obstacles made it necessary to depart from the ideal of acoustically pure, just intonation and to take refuge in compromise. *Mean-tone temperament*, a system developed around 1500, used the device of slightly reducing the size of the perfect fifth, with the result that four superimposed fifths (C–G, G–d, d–a, a–e^1), transposed to the original octave, produced a perfect major third E, while the same note in just intonation would have been slightly sharp. Thus the important major third was quite in tune and the perfect fifth so slightly altered that the change seemed hardly noticeable. The mean-tone system proved highly useful as long as keys with no more than two sharps or flats were employed. The situation changed, however, when musicians ventured to use keys which were further removed from C major in the circle of fifths. As soon as larger numbers of fifths were superimposed upon each other the impurities of this interval became increasingly noticeable and disturbing, and a more efficient and radical method of tuning had to be devised. This was *equal temperament*, a system which divides the octave into twelve exactly equal semitones. Not a single interval—with the exception of the octave—completely coincides with that of just intonation, but none, on the other hand, is so far out of tune as to be unusable. The fifth is only slightly too small ($\frac{2}{100}$ of a semitone, or two "cents," as it is technically called). The major third is worse; it is $\frac{14}{100}$ of a semitone, or 14 cents, too small, but we are so used to this discrepancy that we hardly notice it any more. On the other hand, through equal temperament unlimited modulations are made possible, as all whole tones have the same size of 200 cents, all major thirds the size of 400 cents, and enharmonic changes of notes can take place on any step of the scale.

The principles of equal temperament were known around 1600, but its universal adoption took a surprisingly long time. We are not certain whether Bach's *Well-tempered Clavier* (1722, 1742–44) was based entirely on its principles, and only in the nineteenth century can we observe its adoption in all countries and by all instruments.

Absolute Pitch

So far we have dealt only with the relative frequencies of the different notes within a scale. Let us now examine the question of *absolute pitch*. In earlier times the situation was rather confused. Praetorius complained in 1619: "Be it known that the pitch of organs as well as of other musical instruments often varies a great deal—the wind instruments of various makers differ very much; some are tuned and made high and others low." In Bach's time conditions had not much improved. *Kammerton*, half a tone or a whole tone below our present tuning, was used for instrumental music, and *Chorton*, half a tone higher than our present tuning, for organ music and vocal music with organ. This difference seems to have disappeared in the second half of the century. Mozart's tuning-fork of 1780 had a frequency of 422 for the note a^1, which corresponds to today's $g\sharp^1$, and we may rightly assume that Haydn's and Beethoven's music also sounded a semitone lower in their time than when we play it today. In 1859 the Paris Academy finally established a^1 with a frequency of 435 vibrations per second as the norm. However, even this figure was not definitive. Since stringed and wind instruments sound more powerful and more brilliant the higher they are pitched, orchestras have always shown a tendency to raise their pitch. Thus in 1939 an international conference held in London established a¹ with 440 vibrations per second as the new norm. Nevertheless, the New York Philharmonic orchestra tunes to 441 and the Vienna Philharmonic to 445. It is also characteristic that an electronic organ installed at Carnegie Hall in New York in 1974 is equipped with gadgets which enable the player to change the pitch to anything from 435 to 445, as such alterations might be demanded by visiting orchestras.

Having considered the more general aspects of musical sounds, we will next examine the acoustic phenomena to be observed in specific types of musical instruments.

Acoustics of Stringed Instruments

The vibration of *strings*—as we have explained—is of the transverse kind. Since a string, if it is to sound at all, must be stretched between two points, its vibrations cannot extend beyond these points. Strings therefore produce not progressive but stationary waves, which are thrown back at the fixed points, the "nodes" of the sound wave. The point of the greatest amplitude, halfway between neighboring nodes, is known as the "loop" of the wave.

The pitch of a string is dependent on its length, thickness, and tension, and on the specific gravity of the material of which it is made. If we increase the length of the string, the frequency of vibration and the pitch decrease correspondingly. For example, if we double the length of a string it will sound an octave lower; if we treble the length it will sound a twelfth lower. Similarly, the pitch rises in inverse ratio to the thickness of the string; and, finally, the frequency varies in direct ratio to the square root of the tension, and in inverse ratio to the square root of the specific gravity of the material employed. Thus if c¹ is sounded by a string whose tension is equal to one pound, the tension produced by a four-pound weight will give us the note c², a tension of nine pounds will give us g², and so on. Finally, if the strings are made of materials whose specific gravities stand in the ratios 1 : 4 : 9 : 16, their pitches will be lower by an octave, a twelfth, and a double octave respectively. Since steel has a disproportionately high specific gravity compared with gut, a steel string can be much thinner than a gut string producing the same note. On the other hand, the wrapping of a thin gut string with wire substantially lowers its pitch.

In the majority of stringed instruments the performer can reduce the effective length of the strings either with his finger or with some special contrivance. If the performer shortens a string to $\frac{8}{9}$ of its original length, the frequency of the newly-formed note will stand to the frequency of the original note as $1 : \frac{9}{8}$; the pitch, in other words, will rise by an interval of a whole tone. Similarly, if the stopping of the string reduces it to $\frac{2}{3}$ of its original length, the resulting note will be a fifth higher; and if the length of the string is exactly halved the pitch will rise by an octave.

Harmonics (Flageolet Notes)

If the performer presses his finger only lightly against the string, it will vibrate in fractional parts and so produce unusual sounds, which are called *harmonics* or *flageolet-notes*, because of their likeness to the tones of a flute. If we start by assuming that an unshortened open string is vibrating in the manner shown in Fig. 9, No. 1, then the only nodal points are formed by the two fixed ends of the string. But if a finger is placed lightly on the string at its center a (Fig. 9, No. 2), a new node is set up at this point. The string now vibrates in two equal parts, each of which, being half the length of the whole, sounds an octave higher than the open string. Now if a finger is placed, again only lightly, a third of the way down

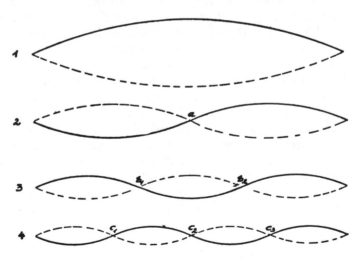

FIG. 9. Diagrams of transverse waves

the effective length, i.e. at point b_1 or b_2, as in Fig. 9, No. 3, the string will be made to vibrate in three equal parts. The resultant harmonic will then correspond to a note with a frequency three times higher than the fundamental tone, i.e. its octave plus a fifth. In the same way a harmonic can be produced of four times the frequency of the fundamental tone (Fig. 9, No. 4), i.e. the double octave, by touching the string lightly at a quarter of its full length at c_1 or c_3.

Even when the string is made to produce ordinary notes, it tends to vibrate in a manner which bears a certain resemblance to the mode of vibration that appears when harmonics are induced. The string will endeavor to produce numerous wave-patterns *simultaneously*: those, for instance, shown in Fig. 9, Nos 1, 2, 3 and 4, as well as several others. The result will be a *combination* wave of great complexity. It must be borne in mind that every elementary wave contained in such a combination wave corresponds to one of the partials in the tone of the stringed instrument, and that the form of the combination wave will therefore depict this tone graphically. Even the fact that some partials represented in the tone sound more strongly, others more weakly, will be reflected in the shape of the combination wave, as the varying amplitudes of the elementary waves leave their imprint on the overall picture of the joint wave.

Tone-Color of Stringed Instruments

A considerable influence on the *color of the tone* is exerted by the choice of the point from which the string is set in vibration; whether the string is bowed or plucked, an arc of vibration forms round the point of contact. Thus if the middle point of a string is bowed or plucked, the arc of vibration occurs in the middle. This means that the harmonics resulting from a nodal point in the middle are lost. The second, fourth, sixth, eighth, and in fact all the even-numbered harmonics are absent, so that the tone produced has a hollow and nasal character. Similarly, when the string is set in vibration at a point corresponding to a third of its length, the third, sixth, ninth, twelfth and fifteenth harmonics are lost. If, however, the string is set in vibration at a point near its fixed end, the vibration will be based on innumerable fractional parts, and will include the higher overtones. The sound in this case will be richer and more expressive than a tone which is poor in harmonics. Thus in the majority of stringed instruments this point is the one chosen.

Thick strings are less capable of vibrating in many fractional parts than thin ones. The sound of thin strings is therefore richer in harmonics and more vigorous. So even for low notes, the use of thick strings is avoided, preference being given to thin strings wound round with wire, which, as we have seen, give a deeper note, but at the same time do not lose the elasticity of thin strings.

If the strings are agitated by a comparatively hard object, such as a metal plectrum (as in the zither), a quill (as in the harpsichord), or a thin, leather-covered hammer (as in the early pianofortes), the close-packed higher overtones are predominant in the sound, which takes on a certain sharpness, or the quality of a metallic tinkle. This effect is especially noticeable in the case of thin metal strings; with the less elastic gut the highest overtones die away more quickly. If, however, we pluck the strings with the bare fingers (as in the guitar), or strike them with felted hammers (as in the modern pianoforte), the first harmonics emerge more strongly than the higher ones. The sound—especially when gut is used—is fuller and softer.

When a stringed instrument is played with a bow, the rosined horsehair of the bow is drawn across the strings, pulling them from their position of rest until their elasticity forces them to fly back. But the bow immediately pulls them sideways again, and the whole process is repeated. This somewhat jerky mode of excitation is, up to a certain point, favorable to the production of the higher overtones, and endows the sound—since the first few overtones are still predominant—with a characteristic plasticity and expressiveness.

Resonance, Sympathetic Strings

In the viola d'amore, the baryton and related instruments, there are strings stretched beneath the finger-board which can neither be shortened by the performer nor reached with the bow. These strings begin to sound, however, without direct intervention, as soon as the notes to which they are tuned occur as partials of any of the notes played on the strings lying above the finger-board. The strings below the finger-board sound throughout the performance and continue to sound after the strings played on by the bow are silent, facts which have a marked influence on the tone of the instrument. This phenomenon is known as *resonance* or *sympathetic vibration*, and the strings in which it is made to occur are called *sympathetic strings*. The explanation of the phenomenon is that the vibrations induced in the upper strings by the bow are transmitted both through the air and through the fixed parts of the instrument. Directly the sound-waves meet a string of the same frequency, this will begin to sound. The phenomenon of resonance is by no means limited to strings. It may be observed in elastic objects of metal, glass or wood, or even in columns of air enclosed in tubes or bulbs.

Sound-board

If we take a tuning-fork, strike it against a hard object, and hold it in the air, we hear a weak but fairly sustained note. If we hold the stem against a table-top after the fork has been struck, the note will not sound for so long, but it will be perceptibly stronger. The vibrations of the fork are now transmitted through the stem to the table-top, and this, because of its much larger surface, sets a greater number of air-particles in motion, thus producing a far stronger note than can be emitted by the tuning-fork alone. The table-top's own sound plays no appreciable part in this; both high and low notes will be impartially reinforced.

This phenomenon is utilized in music, more especially in stringed instruments. The strings by themselves would sound very weak, so they are stretched above an elastic panel of wood, or across a shallow wooden box with air-holes in its upper surface, and this device materially strengthens the sound. Such *sound-boards* and *sound-boxes* facilitate and intensify the spreading of the sound-waves produced by the strings. The shape and material of the sound-box have a decisive influence on the instrument's tone. In the lute, guitar, violin, harpsichord and piano, the form, construction and material of the body largely determine the instrument's tone-quality. Obviously, the size of the sound-board is also of importance. The lower the notes to be played on a stringed instrument, the larger the sound-board must be. In the case of the violin and the 'cello this principle has received due recognition. But if we turn to the viola, which could not be held on the shoulder if it were any larger, we find that the sound-box is too small for the performance required of it. Although the viola goes a full fifth lower than the violin, its body is only about a seventh larger. Thus the fundamental partials in the lower range of the instrument are only incompletely reinforced, which accounts for the viola's faintly hollow and nasal tone-quality.

Acoustics of Wind Instruments

If the *air-column* in a tube with open ends is set in vibration, the strongest motion of the air will take place at these ends, and so an arc or loop of vibration will form here. Since there must be at least one nodal point between two loops, the basic form of vibration would be the one shown in Fig. 10, No. 1. (To simplify their

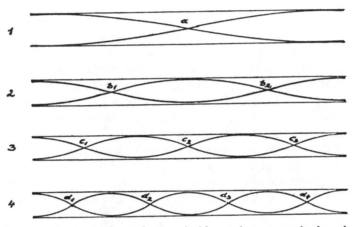

FIG. 10. Diagrams of sound waves inside a tube open at both ends
(presented in the form of transverse waves)

graphic representation and to facilitate comparison with the wave-patterns shown in Fig. 9, the longitudinal waves produced by wind instruments are presented in the form of transverse waves.) The next form of vibration, with two nodal points (b_1 and b_2), is shown in Fig. 10, No. 2, and there can be waves with three (c_1, c_2, and c_3), four (d_1, d_2, d_3, d_4), and even more nodal points.

In our discussion of stringed instruments it was shown that the player can induce the formation of artificial nodes in a vibrating string, and can therefore—without altering the length or tension of the string—produce in succession some of the notes in the series of harmonics. The same series of harmonics can be obtained in a pipe. The way it is done, which is analogous to the production of flageolet-notes on the violin, is described as "overblowing." In the case of a pipe, we have only to alter the method of blowing in order to produce various overtones one after another.

Stopped Pipes

The diagrammatic representation of vibrations in Fig. 10 has to be modified if the pipe is closed at one end, or, to use the technical term, *stopped*. A loop is still formed at the open end, but at the stopped end free vibration is impossible, so a nodal point is formed instead. Diagrammatically, then, we have the pattern shown in Fig. 11, No. 1. If a second nodal point arises we have the pattern

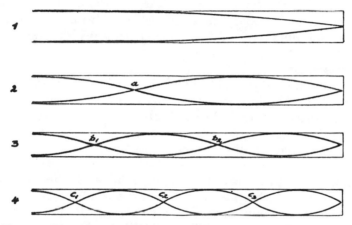

Fig. 11. Diagrams of sound waves inside a tube closed at one end
(presented in the form of transverse waves)

shown in diagram 2; three nodal points yield the pattern shown in diagram 3; and with four nodal points we have the pattern shown in diagram 4. If the distances between the loops of the waves (in physics called half-wave-lengths) in diagrams 1, 2, 3 and 4 are compared, we see that in 2 the half-wave-length is only a third of the half-wave-length in 1; in 3 it is only a fifth; and in 4 only a seventh. The ratios, then, are as $1 : \frac{1}{3} : \frac{1}{5} : \frac{1}{7}$, and the frequencies as $1 : 3 : 5 : 7$. From this we arrive at the important conclusion that in a stopped pipe only the odd-numbered overtones may be obtained, and that their sound contains only odd-numbered harmonics. A further peculiarity of the stopped pipe is that its fundamental tone, and with it the whole series of overtones, lies an octave lower than in an open pipe of the same length. This is shown by comparing the diagrams in Fig. 10/1 and 11/1. In the open pipe (Fig. 10/1) the distance between two loops—that is, the half-wave-length—is fully contained by the pipe; but the stopped pipe, on the other hand (Fig. 11/1), contains only the distance between a loop and a nodal point, i.e. *half* a half-wave-length. Thus the full wave-length of an open pipe is twice the length of the pipe, but in a stopped pipe it is four times the length of the pipe. And since the wave-lengths of an open pipe and a stopped pipe stand in the ratio of 1 : 2, the stopped pipe will sound an octave lower than the open one.

To set the air in a pipe in periodical vibration, and thus make it sound, it is necessary to introduce the "wind" in regular, swiftly-succeeding puffs. This may be done in two different ways.

Flue-Blown Pipes

In *flue-blown pipes*, the wind is directed against a sharp edge placed in the side of the pipe, so that it alternately passes into the tube and is dispersed outside it. In its simplest form this process may be observed in a modern transverse flute. The player blows, through very slightly parted lips, a compressed and flat stream of air against the sharp edge of the mouth-hole or *embouchure*, which is cut in the side of the instrument, close to one end. This stream o air is split by the sharp edge; some of the wind enters the tube, some is dispersed outside it. The air entering the flute causes a compression of the air already there. When the pressure inside the tube is great enough, it overcomes the pressure of the wind directed at the mouth-hole. The compressed air escapes from the tube, carrying with it air from the interior. The air in the tube is now rarefied, so the performer's breath once more passes into the interior of the flute. This process continues uninterruptedly, producing within the pipe the periodic compression and rarefaction of the air necessary to set the air in vibration and produce musical sounds. The recorder and the flue-pipes of an organ also function in this manner, except that in them the flattened stream of air required to make the pipe sound is not given its special form by the musician's lips; its shape and direction are determined by a mechanical device, which compels the wind to pass through a narrow slit before reaching the sharp edge.

Lip-Blown Pipes

The method used to produce sound in flue-blown pipes is fundamentally different from that employed in all other wind instruments. One of the simplest means of creating sound is provided by
the *human lips*. We can observe its application by watching a
player on the trumpet. He pushes the cupped mouthpiece of his
instrument against his compressed lips. He then forces air from
his mouth-cavity through his lips, and a puff of wind passes
through the mouthpiece into the interior of the instrument. At
once the lips, through their elasticity, return to their original
position, almost sealing the mouthpiece of the trumpet again,
until a new access of pressure once more forces them open, sending
a second stream of air into the mouthpiece. This process is repeated continually, and the periodic blasts of air down the tube
produce the necessary compression and rarefaction of the air-
column within the instrument.

The same method of sound-production is employed in the horn,
the trombone, the tuba, the cornet, etc.—in short, in all those
instruments which the musician usually, though not quite
accurately, calls "brass instruments."

Double-Reed-Blown Pipes

In the oboe and bassoon a similar method is adopted, but here
the function of the human lips is assumed by a *double reed*—two
laminae of thin cane (*arundo donax*) bound together at one end
(Fig. 12a and 12b). These laminae are so adjusted that a narrow

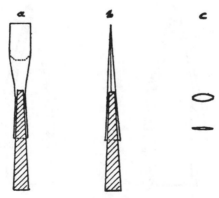

FIG. 12. Diagram of a double cane reed

chink remains open between them. If the performer places the
double reed, which protrudes from the upper end of the oboe or
bassoon, between his lips the elastic reed begins to vibrate under
the pressure of his breath. The slit between the two laminae opens
and closes alternately (Fig. 12c), allowing the air to enter the
instrument in periodic puffs.

The foregoing method of sound-production—by the human
lips in the so-called brass instruments, and by a cane reed in oboe
and bassoon—is based on the acoustic principle of two elastic
bodies beating against each other.

Single-Reed-Blown Pipes

Contrary to this, however, is the *single reed,* used in clarinets and
saxophones. Here a single cane reed—a lamina of *arundo donax*—
is fixed at one end of a frame in such a manner that a narrow
chink remains open between the reed and the frame (Fig. 13). If
the performer takes the reed and the frame (sometimes called the
"beak," because of its external appearance) between his lips, the
elastic reed will begin to vibrate when he blows, and will thus
alternately close and open the slit (Fig. 13a and 13b), so that air,
after passing through the beak, will enter the instrument in
periodic puffs. Thus the single reed of the clarinet performs a
similar service to that of the double-reed of the oboe. It is known
as a *beating reed,* as it "beats" against a frame.

In the reed pipes so far discussed, soft reeds provide the means

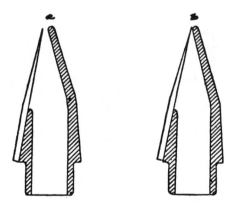

FIG. 13. Diagram of a single cane reed

of setting the air in vibration, while the pitch of the tone depends mainly on the length of the tube attached to the reed. These are known as "heterophonic" reeds, which have only an indirect influence on the production of the tone. In addition there are "idiophonic" reeds, which produce the tone directly. Instruments equipped with these have no tube at all, or a tube which merely reinforces the sound, but has no influence on the pitch. Hardwood or metal reeds are used, and the pitch is determined entirely by the length, thickness and elasticity of the reed itself. We refer to these as instruments with a hard reed. There are again two types of hard reeds: the beating reeds, which, like the clarinet reed, *beat against* a frame; and the *free reeds*, which *move* freely to and fro *through* a frame. We can therefore distinguish the following six types of wind instruments:

1) Flue-vibrated pipes, such as flute, recorder, and the flue-pipes of the organ;
2) Lip-vibrated pipes, such as trumpet, trombone, horn, and tuba;
3) Pipes equipped with heterophonic, "soft," double reeds of *arundo donax*, such as oboe and bassoon;
4) Pipes equipped with a single, beating, heterophonic, "soft" reed of *arundo donax*, such as clarinet and saxophone;
5) Idiophonic, single, "hard," beating reeds, made of metal or hardwood, as used in the organ and regal;
6) Idiophonic, single, "hard," free reeds, made of metal or hardwood, as used in the harmonium and accordion.

Groups 2 and 3 are obviously related, as in both cases a pair of soft, elastic, and vibrating substances (human lips and reeds respectively) cause the production of sound in a tube.

Overblowing
The performer who has caused a tube to emit a tone will next attempt to play notes of different pitch. This can be done in a variety of ways. The most natural is the method of *òverblowing*, already mentioned. By gradually increasing the intensity of the wind-stream the performer may produce within the tube not merely one nodal point, but two, three, four, and more. He

obtains in this way the octave, the twelfth, the double octave, etc., of the fundamental note.

In practice every wind instrument has at its disposal only a limited number of overblown notes or harmonics. If the instrument has a wide bore—that is, if the diameter of the tube is large in comparison with its length—the lower harmonics will be obtainable. As a rule it will be a "full-tube" instrument (like the flute, oboe, or bass tuba), on which the fundamental note can be sounded. However, there are also long and thin instruments, like the trumpet and (French) horn, well suited for the production of the higher overblown notes, on which as a rule the fundamental note cannot be played. They are known as "half-tube" instruments.

The tension of the human lips can be varied within wide limits. If the performer is sufficiently skilful and the tube has the proper narrow bore, a large number of harmonics can be obtained from lip-vibrated wind instruments. Reeds, on the other hand, are much less elastic, so that on the oboe and clarinet—in which, moreover, the tube is comparatively short—only a few harmonics can be obtained. The same may be said of the short flutes, on which overblowing will produce hardly more than the second and third partials.

To produce overblown notes on reed instruments, the frequency of vibration proper to the reed is modified by pressure from the lips or teeth. Overblowing may also be assisted by opening a small vent, known as the *speaker* hole, covered by a key, exactly over one of the nodes of the air-column, which is thus caused to vibrate in fractional parts. If the reed is protected from contact with the mouth, and a speaker hole is lacking, as in the bagpipe and some Renaissance instruments, overblowing is impossible.

In respect to overblowing, the position of the clarinet is peculiar. Acoustically, with its predominantly cylindrical bore, it behaves like a stopped pipe. As a result, overblowing does not produce the even-numbered harmonics. The first is followed by the third, which means that it over-blows to the twelfth and not, as normally, to the octave. Similarly, in the sound of the clarinet the even-numbered overtones are barely audible; they emerge more strongly only with vigorous overblowing. Thus the high notes of the clarinet have a sharp, strident quality, which is entirely absent from the instrument's low notes, with their rather hollow sound. Lastly, the clarinet, in its capacity of stopped pipe, sounds deeper than an oboe of about the same length.

Finger-Holes

To bridge the great intervals lying between the lower natural notes, *finger-holes* were introduced at a very early date. As long as it is closed a finger-hole bored in the wall of a tube does not affect the length of the vibrating column of air; but if open, it allows the air to escape before the end of the tube is reached, the result being analogous to what happens when the performer's finger shortens the length of a string on a stringed instrument. The effect of the finger-holes depends on their size and position; the nearer they are to the bell of the instrument, and the smaller their diameter, the less will be the rise in pitch when they are opened. Conversely, the nearer the mouthpiece they are, and the greater their diameter, the greater will be the rise in pitch brought about by their opening. On earlier instruments finger-holes usually served to produce the notes of the diatonic scale. To sound chromatic notes, the half-closing of holes was employed or "cross fingering." The latter means that the player does not close or open holes successively, which is what is usually done, but that he keeps a hole open between closed ones.

Keys

A great improvement in the use of finger-holes is effected by means of *keys*. Covers made to fit the finger-holes are worked by the performer on the lever principle. He is thus enabled to operate holes lying far apart or too large to be stopped by his finger-tips alone. There are "open keys," which are closed by the pressure of the player's finger, thus lowering the instrument's tone, and "closed keys'," which the performer opens by pressing the lever, thus raising the pitch.

Slides

With lip-vibrated instruments the use of finger-holes to obtain the chromatic scale is acoustically undesirable. When the finger-holes are opened the sound is apt to be ragged, a problem not easily overcome. So different methods had to be developed for this group of instruments. A very early device has been used on the trombone.

Here a metal sleeve, which slides over the main tube, is pulled in and out, thereby altering the length of the whole instrument. As the fundamental notes, the so-called "pedal notes," are partly unobtainable, the largest gap in the series of harmonics is the fifth between the second and third harmonics. This interval is bridged with the help of the seven different *slide positions* available to the trombone player. He has seven series of overtones obtainable which lie a semitone apart from each other. This enables him to play a chromatic scale through a range of about two and a half octaves.

Crooks

A similar result was obtained on (French) horns with the help of *crooks*, inserted between the mouthpiece and the main tube, thus lowering the instrument's series of harmonics (cf. p. 278). Changing crooks, however, took a certain amount of time, which seriously limited the effectiveness of the device.

Valves

A great improvement was achieved through the introduction of the pistons and rotary *valves* invented in the nineteenth century (cf. p. 242f). They enable the player to add a piece of extra tubing immediately, by simply depressing a key. On instruments whose lowest note is the second partial—like trumpets, horns, and cornets—three valves are employed, which lower the pitch by a whole tone, a semitone, and one-and-a-half tones respectively. If, for instance, the first valve is called into play, the air is compelled to make a detour through a supplementary tube just long enough to lower the complete series of natural tones by a whole tone. The other valves work in precisely the same way, and it is also possible to combine two and even three valves. The latter should—in theory, at least—cover the interval of a fifth between the second and third partials. In reality, however, the three sections of extra tubing would not be long enough to sound the expected augmented fourth, and the resulting note would be about a quarter-tone too high. Various devices—such as making the third valve-tube slightly too long—have been employed to compensate for this defect.

Lip-vibrated bass instruments with a wide bore—such as the euphonium and tuba—can be played down to the fundamental note. Here the gap of a whole octave between first and second partials has to be bridged, and an additional valve, lowering the pitch by two-and-a-half tones, is employed. The need to compensate for faulty intonation is particularly great in these instruments, so a fifth, at times even a sixth, valve is introduced.

Transposing Instruments

A notational peculiarity might be mentioned here which arises primarily in connection with wind instruments. During the eighteenth and nineteenth centuries trumpets, horns and clarinets— to mention only some of the most important ones—were regarded as *transposing instruments.* The key resulting from the instrument's fundamental note and its natural series of overtones was always notated in C major, irrespective of the actual pitch. Thus, for instance, a B♭ clarinet (an instrument whose natural tones are derived from the harmonics of the note B♭) is notated in C major, although the pitch is a whole tone lower. If the same instrument played a tune notated in D major, the actual sound would again be a whole tone lower, therefore in C major. Conversely a D trumpet would sound a whole tone higher than it is notated. Thus, for instance, the written notes $c^2 d^2 e^2$ played on a D trumpet would sound $d^2 e^2 f\sharp^2$. Such transpositions are not always indicated. Thus the English horn and the basset horn sound a fifth lower than they are notated, the double-bass an octave lower, and the piccolo flute an octave higher.

The peculiar notation of the transposing instruments simplified matters for earlier performers. When players of the eighteenth and early nineteenth centuries had to use several instruments producing different natural scales, they did not have to transpose, as the notation eliminated this difficulty. With the improvements through the key and valve systems in the nineteenth century, the need to use various sizes of the same instrument was greatly reduced. Such changes were then employed mainly for coloristic reasons.

For the conductor, a score containing parts for several transposing instruments complicates matters. So we find an increasing tendency in twentieth-century scores for all the instruments to be entered as they sound and without transposition.

Acoustics of Bars and Tubes

In addition to strings and pipes, elastic *bars* and *tubes*, vibrating transversely, are used for musical purposes.

In such instruments the frequency of the vibrations depends partly on the material employed, partly on its size. The more elastic the material the higher the frequency; the greater its specific gravity the lower the frequency. If equal-sized bars of lead, clay, tin, brass and iron are suspended side by side, the lead bar will give the lowest note, clay the next lowest, then tin, then brass, then iron. Similarly, boxwood gives a far lower note than pine. Further, with cylindrical bars the frequency rises with the diameter, while it falls with increasing length. On the other hand, the width of a bar of prismatic shape has no effect on its frequency, which is governed by length and thickness; thus, if a prismatic bar whose thickness is half its width is laid on edge, it will sound an octave higher than before. Tubes sound higher than solid cylinders of the same length and diameter; and their pitch rises in proportion as the walls are made thinner.

For best results sounding bars (as in the xylophone or glockenspiel) are supported at two points, each a quarter of their length from the end. Nodes of vibration are formed at these points, while loops are formed at either end and in the center. Tubes, on the contrary, are best suspended by one end (as in tubular bells), forming a node at the fixed end and a loop at the free end. This form of vibration is related to that of the stopped pipe (see Fig. 11).

With bars and tubes the overtones occur in a most complicated numerical ratio, so that the sound has more or less of noise in it. If the overtones are very close together—as in the triangle struck with a metal rod—it is out of the question to talk of pitch; we have simply a very light tinkling sound. But when the overtones lie well apart from each other—as in the xylophone—the pitch is recognizable. The sound is hollow in this case, but is at the same time sharpened by the inharmonious admixture of overtones. Lastly, in the case of suspended tubes, the sound is mellower and fuller, owing to the column of air enclosed in the tube.

Acoustics of Plates

Plates, likewise, vibrate transversely; here the frequency increases with the thickness and the elasticity of the material employed, but is in inverse ratio to the specific gravity of the material and the diameter of the plate. The overtones produced by vibrating plates are mostly inharmonious, so that the result is either pure noise or something very like it. The pitch cannot be determined— at any rate, so far as European gongs and cymbals are concerned. In a gong the nodes of vibration are in the edges, while the loop is at the center. Just the opposite applies to the cymbals; here the node is at the center and the loops at the edges. So gongs are suspended at the edges and hit in the center, whereas cymbals are held in the center while their rims vibrate.

Acoustics of Bells

Bells may be regarded as a variety of curved plates. Their frequencies increase in proportion to decreases in the diameter of the bell and the thickness of the "soundbow" (that part of the bell against which the clapper strikes). The frequency also increases in inverse proportion to the cube of the bell's weight. Thus to double the frequency the weight would have to be reduced to an eighth; to triple it, to a twenty-seventh. The overtones are mostly inharmonious, and the sound of bells is often more noisy than musical. However, bells have been tuned to specific notes with increasing success, as makers have learned to achieve correct pitch for a number of important partials.

Acoustics of Drums

Like every other solid material employed for musical ends, *membranes* also vibrate transversely. Their frequencies decrease in proportion to increases in the length, width and thickness of the membranes. On the other hand, they increase with rises in tension. In the circular membranes most frequently used for musical purposes the overtones come very close together and are inharmonious. The sound is thus indistinct and noisy. In the case of the kettledrum, it is only the cauldron-shaped sound-box, which magnifies certain of the overtones, that proves so favorable to the formation of a musical tone that it is possible to tune the instrument to a given pitch.

Electronic Instruments

The development of physics, and in particular of electronics, has been responsible for the rise of a new class of *electronic instruments*, some of which reinforce the sound of traditional instruments while others create new sounds synthetically. The acoustical details of the processes involved are highly complex and beyond the scope of this book. Some basic information has been supplied along with the discussion of such instruments on p. 267ff.

A SELECTED BIBLIOGRAPHY

ADLUNG, J.: Musica mechanica organoedi. Berlin, 1768; new ed. Berlin, 1961.

AGRICOLA, M.: Musica instrumentalis deudsch. Wittenberg, 1529; repr. in *Publikat. d. Gesellsch. f. Musikforsch.*, 1896.

ALMENRÄDER, K.: Abhandlung über die Verbesserung des Fagotts. Mainz, c. 1820.

ALTENBURG, J. E.: Versuch einer Anleitung zur heroisch-musikalischen Trompeter und Paukenkunst. Halle, 1795; reprint Amsterdam, 1966.

ALTENBURG, W.: Die Klarinette. Heilbronn, 1904.

AMAT, J. C.: Guitarra española. Barcelona, 1586.

ANDERSSON, O.: The Bowed Harp. London, 1930.

APEL, W.: The History of Keyboard Music to 1700, trans. H. Tischler, Bloomington, 1972.

ARBEAU, T.: Orchésographie. Langres, 1589. Eng. transl. London, 1925.

ARNAUT, H.: Les traités d'Henry Arnaut de Zwolle et des divers anonymes. Edited by G. Le Cerf and E. R. Labande. Paris, 1932; new ed. Kassel, 1972.

ARNOLD, E. T.: Die Viola pomposa, in *Zeitschrift für Musikwissenschaft* XIII, 1930.

AUERBACH, C.: Die deutsche Clavichordkunst des 18. Jahrhunderts. Kassel, 2nd ed. 1953.

BACH, C. P. E.: Versuch über die wahre Art das Clavier zu spielen, Berlin, 1753; Engl. translation by W. J. Mitchell, New York, 1949.

BACHMANN, W.: Die Anfänge des Streichinstrumentenspiels. Leipzig, 1964.

BAINES, A.: Fifteenth century Instruments in Tinctoris's 'De Inventione et Usu Musicae', *Galpin Society Journal*, III, 1950.

Woodwind instruments and their History. London, 1957.

European and American Musical Instruments. New York, 1966.

BARNES, W. H.: The Contemporary American Organ. Glen Rock, [8]1964.

BATE, Ph.: The Oboe. New York, 1956.

The Flute. London, 1969.

BECKER, H.: Zur Entwicklungsgeschichte der . . . Rohrblattinstrumente. Hamburg, 1966.

BELLOW, A.: History of the Guitar. New York, 1970.

BERLIOZ, H.: Traité d'instrumentation, Paris 1844. Enlarged Ger. version by R. Strauss, Leipzig, 1905. Eng. translation of the Strauss version, New York, 1948.

BERMUDO, J.: Declaración de instrumentos musicales. Osuna, 1555; repr. Kassel, 1957.

BÉSARD, J.-B.: Isagoge in artem testudinariam. Augsburg, 1614.

BESSARABOFF, N.: Ancient European Musical Instruments. Boston, 1941.

BLANDFORD, W. F. H.: The Bach Trumpet. *Monthly Musical Record*, 1935.

Handel's Horn and Trombone Parts. *Musical Times*, 1939.

BOEHM, T.: Die Flöte und das Flötenspiel. Munich, 1871; Engl. translation, Cleveland, 1922.

BONANNI, F.: Gabinetto Armonico. Rome, 1722; repr. New York, 1964.

BORJON, C. E.: Traité de la musette. Lyons, 1672.

BOTTÉE DE TOULMON, A.: Des instruments de musique en usage au moyen-âge. *L'Annuaire historique*, 1838.

BOWERS, Q.: Encyclopedia of automatic musical instruments. Vestal, N.Y., 1972.

BOYDEN, D.: The History of Violin Playing. London, 1965.

BRAGARD, R.: Les instruments de musique dans l'art et l'histoire. Paris, 1967; Engl. tr. New York, 1968.

BRÖCKER, M.: Die Drehleier: Ihr Bau und ihre Geschichte. Düsseldorf, 1973.

BRÜCKER, F.: Die Blasinstrumente in der altfranzösischen Literatur. Giessen, 1926.

BUCHNER, A.: Musical Instruments through the Ages. London, 1961.

BUHLE, E.: Die musikalischen Instrumente in den Miniaturen des frühen Mittelalters. Band I: Die Blasinstrumente. Leipzig, 1903.

Die Glockenspiele in den Miniaturen des frühen Mittelalters. *Festschrift, Liliencron*, Leipzig, 1910.

CARSE, A.: The History of Orchestration. London, 1925.

Musical Wind Instruments. London, 1939, New York, 1975.

The Orchestra in the XVIIIth Century. Cambridge, 1940.

CERONE, P.: El Melopeo. Naples, 1613.

CHAVEZ, C.: Toward a New Music. New York, 1937.

CHLADNI, E. F. F.: Beyträge zur praktischen Akustik. Leipzig, 1821.

CHORON, A. E. and FRANCOEUR, L. J.: Traité général des voix et des instruments d'orchestre. Paris, 1813.

CHOUQUET, G.: Le musée du conservatoire national de musique. Paris, 1884.

CLAPPÉ, A. A.: The Wind-Band and its Instruments. New York, 1911.

CLEMENCIĆ, R.: Old Musical Instruments. New York, 1968.

CLUTTON, C. and NILAND, A.: The British Organ. London, 1963.

CORRETTE, M.: Méthode pour apprendre aisément à jouer à la flûte traversière. Paris, 1735.

Méthode pour apprendre le Violoncelle. Paris, 1741.

CORVELLI, L.: Gli strumenti musicali in Italia. Bologna, 1967.

COUSSEMAKER, E. H.: Essai sur les instruments de musique au moyen-âge. In *Annales Archéologiques*, 1845–1851.

CRANE, F.: Extant Medieval Musical Instruments. Iowa City, 1972.

CROSBY BROWN Collection of Musical Instruments in the Metropolitan Museum. Catalogue. New York, 1904–1905.

DAY, C. R.: Catalogue of the Musical Instruments . . . at the Royal Military Exhibition, London, 1960.

DENIS, V.: De muziekinstrumenten in de Nederlanden . . . Leuven, 1944.

DIRUTA, G.: Il transilvano. Venice, 1597, ⁵1625.

DONNINGTON, R.: The Instruments of Music. New York, ³1962.

DORF, R. H.: Electronic Musical Instruments. Mineola, 1958.

DUFOURCQ, N.: Documents inédits relatifs à l'orgue français. Paris, 1934–35.

DUPONT, W.: Geschichte der musikalischen Temperatur. Nördlingen, 1955.

EICHBORN, H. L.: Die Trompete in alter und neuer Zeit. Leipzig, 1881.
Das alte Klarinblasen auf Trompeten. Leipzig, 1894.
Die Dämpfung beim Horn. Leipzig, 1897.
EISEL, J. P.: Musicus autodidacticus. Erfurt, 1738.
ENGEL, C.: A Descriptive Catalogue of the Musical Instruments in the South Kensington Museum. London, 1870.
EUTING, E.: Zur Geschichte der Blasinstrumente im 16. und 17. Jahrhundert. Berlin, 1899.
FANTINI, G.: Modo per imperare a sonare di tromba. Frankfurt, 1638; repr. Milan, 1934.
FISCHHOF, J.: Versuch einer Geschichte des Clavierbaues. Vienna, 1853.
FITZPATRICK, H.: The Horn . . . London, 1970.
FLOOD, W. H. G.: The Story of the Bagpipe. London, 1912.
FLORENCE, Galleria degli Uffizi: Mostra di strumenti musicali in disegni delli Uffizi. Florence, 1952.
FLORENCE, Conservatorio di musica Luigi Cherubini. Gli strumenti musicali. Florence, 1969.
FORSYTH, C.: Orchestration. London, ³1936.
FRIEND, D.: Learning Music with Synthesizers. Milwaukee, 1974.
FROTSCHER, G.: Geschichte des Orgelspiels. Berlin, 1935-36.
GAFFORI, F.: De harmonia musicorum instrumentorum . . . Milan, 1518.
GALILEI, V.: Dialogo della musica antica e moderna. Florence, 1581.
GALPIN, F. W.: Notes on a Hydraulus. *The Reliquary*, 1904.
Old English Instruments of Music. London, 1910, ⁴1965.
A Textbook of European Musical Instruments. London, 1937.
GANASSI, S.: La Fontegara. Venice, 1535; repr. Bologna, 1969.
Regola rubertina. Venice, 1542-43; repr. Bologna, 1970.
GEIRINGER, K.: Musikinstrumente, in Adler's *Handbuch der Musikgeschichte*. Berlin, ²1930.
Vorgeschichte und Geschichte der europäischen Laute, in *Zeitschrift für Musikwissenschaft*, 1927.
Alte Musikinstrumente (a catalogue of the Salzburg Museum). Leipzig, 1933.
GERBERT, M.: De cantu et musica sacra. Saint Blasien, 1774.
GERLE, H.: Musica Teutsch. Nürnberg, 1532.
GEVAERT, F. A.: Nouveau traité d'instrumentation. Paris, 1885.
GLAREANUS, H.: Dodecachordon. Basel, 1547, trans. A. Miller, Amer. Inst. of Musicol, Rome, 1965.
GRANOM, L. C. A.: Instruction for Playing on the German Flute. London, 1766.
GREETING, T.: New Lessons for the Flageolet. London, 1661.
GREGORY, R.: The Horn. London, 1969.
GRILLET, L.: Les ancêtres du violon et du violoncelle. Paris, 1901.
HAMMERICH, A.: Musikhistorik Museum. Copenhagen, 1909 ff.
HARDING, R. E. M.: The Pianoforte. Cambridge, 1933.
HARRISON, F. L.: European Musical Instruments. New York, 1964.
HAYES, G.: Musical Instruments, in *New Oxford History of Music* III, London, 1960, and IV, London, 1968.
HAYES, G. R.: The Viols and Other Bowed Instruments. London, 1928-30.

HECKEL, W.: Der Fagott. Leipzig, ²1931.

HEINITZ, W.: Instrumentenkunde. Wildpark Potsdam, 1929.

HESS, J.: Disposition der merkwaardigste Kerk-Orgelen . . . No, pl. 1774; repr. Utrecht, 1945.

HICKMANN, E.: Musica instrumentalis. Baden-Baden, 1971.

HICKMANN, H.: Das Portativ. Kassel, 1936.

HILL, W. H., with HILL, A. F. and HILL, A. E.: Antonio Stradivari. London, 1902.

HINDLEY, G.: Musical Instruments. London, 1971.

HIPKINS, A. J.: The Pianoforte and Older Keyboard Instruments. London, 1896.

HORNBOSTEL, E. M., with SACHS, C.: Systematik der Musikinstrumente. *Zeitschrift für Ethnologie*, 1914.

HOTTETERRE, J. M.: Principes de la flûte traversière . . . Paris, 1707; repr. Kassel, 1965; Engl. tr. New York, 1968.

HOWARD, A.: The Aulos or Tibia. *Harvard Studies*, 1893.

HOWE, H. S.: Electronic Music Synthesis. New York, 1975.

HUBBARD, F.: Three Centuries of Harpsichord Making. Cambridge, Mass., 1965.

HUCHZERMEYER, H.: Aulos und Kithara. Münster, 1931.

HUMMEL, J. N.: Anweisung zum Pianofortespiel. Vienna, 1828.

HUTH, A.: Les Instruments Radio-Électriques, in *La Nouvelle Encyclopédie Française*, 1935.

JAHN, F.: Die Nürnberger Trompeten- und Posaunenmacher im 16. Jahrhundert. *Archiv für Musikwissenschaft*, 1925.

JAMES, P.: Early Keyboard Instruments. London, 1930, ²1960.

JUDENKUNIG, H.: Ain schone kunstliche underweisung . . . auff der Lautten und Geygen. Vienna, 1523; repr. Hofheim, 1960.

KASTNER, G.: Traité général de l'instrumentation. Paris, 1837, 1844.
  Manuel général de musique militaire. Paris, 1841.
  Les danses des morts. Paris, 1852.

KENDALL, A.: The World of Musical Instruments. London, 1972.

KINKELDEY, O.: Orgel und Klavier in der Musik des 16. Jahrhunderts. Leipzig, 1910.

KINSKY, G.: Katalog des musikhistorischen Museums von W. Heyer in Köln. Leipzig, 1910, 1912.
  Doppelrohrblattinstrumente mit Windkapsel, in *Archiv für Musikwissenschaft*, 1925.
  Geschichte der Musik in Bildern. Leipzig, 1929.

KIRCHER, A.: Musurgia universalis. Rome, 1650; new eds. Rochester, 1958; Hildesheim, 1972.

KLOSÉ, H. E.: Méthode de la clarinette. Paris, 1843; new ed. Paris, 1942.

KOERTE, O.: Laute und Lautenmusik bis zur Mitte des 16. Jahrhunderts. Leipzig, 1901.

KÖLBEL, H.: Von der Flöte. Kassel, ²1966.

KOLNEDER, W.: Das Buch der Violine. Zürich, 1972.

KOOL, J.: Das Saxophon. Leipzig, 1931.

KUNITZ, H.: Instrumenten-Brevier. Wiesbaden, ²1971.

LABORDE, J. B. de: Essai sur la musique. Paris, 1780.

LANGWILL, L. G.: The Bassoon and Double Bassoon. London, 1948.

LAVOIX, H.: Histoire de l'instrumentation. Paris, 1878; repr. Bologna, 1972.

LE BLANC, H.: Défense de la basse de viole . . . Amsterdam, 1740.

LEFEVRE, J. X.: Méthode de la clarinette. Paris, 1802.

LE ROY, A.: Instruction pour apprendre la tablature de cistre. Paris, 1565.

LICHTENWANGER, W.: The Dayton C. Miller Flute Collection . . . Washington, D.C., 1961.

LÖHLEIN, G. S.: Anweisung zum Violinspielen . . . Leipzig, 1774.

LOVILLO, J. G.: Las Cantigas. Madrid, 1949.

LÜTGENDORFF, A. L. v.: Geigen- und Lautenmacher . . . Frankfurt a.M., ⁶1922.

LUITHLEN, V.: Katalog der Sammlung alter Musikinstrumente. Vienna, 1966.

LUNELLI, R. and ELIS, A.: Der Orgelbau in Italien. Mainz, 1956.

LUSCINIUS, O.: Musurgia. Strasbourg, 1536.

MACE, T.: Musick's Monument. London, 1676.

MAHILLON, V. C.: Catalogue . . . du musée instrumental . . . de Bruxelles. Ghent-Bruxelles, 1880–1922.

MAHRENHOLZ, C.: Die Berechnung der Orgelpfeifenmensuren. Kassel, 1938.

MAJER, J. F. B. C.: Museum musicum. Halle, 1732; repr. Kassel, 1954.

MANDYCZEWSKI, E.: Katalog der Sammlung alter Musikinstrumente der Gesellschaft der Musikfreunde. Vienna, 1912.

MARCUSE, S.: Musical Instruments: A Comprehensive Dictionary. New York, 1964, ²1975.

A Survey of Musical Instruments. New York, 1975.

MARESCHALL, S.: Porta musices. Basel, 1589.

MARPURG, F. W.: Historisch-critische Beyträge. Berlin, 1754–78.

Die Kunst das Clavier zu spielen. Berlin, 1750, ⁴1762.

MARX, J.: The Tone of the Baroque Oboe, in *The Galpin Society Journal*, 1951.

MATTHESON, J.: Das neu eröffnete Orchestre. Hamburg, 1713.

Der vollkommene Kapellmeister. Hamburg, 1739; repr. Kassel, 1954.

MEIEROTT, L.: Die geschichtliche Entwicklung der kleinen Flöten-typen. Tutzing, 1974.

MELKUS, E.: Die Violine. Bern, 1973.

MERSENNE, M.: Harmonie universelle. Paris, 1636–37; new ed. Paris, 1963.

The book on music. instr. in Engl. translat. by R. Chapman, The Hague, 1957.

MORLEY-PEGGE, R.: The French Horn. New York, 1973.

MOZART, L.: . . . Violinschule. Augsburg, 1756; repr. Mainz, 1950; Engl. tr. London, 1948.

MUDARRA, A. de: Libros de musica . . . para vihuela. Seville, 1546.

MUNROW, D.: Instruments of the Middle Ages and the Renaissance, London, 1976.

MUSTEL, A.: L'Orgue expressive. Paris, 1903.

NEF, K.: Katalog der Musikinstrumente . . . in Basel. Basel, 1906.

Geschichte unserer Musikinstrumente. Leipzig, 1926.

NELSON, S. M.: The Violin and Viola. London, 1972.

NEUPERT, H.: Das Cembalo. Kassel, ³1956.

Das Klavichord. Kassel, ²1956.

NORLIND, T.: Systematik der Musikinstrumente. Hanover, 1939.

OCHSE, O. C.: The Organ in the United States. Bloomington, 1975.

ORTIZ, D.: Tratado de glosas sobre cláusulas . . . en la música de violones. Rome, 1553.

PANUM, H.: Harfe und Lyra im alten Nordeuropa. *Sammelbände der internationalen Musikgesellschaft*, 1905–06.
Stringed Instruments of the Middle Ages. London, 1939.

PAPE, W.: Instrumenten Handbuch. Cologne, 1971.

PARENT, D.: Les instruments de musique au XIVᵉ siècle. Paris, 1925.

PERROT, J.: L'orgue. Paris, 1965; Engl. tr. London, 1971.

PETRI, J. S.: Anleitung zur praktischen Musik. Leipzig, 1767; repr. Giebing, 1969.

PICCININI, A.: Intavolatura di liuto e di chitarone. Bologna, 1623.

PIERRE, C.: Les facteurs d'instruments de musique. Paris, 1893.

PISTON, W.: Orchestration. New York, 1955.

PLAYFORD, J.: A Musical Banquet: Lessons for Lira Viol. London, 1651.

POHL, C. F.: History of the Glass Harmonica. London, 1862.

PONTECOULANT, L. A.: Organographie. Paris, 1861; repr. Amsterdam, 1972.

PRAETORIUS, M.: Syntagma musicum, II (with vol. of illustrations of musical instruments). Wolfenbüttel, 1618; repr. Kassel, 1958–59.

PRICE, F. P.: The Carillon. London, 1933.

PRINTZ, C.: Historische Beschreibung der Edelen Sing- und Kling-Kunst. Dresden, 1690.

QUANTZ, J. J.: Anweisung die Flöte traversiere zu spielen. Berlin, 1752.

QUOIKA, R.: Vom Blockwerk zur Registerorgel. Kassel, 1966.

RAMOS DE PAREJA, B.: De musica practica. Bologna, 1482; repr. Leipzig, 1901.

RENSCH, R.: The Harp. London, 1969.

RIMBAULT, E. F.: The Pianoforte. London, 1860.

RIMSKY-KORSAKOV, N. A.: Foundations of Orchestration. New York, 1933.

RIPIN, E. M.: The Instrument Catalogs of Leopoldo Franciolini. Hackensack, 1974.

ROCKSTRO, R. S.: A Treatise on . . . the Flute. London, 1890; ²1928.

ROUSSEAU, J.: Traité de la viole. Paris, 1687; repr. Amsterdam, 1965.

RÜHLMANN, J.: Die Geschichte der Bogeninstrumente. Braunschweig, 1882.

RUSSEL, R.: The Harpsichord and Clavichord. London, 1959, ²1973.
with BAINES, A.: Catalogue of Musical Instruments in the Victoria and Albert Museum. London, 1968.

SACHS, C.: Reallexikon der Musikinstrumente. Berlin, 1913; repr. Hildesheim, 1962.
Katalog der Sammlung alter Musikinstrumente . . . zu Berlin. Berlin, 1922.
Geist und Werden der Musikinstrumente. Berlin, 1929; repr. Hilversum, 1965.
Handbuch der Musikinstrumentenkunde. Leipzig, 1920, ²1930.
The History of Musical Instruments. New York, 1940.

SAUERLANDT, M.: Die Musik in 5 Jahrhunderten der europäischen Malerei. Leipzig, 1922.

SCHAEFFNER, A.: Origine des instruments de musique. The Hague, ²1968.

SCHLESINGER, K.: The Instruments of the Modern Orchestra and . . . the Precursors of the Violin Family. London, 1910.

The Greek Aulos. London, 1939.

SCHLICK, A.: Spiegel der Orgelmacher. Heidelberg, 1511; repr. Mainz, 1959.

SCHLOSSER, J.: Alte Musikinstrumente. Vienna, 1920.

SCHMITZ, H. P.: Querflöte und Querflötenspiel. Kassel, 1958.

SCHNEIDER, W.: Beschreibung der musicalischen Instrumente. Leipzig, 1834.

SCHULTZ, H.: Instrumentenkunde. Leipzig, 1931, ²1956.

SCHWEITZER, A.: Deutsche und französische Orgelbaukunst. Leipzig, 1906, ²1927.

SEEBASS, T.: Musikdarstellung und Psalterillustration im frühen Mittelalter. Bern, 1973.

SIMPSON, C.: The Division Viol. London, 1659; repr. Rochester, 1957 (microcard).

SKINNER, E. M.: The Modern Organ. New York, 1915, ⁶1945,

SMITHERS, O. L.: The Music and History of the Baroque Trumpet before 1721. London, 1973.

SPEER, D.: Unterricht der musicalischen Kunst. Ulm, 1687.

STAUDER, W.: Alte Musikinstrumente. Braunschweig, 1973.

STELLFELD, J. A.: Antwerpsche clavicimbel- en orgelbouwers. The Hague, 1842.

SUTTON, J.: Organs Built in England from the Reign of King Charles II to the Present Time. London, 1847.

TERRY, C. S.: Bach's Orchestra. London, 1932, ²1958.

TEUCHERT, E. and HAUPT, E. W.: Musikinstrumentenkunde. Leipzig,.1910.

THIBAULT, G. with JENKINS, J. and BRAN-RICCI, J.: Eighteenth Century Musical Instruments. London, 1973.

THON, C. F. G.: Abhandlungen über Klavier-Saiteninstrumente. Weimar, 1843.

TINCTORIS, J.: De inventione et usu musicae (c. 1484). Edited by C. Weinmann, Regensburg, 1917.

TOLBECQUE, A.: L'art du luthier. Niort, 1903.

TOURNIER, M. L.: La Harpe. Paris, 1959.

TRICHET, P.: Traité des instruments de musique (c. 1640). Edited by F. Lesure, Neuilly-sur-Seine, 1957.

TROMLITZ, J. G.: Unterricht die Flöte zu spielen. Leipzig, 1791; repr. Amsterdam, 1973.

VALENTIN, E.: Handbuch der Instrumentenkunde. Regensburg, 1954.

VENTZE, K.: Die Boehmflöte. Frankfurt a.M., 1966.

VIDAL, F.: Galoubet et Tambourin. Avignon, 1869.

VINCENTINO, N.: L'antica musica ridotto alla moderna prattica. Rome, 1555; repr. Kassel, 1959.

VIRDUNG, S.: Musica getutscht. Basel, 1511; repr. Kassel, 1970.

VOLBACH, F.: Die Instrumente des Orchesters. Leipzig, 1913.

WALTHER, J. G.: Musicalisches Lexicon. Leipzig, 1732; repr. Kassel, 1953.

WANZLÖBEN, S.: Das Monochord . . . Halle, 1911.

WARMAN, J. W.: The Hydraulic Organ . . . *Proc. of the Music. Assoc.* 1903–04.

WEIGEL, J. C.: Musicalisches Theatrum (c. 1713). Kassel, 1961.

WELCH, C.: History of the Boehm Flute. London, [3]1896.
  Six Lectures on the Recorder. London, 1911.
WELCKER VON GONTERSHAUSEN, H.: Der Klavierbau. Frankfurt a.M., [4]1870.
WELLESZ, E.: Die neue Instrumentation. Berlin, 1928–29.
WERCKMEISTER, A.: Erweiterte und verbesserte Orgelprobe. Quedlinburg,
  1698; repr. Kassel, 1970.
WIDOR, C.-M.: La technique de l'orchestre moderne. Paris, [2]1906; Engl.
  tr. London, [2]1946.
WINTERNITZ, E.: Keyboard Instruments in the Metropolitan Museum of
  Art. New York, 1961.
  Musical Instruments of the Western World. New York, 1967.
  Musical Instruments and their Symbolism. New York, 1967.
WOLTERS, K.: Das Klavier. Bern, 1969.
ZACCONI, L.: Prattica di musica. Venice, 1592, 1622.
ZAGIBA, F.: Musikgeschichte Mitteleuropas von den Anfängen bis zum Ende
  des 10. Jahrhunderts. Vienna, 1976.
ZUTH, J.: Handbuch der Laute und Guitarre. Vienna, 1926–28.

INDEX OF PERSONS

INDEX OF INSTRUMENTS

Numbers in italics refer to main entries